Introduction

(Student Edition)

First Edition

Rachna Verma

Arvind Kumar Verma

MBM Engineering College
JNV University, Jodhpur, Rajasthan,
India

Introduction to Scilab(Student Edition)

Copyright © 2018 Dr. Rachna Verma and Dr. Arvind Kumar Verma

ISBN: 9781720005704

First published in India by Dr. Rachna Verma and Dr. Arvind Kumar Verma

All rights reserved. No part of this publication may be reproduced or distributed in any form or by any means, or stored in a data base or retrieval system, without the prior written permission of the authors.

Cover (illustration) by Dr. Rachna Verma

Set by Dr. Rachna Verma

Printed by kdp.amazon.com

This book provides a comprehensive, hands-on introduction to Scilab, a powerful, open-source scientific and technical computing environment. Starting with basic concepts, the book lucidly builds advanced Scilab concepts one needs for solving real-life industrial and academic research problems. The book contains a large number of illustrative examples and practice problems. The book is well suited as a textbook for learning Scilab for science and engineering students. It is sold under the express understanding that the information contained in this book is accurate to the best of authors' knowledge. However, the authors will not be held responsible for the consequences of any actions based on the content of the book for any purpose.

Dedicated to
Scilab Developers

Contents

    Preface

1   Introduction to Scilab   1
    1.1   What is Scilab?   1
    1.2   Installing Scilab   2
          1.2.1   Installing Scilab under Windows   3
          1.2.2   Installing Scilab under Linux   3
          1.2.3   Installing Scilab under Mac OS   3
          1.2.4   Installing/Uninstalling Toolboxes   5
    1.3   Starting and Ending a Scilab Session   5
    1.4   Scilab Environment   6
          1.4.1   Console window   8
          1.4.2   Command History window   9
          1.4.3   Variable Browser window   10
          1.4.4   File Browser window   10
          1.4.5   SciNotes window   11
          1.4.6   Graphics window   11
    1.5   Getting Help in Scilab   19
    1.6   Some Useful Scilab commands   20

2   Basics of Scilab   23
    2.1   Introduction   23
    2.2   Character Set   23
    2.3   Data types   24
          2.3.1   Integer data type   24
          2.3.2   Real data type   28
          2.3.3   Complex data type   28
          2.3.4   Boolean data type   30
          2.3.5   String data type   30
    2.4   Constants and Variables   32
          2.4.1   Constants   32

		2.4.2 Variables	34
	2.5	Operators	37
		2.5.1 Arithmetic operators	37
		2.5.2 Relational operators	39
		2.5.3 Logical operators	40
	2.6	Scilab Expressions	41
	2.7	Hierarchy of Operations	43
	2.8	Built-in Functions	46
3	Vectors and Matrices		51
	3.1	Introduction	51
	3.2	Matrices, Vectors and Scalars	51
	3.3	Creating Matrices from Values	52
	3.4	Creating the Empty Matrix	55
	3.5	Creating Large Matrices from Values	55
	3.6	Creating Row Vectors And Column Vectors from Values	56
	3.7	Creating Scalars from Values	56
	3.8	Creating Evenly Spaced Row Vectors	57
	3.9	Creating Evenly Spaced Column Vectors	58
	3.10	Creating Special Matrices	59
	3.11	Creating Sparse Matrices	62
	3.12	Size of a Matrix	64
	3.13	Accessing Matrix Elements	65
	3.14	Creating Sub-Matrices	66
	3.15	Creating Multi-Dimensional Array	68
		3.15.1 Using Scilab functions	68
		3.15.2 Extending dimensions of arrays	69
		3.15.3 Using the cat function	70
	3.16	Operations on Matrices and Arrays	71
		3.16.1 Arithmetic matrix operations	71
		3.16.2 Arithmetic array operations	72
		3.16.3 Relational operations	76
		3.16.4 Boolean (logical) operations	77

		3.17	Matrix Manipulations	77
		3.17.1	Reshaping a matrix (an array) as a column vector	78
		3.17.2	Reshaping a matrix as a differently sized matrix	79
		3.17.3	Changing the size of a matrix	80
		3.17.4	Appending a row or column to a matrix	81
		3.17.5	Deleting rows and columns of a matrix	82
	3.18		Some Useful Matrix Commands	82
4	Polynomials			89
	4.1		Introduction	89
	4.2		Polynomial Creation	89
	4.3		Polynomial Evaluation	91
	4.4		Roots of a Polynomial	92
	4.5		Polynomial Arithmetic Operations	93
	4.6		Polynomial Differentiation and Integration	93
	4.7		Polynomial Curve Fitting	95
5	Scilab Graphics			101
	5.1		Introduction	101
	5.2		Two Dimensional Plots	101
		5.2.1	Adding labels and title	103
		5.2.2	Activating and deactivating grid	104
		5.2.3	Adding texts to a plot	105
		5.2.4	Plotting multiple curves	106
		5.2.5	Adding legends	109
		5.2.6	Interactively editing a figure	111
		5.2.7	Editing a plot through the console window	113
	5.3		Sub-Plots	117
	5.4		Creating Commonly Used 2D Plots	119
		5.4.1	Logarithmic plots	119
		5.4.2	Polar plots	120
		5.4.3	Area plots	120
		5.4.4	Bar charts	124
		5.4.5	Histogram plots	126

		5.4.6 Pie charts	127
		5.4.7 Stair-step plots	128
		5.4.8 2D contour plots	131
	5.5	Three-Dimensional Plots	131
		5.5.1 3D plots	132
		5.5.2 3D parametric curves	138
		5.5.3 3D mesh and surf plots	138
		5.5.4 3D contour Plots	142
		5.5.5 3D scatter Plots	143
6	Programming in Scilab		149
	6.1	Introduction	149
	6.2	Scilab Programs	149
	6.3	Scilab Editor	150
	6.4	Scilab Keywords	152
	6.5	Predefined Variables	153
	6.6	Constants, Variables and Expressions	154
	6.7	Input and Output Statements	154
		6.7.1 Assignment statements	154
		6.7.2 Interactive input	155
		6.7.3 Output functions	163
	6.8	Control Structures	167
	6.9	Looping	167
		6.9.1 for loop	168
		6.9.2 while loop	171
		6.9.3 break and continue statements	172
	6.10	Branching control structures	173
		6.10.1 if-elseif-else statements	174
	6.11	select-case-else statements	176
	6.12	File Handling	177
		6.12.1 File opening and closing functions	178
		6.12.2 Formatted input/output functions	181
		6.12.3 Importing data from Excel files	191

		6.12.4 Reading/writing CSV files	193
	6.13	Scripts and Functions	194
		6.13.1 Script programs	195
		6.13.2 Function programs	196
		6.13.3 Inline functions	198
		6.13.4 Global and local variables	199
		6.13.5 Recursive functions	201
		6.13.6 Nesting of functions	201
		6.13.7 Variable number of arguments in functions	203
		6.13.8 Multiple evaluation of a function	205
		6.13.9 Executing a program file	206
	6.14	Error Handling	209
		6.14.1 try-catch statement	212
	6.15	Program Debugging	215
	6.16	Scilab Code Conventions	222
7	Numerical Methods Using Scilab		227
	7.1	Solutions of Algebraic and Transcendental equations	227
		7.1.1 Bisection method	227
		7.1.2 False position method	230
		7.1.3 Newton-Raphson method	233
	7.2	Interpolation	236
		7.2.1 Newton's formula for interpolation	236
		7.2.2 Lagrange's interpolation formula	239
	7.3	Numerical Differentiation	242
	7.4	Numerical Integration	244
		7.4.1 Trapezoidal rule	245
		7.4.2 Simpson's 1/3 rule	245
	7.5	Solution of Linear Systems of Equations	247
		7.5.1 Matrix inversion method	248
		7.5.2 Gauss elimination method	249
		7.5.3 Iterative method	252
	Appendix I : Commonly Used Scilab Functions		261

Preface

Scilab is a very powerful, free and open-source software package for scientific and technical computation, visualization and programming. It includes a large number of general purpose and specialized functions, using state of the art algorithms, for numerical computation. These functions are organized in libraries called toolboxes that cover areas such as simulation, optimization, image processing, control and signal processing. With easy to use high level programming language and huge library of functions, Scilab reduces considerably the burden of programming for scientific and technical applications. It can also be interactively used as a very powerful scientific calculator. Since Scilab is available free of cost to everyone across the globe and is continuously upgraded by a strong team of open source developers, it is suitable for all undergraduate students, researchers, professors and professionals in any field of Science and Engineering. Further, many commercial developers are also using it to reduce their project cost and has reported many successful applications.

This book is written following several years of teaching the software to our students in introductory courses in numerical methods. The basic objective to write this book is to teach Scilab in a friendly, non-intimidating fashion, without any previous programming experience. Therefore, the book is written in simple language with many sample problems in mathematics, science, and engineering. Starting from the basic concepts, the book gradually builds advanced concepts, making it suitable for freshmen and professionals. The source codes of all the examples presented in this book can be downloaded from https://github.com/arvindrachna/Introduction_to_Scilab.

There are a few books available for teaching Scilab, but most of these books are written in French. The basic motivation to write this book is to spread the awareness and use of Scilab, a state of the art and very powerful open source software for technical and scientific computation, across the globe. The book deals with the latest version of the software.

For promoting outcome based learning, each chapter of the book starts with chapter objectives and lucidly introduces the basic concepts, with sample examples, to achieve those objectives. Each chapter concludes with a summary and a list of key terms to recapitulate the learned concepts. Finally, the chapter ends with exercise problems so as students can apply the concepts learned in the chapter.

The book consists of seven chapters. The first chapter gives a focused introduction to Scilab and explains how one can install the software on ones machine. The second chapter introduces the core concepts of Scilab, a matrix based technical computing environment. This chapter also introduces how the software can be used in its interactive mode to solve scientific and technical problems. The third chapter introduces how to create and manipulate vectors and matrices in Scilab. It also introduces array and matrix operators. The fourth chapter explains how polynomials can be processed in Scilab. Polynomial operations, differentiation and integration are also introduced. The fifth chapter explains graphics capabilities of Scilab. Various 2D and 3D graphics functions are explained in this chapter. The sixth chapter is focused on the programming capabilities of the software. Various programming constructs are explained with examples. The last chapter explains basic numerical methods and how to create Scilab programs for them. This chapter helps students to apply the learned concepts to actual numerical method problems. The book ends with an appendix of commonly used Scilab commands and functions.

We would like to thank several of our colleagues at MBM Engineering College, especially Professor Sunil Rajotia of Mechanical Engineering Department, for proof reading few chapters of the book and suggesting modifications. We also appreciate the support and motivation of Professor K. R Chowdhary of Computer Science and Engineering Department. Special thanks are due to Professor R.S. Anand, Department of Electrical Engineering, IIT Roorkee, for motivating us to write this book.

We also thank our parents for inculcating passion for learning and encouraging work harder. We also thank our kids Aviral and Abhinav for their patience during the writing of this book.

We hope that the book will be useful in lucidly building expertise in Scilab to the readers. We sincerely welcome any suggestion to further improve the book.

Rachna Verma
Arvind Kumar Verma

About the Authors

Dr. Rachna Verma is working as an Assistant Professor, Department of Computer Science and Engineering, MBM Engineering College, JNV University, Jodhpur, Rajasthan, India. She received her BSc (Math Honours) form Delhi University, India and MCA and PhD from JNV University, Jodhpur, India. She has fifteen years of teaching experience. She teaches numerical methods, computer programming and computer graphics and has research interest in computer vision and image processing.

Dr. Arvind Kumar Verma is working as a Professor, Department of Production and Industrial Engineering, MBM Engineering College, JNV University, Jodhpur, Rajasthan, India. He received his BE (Industrial Engineering) and ME (Production and Industrial Systems Enginnering) from IIT Roorkee, India and obtained his PhD in CAD/CAM from MBM Engineering College, Jodhpur, Rajasthan, India. He has 23 years of teaching experience. He teaches numerical methods, CAD/CAM, robotics, computer programming. He has research interest in robotic vision, machinigng feature recognition and numerical computation.

x

Chapter 1
Introduction to Scilab

Learning Objectives
- History of Scilab
- Installation of Scilab
- Familiarization with the Scilab environment
- Getting help in Scilab

1.1 What is Scilab?

Scilab is a free and open source software package for high-performance numerical computations and visualisation for engineering and scientific applications. It provides an interactive computation and visualisation environment along with a large number of easy to use built-in functions for technical and scientific computations, powerful 2-D and 3-D graphics and animations. Further, it is also a high level programming language with advanced data structures to implement complex computations, to develop new features and to modify/extend the existing features.

Scilab stands for **Sci**ence **lab**oratory. It is available as an open source software package, freely downloadable, under the CeCILL license (GPL compatible) for GNU/Linux, Mac OS and Windows for both 32 bits and 64 bits platforms. The first version of Scilab (originally named as Balise) was developed in 1980's as a Computer Aided Control System Design (CACSD) software by INRIA (A French Institute for Research in Computer Science and Control). The development was mainly led by Francois Delebecque and Serge Steer with the purpose of providing an easy to use and an advanced software tool for the researchers in Automatic Control Systems. They were inspired by the versatility and power of Matlab, a commercial technical computing language, developed by Cleve Moler of the Math Works, Inc. At the beginning of 1990's Balise was renamed as Scilab. Further development of Scilab was jointly carried out by researchers from INRIA and ENPC (National School of Bridges and Roads, France). They formed the Scilab Group who's members were Jean-Philippe Chancelier, Francois Delebecque, Claude Gomez, Maurice Gaursat, Ramine Nikoukhah and Serge Steer. In 1994, INRIA decided to distribute Scilab as a free open source software package. With this, the popularity of Scilab increased, and a large number of industries and academic institutions have shown their interest in Scilab. Considering this, in 2003, the Scilab Consortium (http://scilabsoft.inria.fr/consortium/consortium.html) was created for the rapid and sustained development of Scilab. In 2010, Scilab Enterprises Company was founded with the support of INRIA to guarantee the future of Scilab. Now Scilab Enterprises offers professional services and support on Scilab and is fully responsible for its further development under open source business model. The latest version of Scilab can be downloaded from www.scilab.org for various platforms.

Scilab is a very powerful programming language with a very rich library of scientific and engineering functions. From the software point of view, it is an interpreted programming language. It provides an Integrated Development Environment (IDE) for programming and supports features and programming constructs that are commonly available in general purpose programming languages like java, C and C++. It also has easy to use built-in tools for creating Graphical User Interfaces (GUI) for Scilab applications. Further, Scilab facilitates faster applications development as users can directly access its library functions and seamlessly embed them into their applications. The Scilab language is designed in such a way that its users can easily extend its capabilities by creating new user-defined data types and writing new library functions as per their requirements. It also allows dynamic interfacing with other programming languages such as C, C++, FORTRAN and Java. These interfacing capabilities facilitate use of external libraries as built-in features of Scilab.

Figure 1.1 shows the main features and capabilities of Scilab software. It has excellent and extensive built-in tools for linear algebra computations, data analysis and statistics, 2-D and 3-D visualisations, control systems design and analysis, signal processing, optimisation, numerical solutions of ordinary differential equations, dynamic systems modelling and simulation and many more. All the built-in tools use state of the art algorithms. Further, users can develop their own functions with the help of the programming environment provided in Scilab. There are several optional toolboxes available from various Scilab developers for specific applications, which can be downloaded free of cost from their websites. These toolboxes are collections of functions written for specific applications, such as image processing, control system design, statistics, neural network, fuzzy logic and many more. The list of toolboxes is growing with time. Scilab can be easily interfaced with the LabVIEW software, a visual programming language from National Instruments, for rapid development of applications in instrumentations and other related areas.

1.2 Installing Scilab

It is very easy to install Scilab on your computer. For this, you can download Scilab binaries directly from the Scilab homepage http://www.scilab.org for some popular operating systems, such as Windows, Linux, etc., for both 32-bit and 64-bit versions. For advanced users and developers, the source code of Scilab can also be downloaded from the website, which can be compiled using a C++ compiler to create the binary for a specific platform. To compile the Scilab source code, a set of prerequisite binary files is required, which can be downloaded from the

Scilab website. For more details about compiling the source code, users can consult the Scilab website.

1.2.1. Installing Scilab under Windows

The various versions of Scilab are distributed as a self extracting Windows binary application, which automatically installs the application on the user's computer. During the installation, options for a language selection and an installation location are requested from the user. By default, English language is selected and the program is installed in the folder **C:\Program Files\scilab-5.4.1** (Your Scilab version may be different).

1.2.2. Installing Scilab under Linux

For Linux operating system, the binary version is available as a .tar.gz file, which can be unzipped in a target folder. To install Scilab, locate the binary file in the **<path>/scilab-5.x.x/bin/Scilab** and execute it to start Scilab. The console under Linux is exactly the same as it appears in Windows. Scilab is also available as a package and can be installed as a standard Linux package.

1.2.3. Installing Scilab under Mac OS

For Mac OS, the binary versions are available as a .dmg file. Scilab is installed by using the Mac OS installer. The console under Mac OS is also exactly the same as it appears in Windows.

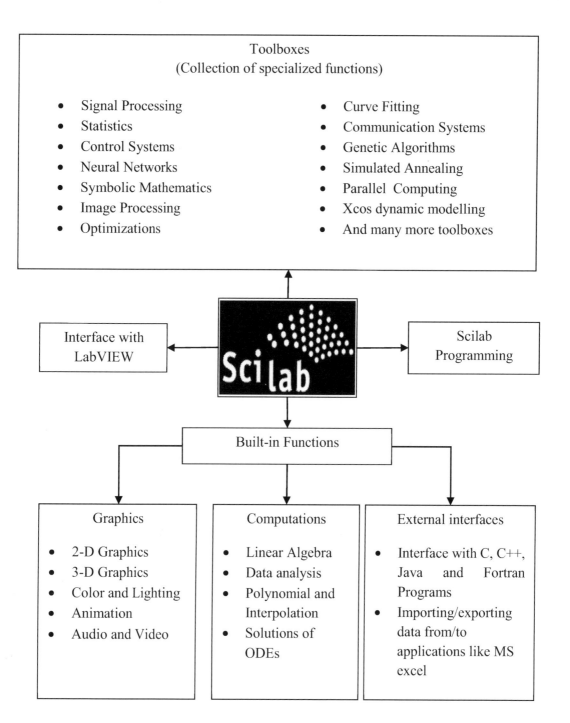

Fig. 1.1: Schematic diagram of the Scilab's main features

1.2.4. Installing/Uninstalling toolboxes

To include the functionalities of the new developments in various areas of science and technology, new toolboxes, also called packages, are being developed for inclusion in Scilab. To facilitate rapid development, Scilab maintains an updated repository for all Scilab external modules ("Toolboxes") and provides an easy mechanism, called **ATOMS** (AuTomatic mOdules Management for Scilab), to install required new toolboxes in Scilab. Following are the two ways to install new toolboxes:

(a) Installation with Internet connection

On a computer with an Internet connection, the following steps are used to install a package:
1. Launch Scilab
2. Click Applications-> Module Manager-ATOMS in the Menu Bar
3. Click on All modules -ATOMS on the left window. This will populate the left window with all the available modules.
4. Select the module and click Install.
5. Close Scilab and restart. The module is loaded now.

(b) Installation without Internet connection

On a computer without internet connection, a new toolbox can be installed from the compiled binary file, which can be directly downloaded from the website **http://atoms.scilab.org/**, of the toolbox with the help of the **atomsInstall** command. For example, the command **atomsInstall ("E:\Download\CPGE_1.0-1.bin.zip")** installs CPGE toolbox in Scilab. The binary of the toolbox is directly downloaded and stored at the specified path.

Installed toolboxes can be removed from Scilab with the **Remove** option of **Applications-> Module Manager-ATOMS**, once the installed toolbox is selected. Alternatively, with the help of the **atomsRemove command**, an installed toolbox can be removed. For example, the command **atomsRemove (["toolbox_4" "1.0"]);** removes version 1.0 of the toolbox_4. If the version is not specified, all versions of the toolbox are removed. For example, the command **atomsRemove (["toolbox_4"]);** removes all versions of the toolbox toolbox_4. The **atomsGetInstalled** command lists all the installed toolboxes of Scilab in the console window.

1.3 Starting and Ending a Scilab Session

Once Scilab is properly installed on a window based computer, a Scilab session can be started either through the start menu or using the shortcut of Scilab on the desktop. To start a Scilab session through the start menu, the following steps are used:

1. Click on the 'start' button on the computer desktop (mostly located at the lower left corner)
2. Select the option 'All Programs' which in turn will show all the programs installed on the computer.
3. Select Scilab-5.4.1 from the displayed options (your version may be different depending on which version you have installed).
4. Next, select either the Scilab console mode or the Scilab window mode. In the console mode, no GUI interface is available, whereas in the window mode full GUI support is available. For the beginners, it is recommended to use the window mode as it is easy to use and all the help is available on just a mouse click. In this book, the window mode is used to write the examples. The advantage of the console mode is its execution speed, but it requires users to remember all the commands.

The Scilab-5.4.1 icon, a shortcut on the computer desktop, can be used to start a Scilab session in the window mode by double clicking. A Scilab session can also be started by double clicking on any Scilab generated file, such as .sci or .sce (these extensions are explained in later chapters) and opens the concerned window. Figure 1.2(a) shows a Scilab session in the console mode, and Figure 1.2(b) shows a Scilab session in the window mode, in their default forms.

To end a Scilab session, select the **File/Quit'(or File->quit)** option from the dropdown menu in the Scilab menu bar, type **'quit'** or **'exit'** in the command Window at the command prompt, or click on the close button of the Scilab main window.

1.4 Scilab Environment

Scilab provides an integrated environment for all the activities that can be performed in Scilab. The environment consists of the following major components:
- Console window
- Command History window
- Variable Brower window
- File Brower window
- Graphics window
- SciNotes window

Figure 1.2(b) shows the default Scilab environment which consists of a Console window, File Brower window, Variable Brower window and Command History window. The Graphics window is used by Scilab to show various types of plots and is opened by Scilab automatically when it is needed. The SciNotes window is used to write Scilab programs. Scilab uses Flexdock concept to manage its environment. The Flexdock system allows dragging and dropping a source window at various positions, such as the top, bottom, left, and right positions in the target window. All the windows in Scilab are dockable and can be resized and repositioned on the desktop, as desired by a user.

Fig. 1.2(a): The initial default screen of Scilab in the Console mode

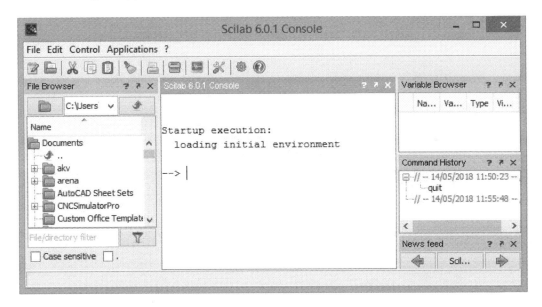

Fig. 1.2(b): The initial default screen of Scilab in the window mode

These windows can be docked in the main window of Scilab or can be undocked and made to float outside the main window on the desktop. Figure 1.3 shows all the Scilab windows docked in the main window, and the individual windows are highlighted using their names in the dashed rectangles. Any window of Scilab can be chosen to be the target window and all the other windows can be docked into it. In order to dock one window into another, drag the source window into the target window. To do this, click and hold down the left mouse button on the title bar of the source window (Figure 1.4(b)) and before releasing the mouse, move the mouse pointer over the target window (Figure 1.4(a)). During the window docking process, when the mouse is moved over the target window, a dotted window, called phantom window, would show the docking position of the source window in the target window depending upon the location of the mouse pointer. Move around the mouse pointer at various locations in the target window to select the desired docking position and then release the mouse button. Figure 1.4 shows the docking process of the SciNotes window into the Console window. To undock a window, simply click on the round arrow in the title bar of the concerned window as indicated in Figure 1.4(c). To close a docked window, click on the cross in the title bar of the concerned window as indicated in Figure 1.4(c). The Flexdock system also has the facilities to create tabbed windows, which can be achieved by releasing the source window over the centre of the target window. The tabbed Console and SciNotes windows are shown in Figure 1.4(d). To remove a tabbed window from the tab, click and drag the concerned tab and release it at any dockable position. It is also possible to have some windows docked and the other windows tabbed in the same target window.

1.4.1. Console window

The Console window is the most widely used window of Scilab. It is the main interface between a user and Scilab to interactively use the vast library of built-in functions and features of Scilab. It also shows the results of any activity performed in Scilab. The Console window has a command prompt, shown as '-->', and a cursor where commands are typed and executed instantaneously on pressing the 'Enter key' of the keyboard. For example, if we want to evaluate the expression '**10 * 5 - 7**', it is typed at the command prompt and evaluated on pressing the enter key. If the result of an expression is not assigned to any variable, Scilab uses '**ans**' as a default variable to store the result. However, it is a better practice to assign the result of a command to a variable. For example, in the statement '**r=10 * 5 – 7**', the result is assigned to the variable '**r**'. By default, Scilab displays the result of every expression it executes, but the display of the result can be suppressed by putting a semi-colon (**;**) at the end of the expression, such as '**r = 10 * 5 - 7;** '. These are illustrated in Figure 1.5.

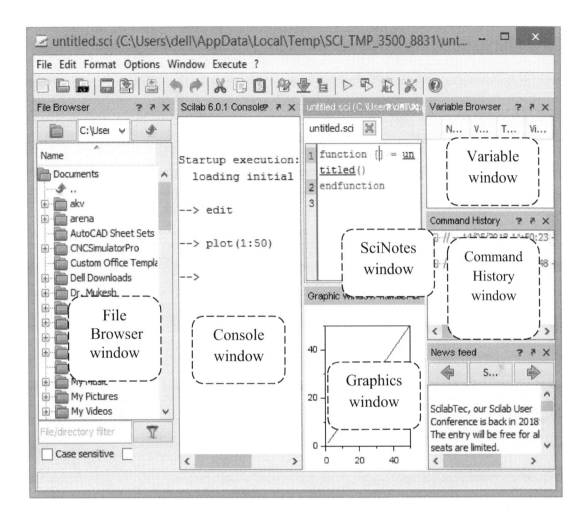

Fig. 1.3: Various Scilab windows docked in the main window

1.4.2. Command History window

The Command History window maintains a list of all the commands entered in the Console window of Scilab. The list is maintained for all the previous Scilab sessions till a user clears the list. The list is separated by date and session for easy reference. Any command listed in the Command History window can be executed by double clicking on it. A group of contiguous commands can be selected by first clicking the left mouse button on a command and then holding the SHIFT key and clicking again on another command. The commands in between these two clicks will be selected. Similarly, non-contiguous commands can be selected by holding the

CTRL key and clicking on commands to be selected one by one. Kindly note, in case of non-contiguous selection, the clicking sequence is important, and commands will be processed in that sequence only. Once the commands are selected from the Command History window, it can be evaluated in the console window by the right click on the selection and selecting **'Evaluate Selection'** option in the popup menu. The popup menu has an **'Edit in SciNotes'** option to create a Scilab program from the selected commands which can be saved and edited as a normal Scilab program and executed later on in the console window. Further, there are options for **Copy, Cut, Delete** and **Clear History** in the popup menu. All the above tasks can be also performed through the Edit option of the main menu of the Command History window as shown in Figure 1.6. All the commands present in the Command History window can be selected by using CTRL+ A (press and hold CTRL key and then press 'A' key). The Command History window along with the pop-up menu is shown in Figure 1.6. The Command History window can be reset using the command **'resetHistory'** in the console window.

1.4.3. Variable Browser window

The Variable Browser window maintains a list of the active variables (variables created but not cleared by the user) in the current session. For every variable, the Variable Browser window stores the name, dimensions, type and visibility of the variable (more about these aspects of a variable in the next chapter). The Variable Browser window is shown in Figure 1.7(a). All the commands executed from the console command prompt and script files executed from the console share these variables. The contents of a variable can be edited directly by double clicking the variable, which opens a Variable Edit window. The Variable Edit window shows the contents of the variable and provides facilities to edit it as shown in Figure 1.7(b). It also has options to show the data in different formats, such as short format, short scientific format, long format and long scientific format. It also provides commands to create a new variable, create a new variable from the selected part of the current data, create a duplicate of the current variable and export the contents of the variable as comma separated values (CSV). There is also a facility to plot the complete contents or the selected portion of the contents of the current variable in different plotting styles. The operations that can be performed on a variable within this window are shown in Figure 1.7(b).

1.4.4. File Browser window

The File Browser window allows the user to browse the files and directories of the system directly from within the Scilab environment. This is an easy to use file browser with additional options like open a file in SciNotes, execute or load a program in Scilab, open a model with Xcos, etc. It also provides facilities for batch operations that can be performed on a set of files in one go. There is a powerful filtering facility to easily locate files and folders. Further, there is an option for the files, not relevant to Scilab, to be opened with the relevant default applications installed on the computer. Figure 1.8 shows the File Browser window and operations that can be performed in it.

1.4.5. SciNotes window

The SciNotes is a powerful built-in editor of Scilab. It is used to create new or edit existing Scilab programs. It uses different colours to highlight various features, such as keywords, functions, constants, etc., for enhanced visibility and readability. Users can customize colours of the features in the editor through the preference menu as per his/her choice and preferences. Figure 1.9 shows a SciNotes window along with the main operations that can be performed in it. The complete program or the selected portion of a program or the program up-to the caret can be executed from the SciNotes window.

The SciNotes automatically indent programs as per the setting and has auto complete option to increase the program coding speed. The indentation of a previously written program can also be corrected automatically for better legibility.

1.4.6. Graphics window

Graphics windows are used to show the output of all the commands that generate some sort of graphics. Figure 1.10(a) shows a Graphics window, which is created by the following Scilab commands:

```
x = 0: 0.05 : 20
y = sin (x)
plot (x, y)
```

The Graphics window provides many features, such as editing, zooming, rotation, etc., of the plot. As per the requirements of an application, a number of graphics windows can be opened simultaneously. Each window can be edited independently, or a common style can be applied to all of them. The Graphics window provides very elaborate editing facilities as shown in Figure 1.10(b).The Graphics Edit window of a figure, such as Figure 1.10(b), can be opened from the edit menu option of the Graphics window. Readers are encouraged to explore the editing facilities to improve the presentation quality of the images.

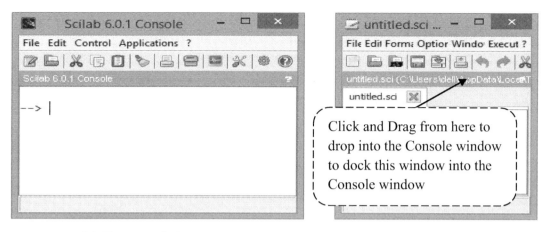

(a) Target window

(b) Source window

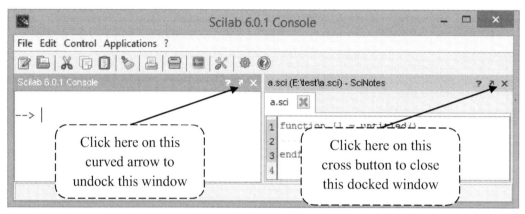

(c) SciNotes window docked into the Console window

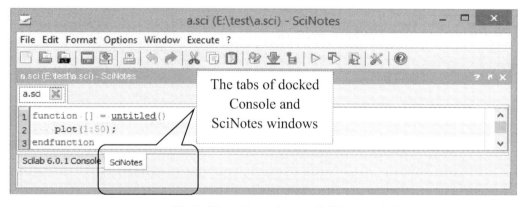

(d) Tabbed Console and SciNotes windows

Fig. 1.4: Docking of windows in Scilab

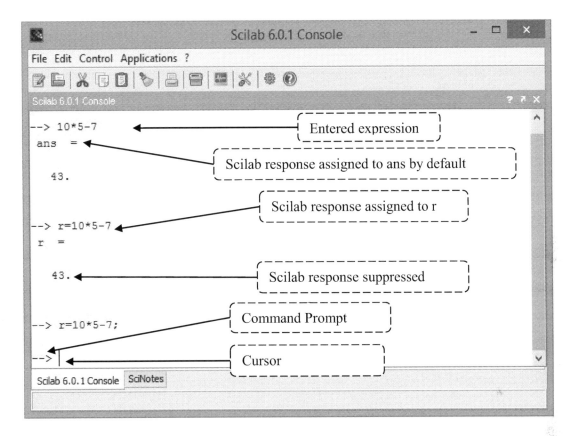

Fig. 1.5: Console window

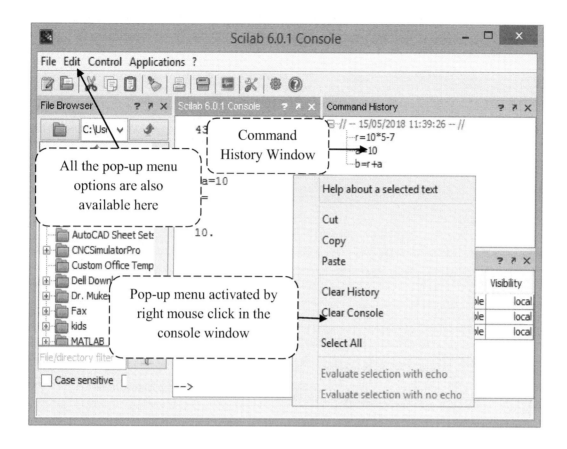

Fig. 1.6: Command History window

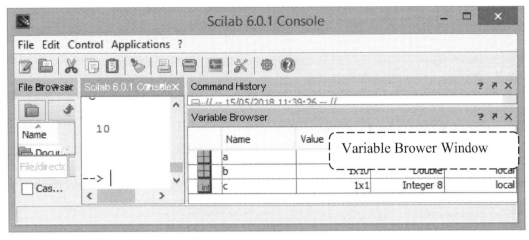

(a) Variable Browser window

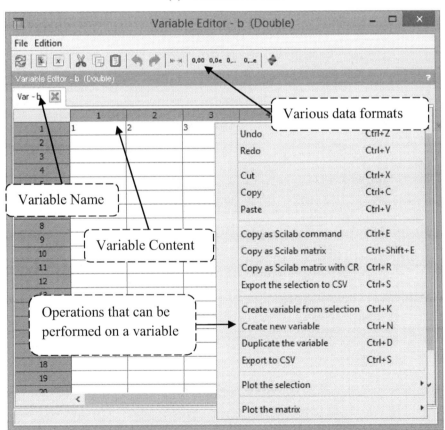

(b) Variable Editor window

Fig. 1.7: Variable Browser window and Variable Editor window

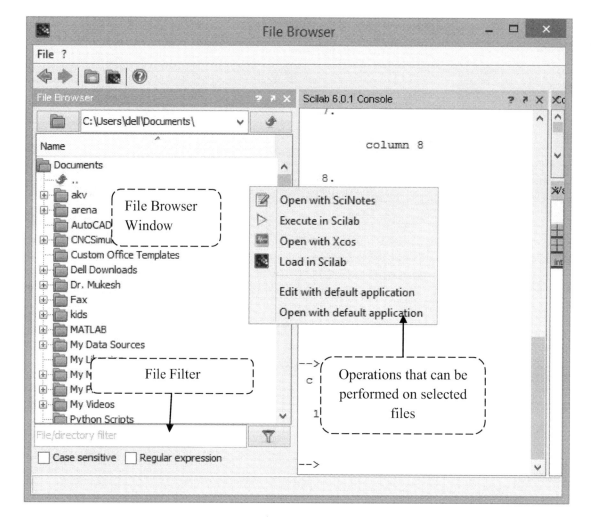

Fig. 1.8: File Browser window

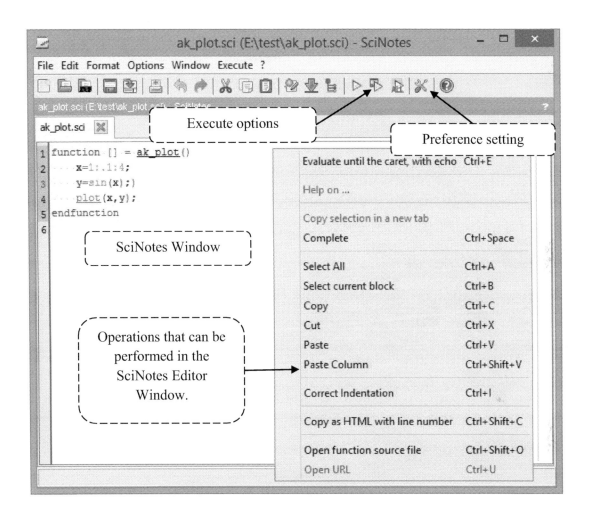

Fig. 1.9: SciNotes editor

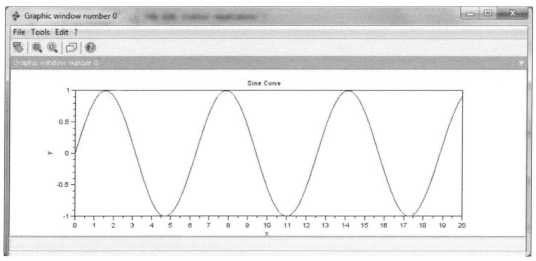

(a) Graphics window

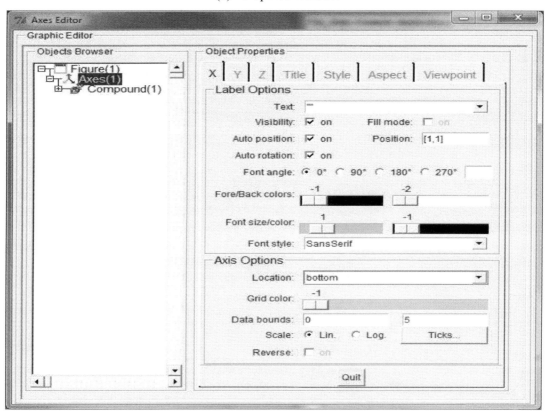

(b) Image editing facilities of the Graphics window
Fig. 1.10: Graphics Edit window

1.5 Getting Help in Scilab

Scilab has a comprehensive help facility for every command, feature and function. The help can be accessed through the help browser that can be opened by clicking on the toolbar button with a question mark on it or by typing *help* at the console command prompt. Figure 1.11 shows the opening screen of the help browser. The help related to a specific command can be obtained by typing help *<command name>* at the command prompt. For example, to get help about the *sin* command, type *help sin* at the console command prompt. Figure 1.12 shows the Scilab help for the **sin** command. Scilab gives description of the command along with a few examples and a list of other related commands. Most of the time, the information provided is sufficient to use the command effectively. However, further help can be obtained from the official Scilab website and various Scilab user's forums.

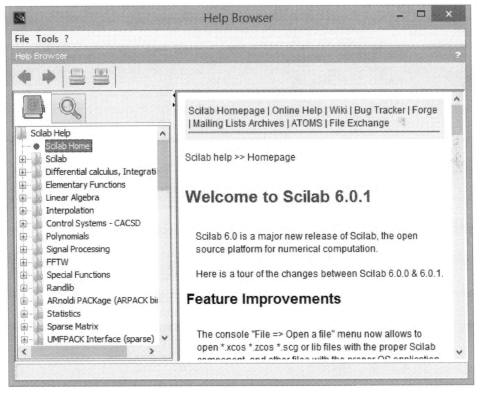

Fig. 1.11: Help browser

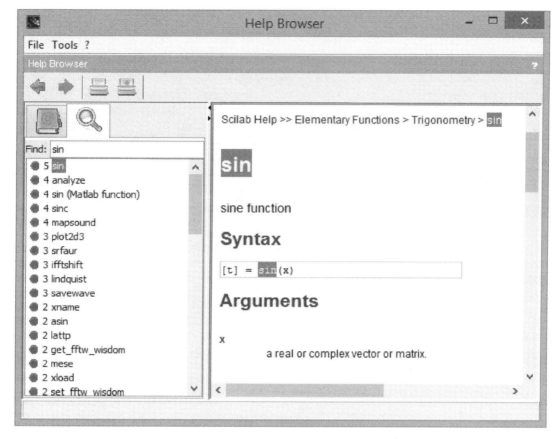

Fig. 1.12: Help about the sin command

1.6 Some Useful Scilab Commands

Some of the commonly used Scilab commands for managing the Scilab environment are listed in Table 1.1. For detailed list of Scilab commands, refer Appendix I.

Table 1.1: Commonly used Scilab commands

A. Date and Time commands	
calendar	Generates calendar of the given year and month.
clock	Returns current time as a date vector.
date	Returns current date as a date string.
datenum	Converts the given date into a serial date number.
now	Returns current date under the form of Unix hour (timestamp).
sleep	Suspends Scilab for the specified time.

tic	Starts a stopwatch timer.
timer	Returns the CPU elapsed time between the current and the previous timer call.
toc	Reads the stopwatch timer.
B. Directory Management Commands	
cd	Changes current directory.
createdir, mkdir	Makes a new directory.
dir or ls	Lists files/directories of the specified path.
isdir	Checks if argument is a directory path.
pwd	Gets current directory.
removedir or rmdir	Removes a directory.
C. Workspace commands	
clear	Kills all the variables of the current Scilab session.
clearglobal	Kills all the global variables of the current Scilab session.
exists or isdef	Checks variable existence in the current workspace.
isglobal	Checks if the specified variable is global.
who	Lists all the variables in the current Scilab session.
who_user	Lists all the user created variables of the current Scilab session.
whos	Lists all the variables in long form.
D. Scilab Termination commands	
quit	Terminates the current Scilab session without confirmation pop-up.
exit or CTRL+Q	Terminates the current Scilab session with confirmation pop-up.

Summary

- Scilab, open source software for high performance numerical computation, visualisation and powerful technical programming language, is widely used for academic and commercial researches. It is used as a substitute to many similar commercial software.
- Scilab is available for all the popular operating systems, such as Windows and Linux, for both 32 bit and 64 bit versions.
- Scilab includes many application specific toolboxes, such as image processing, neural network, etc. Many new toolboxes are being developed by a strong community of Scilab programmers and users.
- New toolboxes can be installed/uninstalled with the help of ATOMS.
- Scilab can be used as a high end scientific and technical calculator and high level technical programming language.

- Scilab provides an integrated environment for all the activities that can be performed in Scilab. The environment consists of the following major components: Console, Command History, Variable Brower, File Brower, Graphics and SciNotes windows.

Key Terms

- ATOMS
- **atomsInstall()**
- **atomsRemove()**
- built-in tools
- Command History window
- Command prompt
- dynamic interfacing
- engineering and scientific applications
- File Brower window
- Flexdock
- Graphical User Interface
- Graphics window

- **help**
- installing Scilab
- Integrated Development Environment
- interactive computation
- numerical computations
- open source
- packages
- SciNotes window
- toolboxes
- Variable Brower window
- workspace

Exercise Problems

1.1 Describe the major components of Scilab.
1.2 Describe the procedure to install Scilab on a Window Machine.
1.3 What do you mean by workspace? How will you see the list of variables available in the current workspace?
1.4 Describe the uses of the History browser window.
1.5 Explain various ways to get help about commands in Scilab.
1.6 What is the purpose of the current directory? Describe processes to change the current directory in Scilab.
1.7 What is the purpose of toolboxes? How will you install a new toolbox?

Chapter 2
Basics of Scilab

Learning Objectives
- Data types supported by Scilab
- Predefined constants
- Variable naming rules
- Operators
- Expression types and their evaluation
- Hierarchy of operators

2.1 Introduction

Scilab is a very powerful, interactive computing tool along with a very rich and easy to use programming language. In interactive mode, Scilab can be used as a scientific calculator to solve various problems, whereas as a programming language, it can be used to write computer programs to solve complex scientific problems. Scilab has a large number of built-in features for solving scientific problems. Firstly, it has a very powerful matrix and vector notations (i.e. matrices and vectors are treated and processed like simple variables without using loops. For example, the multiplication of two matrices A and B can be calculated simply as C=A*B) that makes the Scilab program compact, concise and easy to write and understand. Secondly, all memory management (i.e. memory allocation and memory release during the program execution) are automatically handled by the Scilab memory manager. Finally, it contains a huge collection of built-in functions for various scientific computations. To make effective use of Scilab, this chapter introduces its basics: character set, data types, constants and variables, operators, built-in functions and syntax rules. The basic familiarity of these rules is essential to write commands in interactive mode and to write computer programs.

2.2 Character Set

The character set of Scilab consists of alphabets, digits, special characters and white spaces. Each English alphabet (both capital and small case) is a valid character in Scilab. Further, Scilab is a case sensitive programming language, which means, small case letters are different than corresponding capital letters and are recognised as different symbols. The numeric digits (0 – 9), the special characters (brackets, comma, semicolon, dot, etc.) and the white spaces (space, tab and carriage return) are valid symbols. Table 2.1 shows the valid character set of Scilab.

Table 2.1 : Character set of Scilab

Alphabets	A-Z and a-z
Numerals	0-9
Special Characters	comma, semicolon, dot, [,], (,), {, }, <, >, ?, /, \, +, -, *, &, ^, % , $, #, @, !, ~,single quote('), double quote(")
White Spaces	Space, tab, carriage return

2.3 Data Types

Scilab has a variety of data types to optimize the accuracy, speed and resource requirements for different types of applications. Further, every data type allows storing the data in the form of an array. The array can be of single element, or it can be of n-dimension. The size of an array is only limited by the available stack memory in the computer. By default, the size of the stack is 10,000,000 and can be extended up to 268,435,454 (on 64 bit platforms). The two dimensional version of an array is called matrix in Scilab. Scilab is designed to efficiently process numeric data, complex data and strings. Along with the numeric and string data, it also supports cell and structure data types. Figure 2.1 shows the various data types supported by Scilab. The numeric data type is the most widely used data type in Scilab that includes integer, real and complex types.

2.3.1 Integer data type

In Scilab, integers are further classified as int8, int16, int32, uint8, uint16 and uint32. The number suffixed to an integer type indicates the number of bits used by it to store data. For example, int8 uses eight bits to store data. Similarly, **'u'** is prefixed before an integer type to indicate unsigned numbers. For example, the command **y=uint8(x)** converts the value of a real number **x** into an appropriate unsigned eight bit integer and stores it into **y**. The range of values that an integer type can hold is directly linked with the number of bits it uses to store data. The range of a signed integer type is determined by the expression $[-2^{n-1}, 2^{n-1} - 1]$, and the range of an unsigned integer type is determined by the expression $[0, 2^n - 1]$, where **n** is the number of bits used for its storage. Table 2.2 shows the range of valid values of the various integer types along with the Scilab built-in functions to create them. Programmers should carefully choose a correct type of integers for their problems as unnecessarily large size type may reduce the computational speed and increase storage requirements. However, too small size integer type may result into loss of the data. There are built-in functions which allow conversion of one integer type to another integer type as listed in Table 2.2. The **inttype(x)** function can be used to inquire about the type of an integer variable **x**. Table 2.3 shows integer values returned by the **inttype** function for various types of integers.

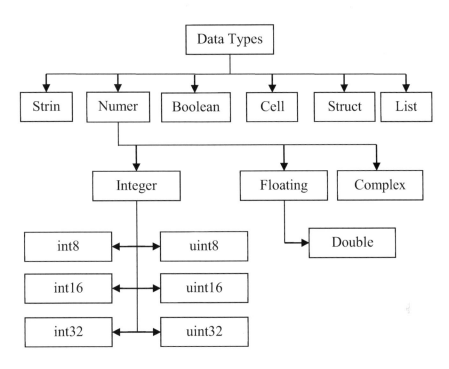

Figure 2.1 shows the various data types supported by Scilab

Table 2.2 : Range of valid values of various numeric data types

Integer Type	Range of valid values	Storage size in bytes	Scilab function
int8	[-128, 127]	1	int8(x)
uint8	[0, 255]	1	uint8(x)
int16	[-32768, 32767]	2	int16(x)
uint16	[0, 65535]	2	uint16(x)
int32	[-2147483648, 2147483647]	4	int32(x)
uint32	[0, 4294967295]	4	uint32(x)

Table 2.3: Types of integers returned by the inttype function

Value returned by inttype(x)	Type of integer
1	8-bit signed integer
2	16-bit signed integer
4	32-bit signed integer
11	8-bit unsigned integer
12	16-bit unsigned integer
14	32-bit unsigned integer

When two integers are added, the types of both the operands are analyzed. Scilab uses the larger integer type out of the two to store the result of computation to avoid any loss of data (see Example 2.1). This concept is applicable to all the binary arithmetic operators. However, if both the operands are of the same type, the result will also be of the same type even though it may result into a loss of data. This is illustrated in Example 2.2, in which two int8 variables "i" and "j" with value **125** each are added, and the result is assigned to a variable 'r'. Although the correct result of the operation is **250,** but Scilab assigns **-6** to the variable **"r"**. This is due to the way Scilab evaluates expressions and assigns data type to the result. In this case, the result is stored in a variable **"r"** that is assigned int8 type by Scilab as both the operands are of int8 type. This results into the incorrect result (**-6**) due to loss of some data (the range of an int8 type integer is [-128, 127]).

The behaviour of integers at the range boundaries deserves a special attention as it differs from software to software. In Scilab, the behaviour is circular, that is, if the largest integer is incremented by one, the result is the lowest integer of the given integer type range. For example, **int8 (127) +int8 (1)** results into **-128**. Similarly, **uint8 (255) + uint8 (1)** results into **0**. This circular behaviour is applicable to all the integer types. This is in contrast with the other mathematical packages, such as Matlab, in which an integer at the upper limit does not change after the increment. For example, in Matlab, **uint8 (255) + uint8 (1) = 255**. Due to this differing treatment of integers at the boundary, users should be careful when converting a program written in one package to the other.

Another important feature of Scilab is floating point integers. By default, Scilab stores every numeric variable or constant (including integral values) as a 64 bit double floating number. This helps in storing the integers in the range $[-2^{52}, 2^{52}]$ (known as safe range in Scilab) accurately without loss of any digit. Further, all the default integer computations falling in the range $[-2^{52}, 2^{52}]$ are exact. The computations outside the safe range are not exact. These features are illustrated in Scilab Example 2.3. Comments are added into the code for easy comprehension.

Example 2.1

```
-->i= int8 (1)
i =
1
--> inttype (i)
ans =
1.
-->j= int16 (2)
j =
2
--> inttype (j)
ans =
2.
-->k=i+j
k =
3
--> inttype (k)
ans =
2.
```

Example 2.2

```
-->i=int8(125)
i =
125
-->inttype(i)
ans =
1.
-->j=int8(125)
j =
125
-->inttype(j)
ans =
1.
-->r=i+j
r =
-6
-->inttype(r)
ans =
1.
```

Example 2.3

```
// Safe range example
--> format (25)  //Sets display format to show the first 25 digits of a variable or a constant
-->a= 2^40 - 12
a =
1099511627764.   // A very large number that can not be stored in any Scilab integer type
-->b= 2^45 + 3
b =
35184372088835. // Another very large number
-->c = a + b
c =
36283883716599. //Exact result as the result is within the safe limits.

// Outside safe range example
```

```
--> format (25)
- - >(2^53 + (1:5)) '  //2^53 is outside the safe range
ans =
  9007199254740992.
  9007199254740994.
  9007199254740996.
  9007199254740996.
  9007199254740996.
// above results are unexpected and wrong as all the numbers are even despite the
//addition of some even and odd number pairs.
```

2.3.2 Real data type

Scilab only supports double precision real numbers and uses IEEE 754 standard to represent them. The term precision refers to the number of decimal digits accurately calculated in an expression and stored in a variable. In Scilab, all the real number calculations are carried out with a minimum 15 decimal places accuracy. Table 2.4 shows the range of the real data type.

Table 2.4 : Real number

Type	Valid Range	Storage size in bytes	Scilab Function
Double	[$\pm 2.23 \times 10^{-308}$ to $\pm 1.80 \times 10^{+308}$]	8	double(x)

2.3.3 Complex data type

In engineering and scientific problems, complex numbers are widely used. To cater these needs, Scilab is designed to process complex numbers as efficiently as real number computations. Scilab stores a complex number as an ordered pair of two floating point numbers. The first number represents the real component, and the second represents the imaginary component of a complex number. The predefined variable '**%i**' represents the mathematical imaginary number "*i*" (iota) which satisfies $i^2 = -1$. The complex number **2 + *i* 3** can be created by the command **a= 2+ 3 * %i** , **a= 2 + %i * 3** or **a =complex (2, 3)**. Table 2.5 lists some functions commonly used to manage complex numbers. Example 2.4 shows the applications of these functions. Most of the elementary mathematical functions of Scilab are overloaded to process complex numbers.

Table 2.5: Commonly used functions for handling complex numbers

Function	Purpose of the function
complex(a, b)	To create a complex number with 'a' as its real part and 'b' as its imaginary part.
real(x)	To get the real part of a complex number.
imag (x)	To get the imaginary part of a complex number.
imult(x)	Efficiently multiplies a complex number by i *(iota)*.
isreal(x)	Returns true if 'x' is a real number and returns false if 'x' is a complex number.
conj(x)	To get the complex conjugate of a complex number.

Example 2.4 : Creating and processing complex numbers

```
-->x=1+%i    // Creates a complex variable, x
 x  =
    1. + i
-->y=complex(2,3) // Creates a complex variable, y
 y  =
    2. + 3.i
-->isreal(x)   // Tests whether the variable x is a complex variable or a real variable
 ans  =
  F
-->real(x)  // Gets the real part of the complex variable x
 ans  =
    1.
-->imag(x) // Gets the imaginary part of the complex variable x
 ans  =
    1.
-->imult(y) // Multiplication of i with the complex variable y
 ans  =
  - 3. + 2.i
-->conj(y)  // Gets the complex conjugate of the complex variable y
 ans  =
    2. - 3.i
```

2.3.4 Boolean data type

Boolean data type is designed to store and process logical true or false values. In Scilab, logical true is represented with **%t** or **%T** and false with **%f** or **%F**. Boolean variables can be created by either assigning them Boolean values or executing logical expressions. For example, the expression **b=%T** creates a Boolean variable **b** with true value. Similarly, the expression **b= 10>15** creates a Boolean variable **b** with false value. Numerically, **%T** is equal to **1**; **%F** is equal to **0**. Boolean variables can be used in arithmetic expressions.

2.3.5 String data type

In Scilab, a group of characters written within a pair of doublequotes (") or a pair of singlequotes (') is a string. For example, "Scilab is a very powerful technical computing system." and ' It is widely used by Scientists and Engineers for Technical and Scientific computations.' are examples of strings. Like any other data types, a number of strings can also be stored in a matrix form. Strings can be joined together by using the concatenation operator ("+"). For example, the expression *"String 1" + " String 2"* evaluates to *"String 1 String 2"*. Scilab provides a number of functions to process strings. Commonly used string processing functions are shown in Table 2.6. Example 2.5 shows a few illustrative examples of use of these functions. The comment lines are added in the examples for easy comprehension and elucidation.

Table 2.6 : String processing functions

Function	Purpose of the function
string(x)	Converts a matrix of any data type to a matrix of string type.
strsplit(s)	Splits a string into a vector of character strings.
length(s)	Returns number of characters in the argument string. If the argument is a matrix of strings, it will return a matrix of the number of characters in the corresponding string in the matrix. For the other data types, it will simply return the number of elements in the matrix.
part(s, r1: r2)	Extracts the part of the string "s" from the index **r1** to **r2**.
evstr(s)	Evaluates the string "s" as a Scilab script and returns the result.
execstr(s)	Executes the string "s" as a Scilab script and does not return the result.
strsubst (s,s1,s2)	Searches the string "**s1**" into the string "s" and substitutes it with the string "**s2**".
strcat(s)	Concatenates all the entries of the string matrix "s" into a single string.
strindex(s,s1)	Searches the occurrences of the string "**s1**" in the string "s" and returns the positions of its occurrences from the start.

Example 2.5: String processing

```
//Create a matrix of random numbers of size 2x2 and convert it to a matrix of strings.
-->s=string(rand(2,2)) // String matrices are shown using the exclamation mark(!)
 s  =
!0.3616361  0.5664249  !
!                      !
!0.2922267  0.4826472  !
-->length(s)  //Calculates the number of characters in each string of the matrix "s"
 ans  =
   9.  9.
   9.  9.
-->strcat(s)  //Concatenates each string of the matrix "s" into a single string
 ans  =
 0.36163610.29222670.56642490.4826472
-->s1=strsubst(ans,"0.",", 0.") // Replaces "0." with ",0." in the string 'ans'
 s1  =
 , 0.3616361, 0.2922267, 0.5664249, 0.4826472
-->length(s1)  // Calculates the number of characters in the string 's1'
 ans  =
   44.
-->s2=part(s1,2:44) //Extracts the part of the string s1 from the 2nd character to the 44th character
 s2  =
  0.3616361, 0.2922267, 0.5664249, 0.4826472
-->strindex(s2,",") //Gets the locations of the occurrences of the string "," in the string 's2'
 ans  =
   10.  21.  32.
-->evstr("1+2")  // Evaluates the string "1+2" as a Scilab expression and return the result
 ans  =
   3.
-->execstr("a=1+2") // Executes the expression "1+2" and store the result in the variable 'a'
```

2.4 Constants and Variables

2.4.1 Constants

Constants refer to fixed values that do not change during the execution of a program. Scilab supports various types of constants such as string, integer, real and Boolean constants. Table 2.7 shows various types of constants along with some illustrative examples. For the purpose of display only, integers can also be shown in the binary, octal and hexadecimal formats. Table 2.8 shows the Scilab functions for converting decimal integers into other formats and vice-versa along with some illustrative examples. However, all the calculations in Scilab are carried out in the decimal form of the integers, and other integer forms cannot be directly used in calculations. The **string** function can be used to convert any data type to the string format representation.

Scilab has some predefined constants which are shown in Table 2.9. It is strongly recommended that these predefined symbolic constant names should not be used for any other purpose, such as naming variables or naming functions, in a program.

Table 2.7 : Types of Constants

Constant type	Description	Examples
String	Anything written between a pair of doublequotes (") or a pair of singlequotes (') is a string.	'Scilab', "programming tool"
Integer	Whole numbers are integer constants.	12, 100
Double	Numbers with a fraction and a decimal point are double numbers. The double can be written either in the simple form or in the scientific form. Letters **'e', 'E','d' or 'D'** can be used in the scientific form.	10.5, 1.23e10, 2.25d-2
Complex	In Scilab, a complex number is in the form of "**real+%i*img**" or "**real+img*%i**", where "**real**" and "**img**" are two real numbers and represent the real and the imaginary part of the complex number respectively. Mathematically, **%i** represents $\sqrt{-1}$.	10+%i*20, 2.3+%i*5.2 10+20*%i
Boolean	There are only two Boolean constant TRUE and FALSE. The symbol **%t** or **%T** represents TRUE and **%f** or **%F** FALSE.	%t, %f

Table 2.8: Conversion of integers from one form of representation to the other

Function name	Description	Example
str=dec2bin(n)	Converts a decimal integer to the equivalent binary string	-->str=dec2bin(100) str = 1100100
str=dec2oct(n)	Converts a decimal integer to the equivalent octal string	-->str=dec2oct(100) str = 144
str=dec2hex(n)	Converts a decimal integer to the equivalent hexadecimal string	-->str=dec2hex(100) str = 64
n=bin2dec(str)	Converts a valid binary string to the equivalent decimal integer	-->str=bin2dec('110010') str = 50.
n=oct2dec(str)	Converts a valid octal string to the equivalent decimal integer	-->str=oct2dec('62') str = 50.
n=hex2dec(str)	Converts a valid hexadecimal string to the equivalent decimal integer	-->str=hex2dec('32') str = 50.

Table 2.9: List of predefined constants

Constants	Description
SCI	Contains the value of the root path of Scilab.
SCIHOME	Contains the path to preferences and history files of your Scilab session.
TMPDIR	Contains the temporary directory path.
home	Gives the current user directory, where, by default, files are saved.
%eps	Epsilon (floating-point relative accuracy).
%i	Represents $\sqrt{-1}$, i.e. *iota* used in complex numbers.
%inf	Infinity value.
%nan	Not-a-number.
%pi	Represents the value of π.

2.4.2 Variables

Variables refer to data objects that can change their values during the program execution. Technically, Scilab is an interpreted language, which implies that there is no need to declare a variable before using it. Variables are created when they are assigned values for the first time. In Scilab, the "=" operator is used to assign values (variables are in the left of the equal operator and values in the right) as shown in Example 2.6. In this example, a variable "**x**" is created, and its value is set to **1**. By default, Scilab displays the contents of a variable every time it is assigned new values. The display of the contents can be suppressed by putting a semicolon (**;**) after the statement as shown in Example 2.6.

Example 2.6

```
-->x=1   //Creates a variable x with the value 1 and displays the result
 x =
    1.
-->y=2; // Creates a variable y with the value 2 and the display of the content of y is suppressed
-->
```

2.4.2.1. Rules for naming variables in Scilab

Following are the rules for naming variables in Scilab:
1. The permitted characters to be used in naming variables are: (a) All the letters from "**a**" to "**z**" and from "**A**" to "**Z**", (b) All the digits from "**0**" to "**9**", and (c) the additional characters **"%", "_", "#", "!", "$", "?"**. However, the character "**$**" alone should not be used as a user defined variable name as it is used to extract the last index of rows and columns of a matrix. Another important point, Scilab is a case sensitive language, i.e. a small case letter is different from the corresponding upper case letter. For example, **A** and **a** are two different variables.
2. Variable names must begin with a letter or one of the following special characters: **'%', '_', '#', '!', '$', '?'**. The special character **"%"** can only be used as the first character in variable names and is normally used for the pre-defined Scilab variables. It is recommended that it should not be used to name user variables. The other characters of variable names may be letters, digits and special characters (**'_', '#', '!', '$', '?'**).
3. Names may be as long as programmers want but only the first 24 characters are taken into account. If a variable name exceeds this limit, a warning message is generated by Scilab as shown in Example 2.7. In the future releases of Scilab, this limitation may be dropped.
4. Variable names must be unique in its scope. The scope of a variable is the area of a program where variable is available for use.

5. Keywords, predefined variables and constant names should be avoided as variables names.

Example 2.7: Number of characters in a variable name

-->abcdefghijklmnopqrstuvwxyz = 10   // A variable name with more that 24 characters
Warning :
The identifier : abcdefghijklmnopqrstuvwxyz
has been truncated to: abcdefghijklmnopqrstuvwx.
abcdefghijklmnopqrstuvwx =
     10.
--> //The warning message is generated by Scilab regarding the number of characters in a variable name.
--> // Only the first 24 characters are retained and the remaining are truncated.
-->

Table 2.10 give some examples of valid and invalid variable names. It is recommended that users should give meaningful names to variables for easy comprehension of long programs to him and for the other users. This will also help in reusability of the code in other programs.

Table 2.10 : Examples of valid and invalid variable names

Name	Description
A	Valid.
A,b	Invalid. Contains a comma ",", which is not allowed.
A#b	Valid.
A-2	Invalid. Contains a minus "-", which is not allowed.
for	Invalid. Contains "for", which is a keyword.
sin	Valid, but not recommended as it is a common library function name.
Max Value	Invalid. Contains spaces, which are not allowed.
Max_Value	Valid.
1abc	Invalid. Number is not allowed at the first place.
$abc	Valid.
$$abc?	Valid.
%abc	Valid.
ab%c	Invalid. % is not allowed in the middle.
$	Invalid. $ alone is not allowed as a variable name.
$$	Valid.

2.4.2.2. Dynamic nature of variables

It should be noted that Scilab is not a typed language, that is, it is not required to declare the type of a variable before setting its content. Moreover, the type of a variable can be changed during the life of the variable. As stated earlier, a variable is created simply by assigning a value to it. The type of a variable is decided by the type of data assigned to it. Thus, the type of a variable can be changed at any time by assigning a different type of data to the variable. This makes the variable type dynamic in Scilab. In other words, Scilab allows to change the type of a variable dynamically at any moment in the program. Example 2.8 shows the dynamic nature of the variable type. In this example, a variable "**x**" is initially created as a real variable by assigning a real data to it. Subsequently, it is changed to a string type variable by re-assigning a string data to it.

2.4.2.3. The "ans" variable

Whenever an expression is evaluated in the Scilab console window and the result of the expression is not assigned to any variable, Scilab uses the "**ans**" variable to store the result. Subsequently, the "**ans**" variable can be used like any other variable. The contents of the "**ans**" variable get changed whenever an expression is evaluated and the result is not assigned to any variable. Hence, the "**ans**" variable should be used only in interactive sessions for simple calculations. However, it can be of a great help to the user who has forgotten to store the result of an interesting computation and do not want to recompute the result. This might be the case after a long sequence of trials and errors, where we experimented several ways to get the result without taking care of actually storing the result. It is a bad practice to rely on the "**ans**" variable for long and complicated computations. Example 2.9 illustrates the use of the "**ans**" variable.

Example 2.8: Dynamic nature of variable data type

```
-->x=1      // Create a real variable.
x =
1.
-->x+1
ans =
2.
-->x="Scilab"   // Change the type of the variable "x" by reassigning a string to it.
x =
Scilab
-->x+" program"
ans =
Scilab program
```

Example 2.9: Use of the "ans" variable

```
-->exp(10)   //The command evaluates  exp(10), which created the ans variable.
 ans  =
    22026.466
-->log(ans)   // use of the ans variable to evaluate the log of the previous result.
 ans  =
    10.
-->
```

2.5 Operators

Scilab has a rich set of operators, which can be classified into three categories:
1. Arithmetic operators that perform arithmetic computations like addition, subtraction, etc.
2. Relational operators that perform comparisons such as "less than", "not equal to", etc.
3. Logical operators that perform logical computations such as AND, OR, NOT, etc.

2.5.1 Arithmetic operators

Some arithmetic operators used in Scilab are listed in Table 2.11 along with some illustrative examples. In the examples, **a = 9** and **b = 6** are used for the evaluation of the expressions. All these operators are designed to process matrices as well as scalars as operands. The matrix and array version of the operators are discussed in detail in the third chapter. These operators are designed to process real and complex numbers with equal efficiency. The basic arithmetic operations over complex numbers are illustrated below using two complex numbers $A = a + i\,b$ and $B = c + i\,d$. The complex conjugate (B') of B is $c - i\,d$.

$A + B = (a + c) + i\,(b + d)$
$A - B = (a - c) + i\,(b - d)$
$A * B = (a * c - b * d) + i\,(a * d + b*c)$
$A / B = (A * B') / (B * B') = ((a * c + b * d) + i\,(b * c - a * d)) / (c^2 + d^2)$

Table 2.11: Arithmetic operators in Scilab

Operator	Operation	Algebraic Form	Scilab Expression	Value of x
+	Addition	a+b	x=a+b	15
-	Subtraction	a-b	x=a-b	3
.*	Element-wise multiplication	a x b	x=a.*b	54

./	Element-wise right division	a/b	x=a./b	1.5
.\	Element-wise left division	b x a^{-1}	x=a.\b	0.6666667
.^	Element-wise exponentiation	a^b	x=a.^b	531441.
+	Unary plus	+a	x=+a	9
-	Unary minus	-a	x=-a	-9

Example 2.10 shows the application of these operators for complex numbers. The complex numbers used in the examples are **p=2+3*i*** and **q=3+4*i***. In Scilab, logical variables can also be used in arithmetic operations. During the evaluation of an arithmetic expression containing logical values, a TRUE value is replaced by **1** and a FALSE value by **0**. For example, the expression **10 + %T** evaluates to **11** and **10+%F** evaluates to **10** in Scilab.

Example 2.10 : Arithmetic operators with complex numbers

```
-->p=2+3*%i    // Create a complex variable
 p  =
    2. + 3.i
-->q=3+4*%i    // Create a complex variable
 q  =
    3. + 4.i
-->p+q         // Addition of two complex numbers
 ans  =
    5. + 7.i
-->p-q         // Subtraction of two complex numbers
 ans  =
  - 1. - i
-->p.*q        // Multiplication of two complex numbers
 ans  =
  - 6. + 17.i
-->p./q        // Right division of two complex numbers, p/q
 ans  =
    0.72 + 0.04i
-->p.\q        // Left division of two complex numbers, q/p
 ans  =
    1.3846154 - 0.0769231i
-->p.^q        // Exponentiation of two complex numbers, p^q
 ans  =
  - 0.2045529 + 0.8966233i
```

```
-->-p    // Unary minus
 ans  =
 - 2. - 3.i
-->+p   // Unary plus
 ans  =
  2. + 3.i
```

2.5.2 Relational operators

Relational operators of Scilab are shown in Table 2.12 along with illustrative examples using two real numbers **a=3** and **b=2**. The result of a relational operator is either **TRUE** or **FALSE** and displayed as **T** or **F**, respectively, in the console window. Relational operators can take matrices as operands and always operate element wise. The matrices used in relational operators must be identical in the shape and size. For complex numbers, the only valid logical operators are "equal to" (==) and "not equal to" (~=) operators, and the other relational operators cannot be used with them. In the previous relational operators, one operand can be of real type and the other can be of complex type. Example 2.11 shows the application of relational operators with complex numbers as its operands.

Table 2.12: Relational Operators in Scilab

Operator	Operation	Algebraic Form	Scilab Expression	Value of x
<	Less than	a<b	x=a<b	F
<=	Less than or equal to	$a \leq b$	x=a<=b	F
>	Greater than	a > b	x=a>b	T
>=	Greater than or equal to	$a \geq b$	x=a>=b	T
==	Equal to	a=b	x=a==b	F
~=, <>	Not equal to	$a \neq b$	x=a~=b	T

Example 2.11 : Relational operators with complex numbers

```
-->p=2+3*%i    //Create a complex number
 p  =
   2. + 3.i
-->q=3+4*%i    //Create a complex number
 q  =
   3. + 4.i
-->r=2+3*%i    //Create a complex number
 r  =
   2. + 3.i
```

```
-->p==q   // Use of "equal to"( == )operator with complex numbers
 ans  =
 F
-->p==r  // Use of "equal to"( == )operator with complex numbers
 ans  =
 T
-->p~=r   // Use of "not equal to"( ~= )operator with complex numbers
 ans  =
 F
-->p>q  // Use of "greater than" (>) operator with complex numbers and the error message
   !--error 144
Undefined operation for the given operands.
check or define function %s_2_s for overloading.
```

2.5.3   Logical operators

Logical operators are used to evaluate logical operations such as "AND", "OR", etc. Table 2.13 shows logical operators of Scilab. The logical AND operation returns true if both the operands are true else it returns false. The logical OR operation returns true if any one or both the operands are true, and if both the operands are false, only then it returns false. The operands of all logical operators must be logical variables, expressions or constants. In Scilab, any value other than **0** is considered as true in a Boolean expression (logical expression). For example, the logical expression **5 & 6** evaluates to **TRUE**, whereas, the logical expression **0 & 5** evaluates to **FALSE**. Logical operators also accept complex numbers as their operands. All the complex numbers with non-zero real and/or imaginary parts are treated as **TRUE**, and the complex numbers with both the real and imaginary parts with zero values are treated as **FALSE**. For example, 1 +3*%i & 2 +4*%i gives **TRUE** and 1 +3*%i & 0+0 * %i gives **FALSE**. Logical operators also accept matrices as their operands and apply logical operations element-wise. Matrix logical operations are discussed in Chapter 3.

Scilab has a number of built-in functions that can apply logical operations at the individual bits of the operands. These are known as bit-level logical operations. In this case, the operands are processed in the binary form, and each bit is treated as a separate value. If a bit is **1**, it is treated as true, otherwise false. Bit level logical functions are shown in Table 2.14 along with some examples. Bit level functions only accept unsigned integers as their arguments and return an unsigned integer as their results. These functions cannot process any other data types.

Table 2.13 : Logical operators

Operator	Description	Expression	Result
&	& (AND) operator performs logical AND operation	%t & %t	T
		%t & %f	F
		%f & %t	F
		%f & %f	F
|	|(OR) operator performs logical OR operation	%t & %t	T
		%t & %f	T
		%f & %t	T
		%f & %f	F
~	~(NOT) operator performs logical NOT operation	~%t	F
		~%f	T

Table 2.14 : Bit level logical functions

Operator	Description	Expression	Result
bitand(a,b)	Applies bit level logical AND operation on a and b.	bitand(3,6)	2
bitor(a,b)	Applies bit level logical OR operation on a and b.	bitor(3,6)	7
bitxor(a,b)	Applies bit level logical Exclusive OR operation on a and b.	bitxor(3,6)	5

2.6 Scilab Expressions

An expression is a combination of operands and operators. In Scilab, operands can be variables, constants and functions that return a value. An expression may consist of one or more operands and zero or more operators. For example, **a + b** is an expression, where "**a**" and "**b**" are operands of the variable type and "**+**" is an operator. Similarly, **a + 1** is also an expression which combines one variable operand and one constant operand. The expression **2 * sin (a) + b** is an expression combining a constant, a library function **sin()** and two variables **a** and **b**. In an expression, adjacent operands must be separated by a valid operator depending on the type of operands. Variables and constants, in expressions, can be scalars or matrices or their combinations. Expressions with matrices as operands are described in Chapter 3.

Expressions in Scilab can be broadly classified as:

- constant expressions,
- integral expressions,
- float expressions,
- relational expressions,
- logical expressions,
- bitwise expressions,
- string expressions and
- compound expressions.

Constant expressions consist only of constant values as operands, such as **10 + 1.5 * 30**. In Scilab, all numerical constant values are, by default, stored as double numbers. To store an integer number in any integer format, an appropriate function must be used. For example, to store **10** as an eight bit signed integer constant, it should be written as **int8(10)**.

Integral expressions consist of only integer constants and integer variables as operands and evaluate to integral values. For example, **int8 (3)/int8 (2)** evaluates to **1,** and the result is stored as an integer number. If an integer expression contains integer operands of different types, the lower size integer operands are upgraded to the higher size integer operands, in term by term fashion, during the evaluation of the expression. The final result type is equal to the largest operand type present in the expression. For example, the expression **int8 (5) + int16 (10)** contains different types of integer operands. Before evaluation, the operand **int8 (5)** is automatically upgraded to **int16 (5),** and the final result **15** is stored as **int16** type.

Float expressions consist of real constants and real variables as operands and evaluate to real values. For example, the expression **3/2** is a float expression and evaluates to **1.5**. It is important to note that a numeric constant written with or without a decimal point is always stored as a double precision real number in Scilab. Hence, all these expressions **3/2, 3.0/2** or **3.0/2.0** evaluates to **1.5**.

Relational expressions consist of one relational operator and two expressions as operands and evaluate to either logical **TRUE** or **FALSE**. For example, the expression **3<10** is a relational expression and evaluates to **TRUE**. In a relational expression, both the operand expressions are evaluated as per their types. For example, **7/2 > 3** is evaluated as **TRUE** as **7/2** evaluates to **3.5** whereas **int8 (7)/int8 (2) > int8 (3)** is evaluated to **FASLE** as **int8 (7)/int8 (2)** evaluates to **3**.

Logical expressions consist of one or more Boolean operators and Boolean variables, constants and expressions as operands. For example, the expression **10>5 & 4<8** is a logical expression and evaluates to **TRUE.** Operands in a logical expression can be of any type except string expressions. For example, the expression **1+2 & 5+4** is a logical expression and evaluates to **TRUE** as any expression that evaluates to a non-zero value is considered **TRUE.** Similarly, the logical expression **1+2 & 5-5** evaluates to **FALSE** as any expression that evaluates to zero is considered **FALSE** in Scilab.

Bitwise expressions consist of bitwise logical operation functions and positive integral expressions as their arguments. For example, **bitand (10, 6)** is a bitwise expression and applies bitwise logical **AND** operation on **10** and **6** and evaluates to **2**.

String expressions consist of strings as operands and one or more concatenation operator (+) and evaluate to strings. The only valid operator in a string expression is '+'. For example **"Scilab" + " " + "is a very versatile programming language"** is a string expression and evaluates to **"Scilab is a very versatile programming language"**. To use the other data types in a string expression as operands, the operands must be explicitly converted to the string type by the **string** function. For example, the expression **"abc:"+ 40** should be written as **"abc: " + string (40)** which will evaluate to **"abc: 40"**.

A compound expression consists of at least one integer type data and one or more float type data in a single expression such as **2.5 + int8 (3)**. A compound expression always evaluates to an integer value. The integer value corresponding to a real number is obtained by simply truncating the fractional portion of it. For example, the real numbers **2.5, 2.8** and **2.1** change to **2**, and the real numbers **-2.5, -2.8** and **-2.1** change to **-2** when they are converted to the integer type. Hence, the previous expression evaluates to **5**. Similarly, **-4.5+int8 (4)** will evaluate to **0**. A compound expression is evaluated as per the precedence order of the operators. The operator precedence is discussed, in detail, in section 2.7. During the evaluation of a compound expression, on the first encounter of an integer data in the expression, the result of the part of the expression evaluated till now is converted to an appropriate integer value and the remaining calculations are carried out as an integer expression by converting non-integer operands to the appropriate integer values. Figure 2.2 shows an example of the evaluation of a compound expression. The first interaction with an **int8** data type during the evaluation of the compound expression is shown within a dashed rectangle in the figure. In a compound expression, the logical values, i.e. **%t** and **%f**, can be used, but only before the first interaction with an operand of integer data type. In other words, once the evaluation is changed to the integer mode, the logical values are not allowed in the expression. For example, the expression **%t+10+int8 (5)** evaluates to **16**. However, the expression **%t+10+int8 (5) +%t** gives an error message: **"!--error 144. Undefined operation for the given operands. check or define function %i_a_b for overloading"**. Scilab has facility to overcome this error message by overloading the operator for the unsupported data types if user desires so.

2.7 Hierarchy of Operations

Generally, several operations are combined into a single expression. An expression is evaluated by executing one operation at a time. The order in which the operations of an expression are executed is called hierarchy of operations or operators precedence order. The rules governing the precedence of operators are an extension of the rules used to evaluate algebraic expressions, which is popularly known as the BODMAS rule. Under the BODMAS rule the order of evaluation of operations is brackets, of, divisions, multiplications, additions and subtractions. The same level of operations is evaluated from the left to the right in an expression. The order in which operators are evaluated in Scilab is given in Table 2.15. Example 2.12 shows some examples of expression evaluation.

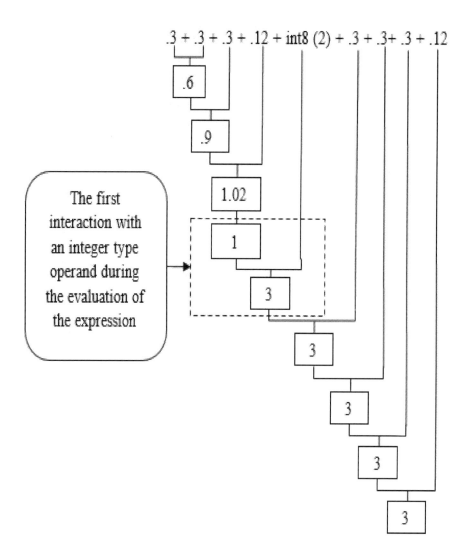

Fig. 2.2: Evaluation of a compound expression

Table 2.15: Operators precedence order

Precedence No.	Operators	Remark
1.	( )	The contents of parentheses ( ) are evaluated first, starting from the innermost parentheses and working/moving outwards one at a time.
2.	+ , -	Unary plus (+) and unary minus (-).
3.	^	Exponentiation (^).
4.	.* , ./ , .\	Multiplication (.*), right division (./) and left division (.\ ).
5.	*,/,\	Matrix multiplication (*), matrix right division (/) and matrix left division (\ ). For scalar data, operators and their dot equivalents have the same meaning.
6.	+ , -	Addition (+) and subtraction (-).
7.	< , <= , > , >= , == , ~=	Less than (<), less than or equal to (<=), greater than (>), greater than or equal to (>=), equal to (==) and not equal to (~=).
8.	~	Logical NOT (~).
9.	&	Logical AND (&).
10.	|	Logical OR (|).
11.	=	Assignment (=).

Example 2.12: Evaluation of expressions

-->2 + 3 * 4 ans = 14.	// The multiplication operation (*) is evaluated first due to its higher precedence than the addition operation (+).
-->2 / 3 + 4 ans = 4.6666667	// The division operation (/) is evaluated first due to its higher precedence than the addition operation (+).
-->2 + 3 / 4 ans = 2.75	// The operation (/) is evaluated first due to its higher precedence than the addition operation (+).

--->2 * (3 + 4) ans = 14.	// Due to parentheses the addition operation (+) is evaluated first as a parentheses operator has higher precedence than a multiplication operator (*).
--->(2 + 3) * 4 ans = 20.	// Due to parentheses the addition operation (+) is evaluated first as a parentheses operator has higher precedence than a multiplication operator (*).
--->(2 + 3) / 4 ans = 1.25	// Due to parentheses the addition operation (+) is evaluated first as a parentheses operator has higher precedence than a division operator (/).
--->3 / (2 + 4) ans = 0.5	// Due to parentheses the addition operation (+) is evaluated first as a parentheses operator has higher precedence than a division operator (/).
->4*3^2/2 ans = 18.	// The exponentiation operation (^) is evaluated first as an exponential operator has higher precedence than a division operator (/) and a multiplication operator (*).

2.8 Built-in Functions

Scilab has a very rich library of mathematical built-in functions to facilitate complex engineering and scientific calculations. A mathematical function is an expression that takes one or more input values and returns one or more output values. Scilab has a large variety of built-in functions related with various disciplines of engineering and science along with commonly used trigonometric, logarithmic, numerical methods and interpolation functions. All the functions are implemented using state-of-the-art algorithms that ensure accurate results and faster calculations. Appendix–I lists some commonly used built-in functions. The syntax of a built-in function is given as below:

function_name (input arguments)

Functions can be used in arithmetic expressions like simple variables. All the functions appearing in an expression are evaluated first. Hence, the arguments of functions are computed first in order to evaluate a function. For example, the expression **a=log (sqrt (x / (y * z))** implements the following mathematical function:

$$a = \log_e \sqrt{\frac{x}{yz}}$$

Example 2.13 illustrates the application of built-in functions to find the length of the third side and area of a triangle when two sides and the included angle are given in an interactive calculation.

Example 2.13: Use of built-in functions

```
-->a=2;
-->b=3;
-->theta=60;
-->theta=theta*%pi/180;
-->c=sqrt(a^2+b^2-2*a*b*cos(theta))
 c =
   2.6457513
-->area=a*b*sin(theta)/2
 area =
   2.5980762
```

Summary

- Scilab is a very powerful, interactive computing tool along with a very rich and easy to use programming language.
- Scilab uses vectors and matrices to store data, which helps efficient vectorised operations and compact programs.
- Scilab supports many data types, such as int8, int16, int32, etc., to optimize the performance and storage requirements.
- Scilab processes complex numbers and real numbers using identical syntaxes. Most of the built-in-functions are capable of handling complex as well as real numbers.
- Scilab does not require explicit type declaration of a variable. The type of a variable is decided by the last assignment to it.
- Scilab supports arithmetic operations, relational operations and logical operations and uses the similar syntaxes for both matrix as well as scalar data.
- Scilab has a huge library of functions, which is evolving further to include new researches, for solving scientific and technical problems. These functions use state-of-the-art algorithms.

Key Terms

- ans
- arithmetic operators
- bit level logical functions
- built-in functions
- character set
- **complex()**
- constants
- data type
- evaluation of expressions
- floating point integers
- **format()**
- hierarchy of Operations
- **inttype()**
- logical operators
- operators
- operators precedence
- predefined constants
- relational operators
- safe range
- special Characters
- **string()**
- syntax rules
- **uint8()**
- variables
- white Spaces

Exercise Problems

2.1 Evaluate the following expressions:
  (a) $2.3 + \dfrac{4}{5} + 3 * 6$
  (b) $3.5 + 7 + int8(5) + 2.3$
  (c) $2/3 * 4/5$
  (d) $3 + \dfrac{3.5 + 2.7}{(4+7)*(2+5)} - 2.1$
  (e) $\ln 3 + \sin 45° + e^{-2}$
  (f) $(3 + 4i) * (2 - 3i)$
  (g) $(3 + 4i)/(2 - 3i)$
  (h) $\dfrac{\sin 30° + i \cos 30°}{\sin 30° - i \cos 30°}$

2.2 Write the Scilab statements corresponding to the following mathematical equations:
  (a) $A = \pi r^2$

(b) $a = \dfrac{b+c}{d+e}$

(c) $x = \dfrac{-b \pm \sqrt{b^2 - 4ac}}{2a}$

(d) $x = ae^{-t\theta}$

(e) $a = |y^2 - z^2| + \sqrt{5yz} + \cos\pi + 2\log_{10} x$

(f) $p = x^5 + 3x^4 + 6x^3 + 2x^2 + 7x + 10$

(g) $A = \log\left(\dfrac{x - \sqrt{x^2 - 1}}{x + \sqrt{x^2 - 1}}\right)$

2.3 Write the Scilab equivalent expressions for the following complex expressions:
   (a) $1 + 2i$
   (b) $\cos(25°) - \sin(25°)i$
   (c) $e^{-i\theta}$

2.4 Evaluate the following expressions for θ =30°, 60°,130°,230°:
   (a) $\sin(\theta)$
   (b) $\cos(\theta)$
   (c) $\dfrac{\sin\theta}{\cos\theta}$
   (d) $3\sin^2\theta + 2\cos^2\theta$

2.5 Evaluate the following expressions:
   (a) $\sin^{-1}\dfrac{\sqrt{3}}{2}$
   (b) $\cos^{-1}\dfrac{1}{2}$
   (c) $\tan^{-1}\sqrt{3}$

2.6 Evaluate the following logical and relational expressions for x=10, y=20 and z=5:
   (a) $x > y$
   (b) $x < y \,\&\, y > z$
   (c) $x > z \,||\, y > x$

Chapter 3
Vectors and Matrices

Learning Objectives
- Methods to create vectors, matrices and arrays
- Creating evenly spaced row vectors
- Creating special test matrices
- Creating sparse matrices
- Creating submatrices
- Creating multidimensional arrays
- Matrix and array operations
- Matrix manipulations

3.1 Introduction

It may seem strange at first, but the fact is that in Scilab everything is a matrix. Every data in Scilab is stored in the form of a matrix irrespective of their type. That is, all real, complex, Boolean, integer, string and polynomial variables are matrices. In mathematics, a matrix is an arrangement of numbers, symbols or letters in rows and columns which is used to solve mathematical problems. The matrix notation adopted by the developers of Scilab is based on the observation that scientific and technical problems formulated using matrix notations usually simplify their solutions and make the solution process efficient. In Scilab, a matrix is a rectangular array of various types of data arranged in rows and columns. Matrices with a single row are called row vectors, and those with a single column are called column vectors. Matrices having only single element are called scalars.

The strength of Scilab is its capability to apply an operation on the complete matrix simultaneously which removes the requirement of repetition of statements in many situations. This feature makes Scilab more efficient than traditional high level programming languages which work on one data at a time. This also makes programs succinct, small in size and more readable.

3.2 Matrices, Vectors and Scalars

The basic data type in Scilab is matrix, which is defined by the number of rows, the number of columns and the type of data. The data types can be real, integer, complex, Boolean, string and polynomial. The size of a matrix is written as **[m, n]**, where **m** represents the number of rows and **n** the number of columns of the matrix. When the number of rows is equal to the number of columns, the matrix is a square matrix; otherwise, it is a rectangular matrix. Vectors are a special case of matrices, where either the number of rows or the number of columns is equal to **1**. When the number of rows is equal to **1** in a matrix, it is called a row vector. The size of a row vector is written as **[1, n]**. When the number of columns in a matrix is equal to **1**, it is called a column vector. The size of a column vector is written as **[n, 1]**. When a matrix consists of only one row and only one column, it is called a scalar. The size of a scalar is written as **[1, 1]**. Simple scalar variables, as defined in traditional programming languages, do not exist in Scilab. Table 3.1 gives examples of a matrix, a row vector, a column vector and a scalar.

Table 3.1: Various types of matrices

Matrix Type	Example
Matrix	$\text{Rows} \begin{bmatrix} 1 & 2 & 3 & 4 \\ 5 & 6 & 7 & 8 \\ 9 & 10 & 11 & 12 \end{bmatrix}$ (Columns)
Row vector	$[1 \quad 2 \quad 3]$
Column vector	$\begin{bmatrix} 1 \\ 2 \\ 3 \end{bmatrix}$
Scalar	$[1]$

3.3 Creating Matrices from Values

Scilab has a simple and efficient syntax to create a matrix with given values. The following is the list of symbols used to define a matrix:
1. Square brackets " [" and "] " mark the beginning and the end of a matrix,
2. Commas " , " separate the values in different columns,
3. Semicolons " ; " separate the values of different rows.

For example, the Scilab code **[1,2,3,4;5,6,7,8;9,10,11,12]** creates the following matrix:

$$\begin{bmatrix} 1 & 2 & 3 & 4 \\ 5 & 6 & 7 & 8 \\ 9 & 10 & 11 & 12 \end{bmatrix}$$

The same code can be written as **[1, 2, 3, 4; 5, 6, 7, 8; 9, 10, 11, 12]** with few spaces, before and after the elements to make the code easy to read. The spaces are automatically removed by the Scilab compiler and the code produces the same result. Space(s) can also be used in place of commas to separate the elements of a matrix column. The previous code can be written as **[1 2 3 4; 5 6 7 8; 9 10 11 12]** with the same result. At least one space or a comma is essential to separate the column elements, and they can be used interchangeably, i.e. some elements may be separated by commas whereas others by space(s). The previous code can also be written as **[1 2, 3 4; 5, 6, 7, 8; 9 10 11, 12]**. However, it is strongly recommended that mixing of spaces and commas should be avoided. For separating rows, '**enter key**' strokes can also be used in place of semi colons. And again, semi colons and '**enter key**' strokes can be mixed up for separating rows. Results produced by the previous code in different formats are shown in Example 3.1.

Matrices with complex numbers as data elements can be created using the same syntax as used for creating matrices from real values. The Scilab code for creating the following complex number matrix is **A=[2+3*%i, 3*%i; 3+5*%i, 5]**, here **%i** is a predefined Scilab constant with value $\sqrt{-1}$ and used to represent '*i*' of a complex number. Note the use of ' * ' symbol in writing complex numbers.

$$A = \begin{bmatrix} 2 + 3i & 3i \\ 3 + 5i & 5 \end{bmatrix}$$

Matrices with expressions and functions as data elements can also be created using the same syntax. The Scilab code to create the following matrix is **B = [2, 5+sqrt(3) ; 2*%pi , log(2)]**.

$$B = \begin{bmatrix} 2 & 5 + \sqrt{3} \\ 2\pi & \log 2 \end{bmatrix}$$

Matrices with strings as data elements can also be created with the same syntax as used for the numbers. The Scilab code to create the following string matrix is **C= ['a', 'b'; 'c','d']** or **C= ["a", "b"; "c", "d"]**. String values are enclosed either within a pair of double quote (**"string value"**) or a pair of single quote (**'string value'**). Example 3.2 shows the creation of these matrices in the Scilab console.

$$C = \begin{bmatrix} 'a' & 'b' \\ 'c' & 'd' \end{bmatrix}$$

Example 3.1 : Creating matrices from values

```
-->[1,2,3,4;5,6,7,8;9,10,11,12]  // The code to create a matrix from the given data
 ans  =
   1.   2.   3.   4.
   5.   6.   7.   8.
   9.  10.  11.  12.
-->[1, 2, 3, 4; 5, 6, 7, 8; 9, 10, 11, 12]   // The previous code with spaces for better readability
 ans  =
   1.   2.   3.   4.
   5.   6.   7.   8.
   9.  10.  11.  12.
-->[1 2 3 4; 5 6 7 8; 9 10 11 12] // Spaces can also be used to separate column elements
 ans  =
   1.   2.   3.   4.
   5.   6.   7.   8.
   9.  10.  11.  12.
-->[1 2, 3 4; 5, 6, 7, 8; 9 10 11, 12]  // Mixing of spaces and commas as separators
 ans  =
   1.   2.   3.   4.
   5.   6.   7.   8.
   9.  10.  11.  12.
-->[1, 2, 3, 4
-->5, 6, 7, 8
-->9, 10, 11, 12]  //Use of enter key strokes to separate the rows in a matrix.
 ans  =
   1.   2.   3.   4.
   5.   6.   7.   8.
   9.  10.  11.  12.
-->[1, 2, 3, 4
-->5, 6, 7, 8;9,10,11,12]  //Mixing of enter key strokes and semi colons to separate the rows.
 ans  =
```

```
1.   2.   3.   4.
5.   6.   7.   8.
9.   10.  11.  12.
```

Example 3.2 : Creating matrices with complex numbers, expressions and string data

```
-->A=[2+3*%i, 3*%i; 3+5*%i, 5]   // Creating a complex number matrix
 A  =
   2. + 3.i    3.i
   3. + 5.i    5.
-->B=[2, 5+sqrt(3) ; 2*%pi , log(2)]  // Creating a matrix from expressions and functions
 B  =
   2.          6.7320508
   6.2831853   0.6931472
-->C= ["a", "b"; "c", "d"]   //Creating a matrix of strings using a pair of double quotes
 C  =
a.  b.
c.  d.
-->C= ['a', 'b'; 'c', 'd']   //Creating a matrix of strings using a pair of single quotes
 C  =
a.  b.
c.  d.
```

3.4 Creating the Empty Matrix

The empty matrix is created by assigning empty square brackets to a variable. For examples **A=** **[]**, where **A** is an empty matrix of size 0x0.

3.5 Creating Large Matrices from Values

Sometimes, the number of elements in a matrix is so large that they cannot fit into a single line of the Scilab console window. To create a matrix in this situation, an ellipsis (…) is used to continue data entry into the next line for the same row. An ellipsis is a set of three consecutive dots. Using ellipses, the data entry can be continued into many lines of the Scilab console. Example 3.3 shows a few examples of data entry of large matrices.

Example 3.3 : Creating a large matrix

```
-->A=[1,2,3,4,5 ...    // An ellipsis is used to continue a row in the next line
-->6,7,8,9,10]
 A  =
   1.   2.   3.   4.   5.   6.   7.   8.   9.   10.
-->A=[1,2,3 ...    // Ellipsis is used to enter data into the multiple lines
-->4,5,5 ...
-->7,8,9,10]
 A  =
   1.   2.   3.   4.   5.   5.   7.   8.   9.   10.
-->A=[1,2,3; 4,5 ...    // An ellipsis is used to type a part of the second row in the next line
-->6; 7,8,9]
 A  =
   1.   2.   3.
   4.   5.   6.
   7.   8.   9.
```

3.6 Creating Row Vectors and Column Vectors from Values

The syntax used for creating matrices is used to create row vectors and column vectors as well. The Scilab code to create the following row vector is **A= [1, 2, 3, 4]**. The code can also be written as **A= [1 2 3 4]**.

$$A = \begin{bmatrix} 1 & 2 & 3 & 4 \end{bmatrix}$$

The Scilab code to create the following column vector is **B= [1; 2; 3; 4]**. The code can also be written using the enter key in place of semicolons.

$$B = \begin{bmatrix} 1 \\ 2 \\ 3 \\ 4 \end{bmatrix}$$

3.7 Creating Scalars from Values

Scalars can be created by simply assigning values to variables. For example, the code **x=10** creates a scalar variable **x** with a value of **10**. Similarly, the codes **c=1+2*%i, s= 'Scilab', i=int8**

(2), b=%t create scalars holding a complex number, a string, an integer and a Boolean value, respectively.

3.8 Creating Evenly Spaced Row Vectors

A row vector with evenly spaced real values can be created using the following syntax:

variable name = start value : step size: end value

For example, the code **V=1:2:10** creates the following row vector. It may be noted that the end value may not be the part of the vector created.

$$V = [1 \quad 3 \quad 5 \quad 7 \quad 9]$$

The start value, the step size and the end value need not be integers and positive values. They can be real values. For example, the code **V=0.5 : 0.25 : 1.5** creates the following row vector:

$$V = [0.5 \quad 0.75 \quad 1 \quad 1.25 \quad 1.5]$$

The code **V= -2 : 1: 2** creates the following row vector:

$$V = [-2 \quad -1 \quad 0 \quad 1 \quad 2]$$

The code **V= 2 :- 1: -2** creates the following row vector:

$$V = [2 \quad 1 \quad 0 \quad -1 \quad -2]$$

If a step size is not specified in the code, +1 is taken as the step size by default. The code **V= 1:5** creates the following row vector:

$$V = [1 \quad 2 \quad 3 \quad 4 \quad 5]$$

If proper values for the start value, the step size and the end value are not specified, the empty matrix may result. The code **V=5:1:2** creates the empty matrix, i.e. **[ ]**.

Evenly spaced row vector can also be created by using **linspace** command, which has the following syntax:

V=linspace (p, q, n)

where **p** is the starting value, **q** is the last value and **n** is the number of elements to be generated in the resultant row vector. The default value of **n** is **100**.

For example, the command **V=linspace (2, 4, 6)** creates the following row vector, which consists of six data points equally spaced between **2** and **4**. The **linspace** command automatically calculates the step size from the input supplied.

$$V = [\,2 \quad 2.4 \quad 2.8 \quad 3.2 \quad 3.6 \quad 4\,]$$

The **linspace** command can also be used with complex numbers as its first two arguments. In this case, the command generates an evenly spaced row vector of complex numbers. For this purpose, Scilab internally generates two evenly spaced row vectors, one from the real parts of the two complex numbers and the other from the coefficients of their imaginary parts. Finally, these two vectors are combined element-wise to create the resultant complex vector. For example, the command **C=linspace (1+2*%i, 4+8*%i, 4)** creates the following complex number row vector:

$$C = [\,1 + 2i \quad 2 + 4i \quad 3 + 6i \quad 4 + 8i\,]$$

Similarly, the command, **logspace (a, b, n)** can be used to create a logarithmically spaced row vector of **n** elements between 10^a to 10^b. For example, the command **x=logspace (1, 4, 4)** gives the following row vector.

$$x = [\,10 \quad 100 \quad 1000 \quad 10000\,]$$

The behaviour of the command **logspace (a, %pi, n)** is unique when the value of the second argument is **%pi**. In this situation, a row vector of **n** elements is created between 10^a to π such that ratio of the adjacent pair of elements of the row vector is same. For example, the command, **x=logspace (1, %pi, 4)** creates the following row vector. The ratio of consecutive adjacent elements is **1.4710137**.

$$x = [\,10 \quad 6.7980334 \quad 4.6213257 \quad 3.1415927\,]$$

3.9 Creating Evenly Spaced Column Vectors

Evenly spaced column vectors can be created by first creating equivalent row vectors and then transposing them. For example, the following column vector can be created by the Scilab code **C= [1:1:5]'** where ' ' ' is a matrix transpose operator that transposes a matrix. A column vector can be transposed into a row vector.

$$C = \begin{bmatrix} 1 \\ 2 \\ 3 \\ 4 \\ 5 \end{bmatrix}$$

3.10 Creating Special Matrices

Scilab has many functions that can be used to generate special matrices of different sizes as per the requirements, such as a 3x3 matrix with all zero elements and a 4x3 matrix of normally distributed random numbers. Table 3.2 lists some of the commonly used special matrix generation functions. The **testmatrix** function is used to generate various test matrices, such as magic matrices, Frank matrices and Hilbert matrices. The syntax of the function is as given below:

A=testmatrix (name, n)

where **name** is an attribute that specifies the name of the matrix to be created, and **n** specifies the size of the output matrix. The attribute **name** can be set to **"magi"**, **"frk"** or **"hilb"** for a magic matrix, an inverse Frank matrix and a Hilbert matrix, respectively. This function always creates a square matrix of size **n x n**.

A magic matrix is a square matrix of size **n x n** of numbers consisting of the distinct positive integers **1, 2, 3 ... n²** arranged in such a fashion that the sum of each row, each column and each diagonal is always the same number. The sum depends on the size of the magic matrix. The following are examples of the magic matrices of size **3 x 3** and **4 x 4**. The sum of elements of each column or each row or each diagonal for **3 x 3** is **15** and for **4 x 4** is **34**. The matrices generated by the Scilab code **testmatrix ("magi", 3)** and **testmatrix ("magi", 4)** are shown below.

-->testmatrix("magi",3)
ans =
  8. 1. 6.
  3. 5. 7.
  4. 9. 2.
	-->testmatrix("magi",4)
	ans =
	  16. 2. 3. 13.
	  5. 11. 10. 8.
	  9. 7. 6. 12.
	  4. 14. 15. 1.

Table 3.2 : Special matrix generation functions

Function	Description	Example
zeros(p, q)	It returns a rectangular matrix of the size p x q with all the elements set to **0**. To generate a square matrix use the same value for p and q.	zeros(3,2) $\begin{bmatrix} 0 & 0 \\ 0 & 0 \\ 0 & 0 \end{bmatrix}$
ones(p, q)	It returns a rectangular matrix of the size p x q with all the elements set to **1**.	ones(2,3) $\begin{bmatrix} 1 & 1 & 1 \\ 1 & 1 & 1 \end{bmatrix}$
eye(p, q)	It returns a rectangular matrix of the size p x q with all the main diagonal elements set to **1** and the other elements set to **0**.	eye(3,4) $\begin{bmatrix} 1 & 0 & 0 & 0 \\ 0 & 1 & 0 & 0 \\ 0 & 0 & 1 & 0 \end{bmatrix}$
rand(p,q, "type")	It returns a rectangular matrix of the size p x q with random values assigned to all the elements from the specified distribution. The most widely used value of the attribute **type** is **"uniform"** (Random numbers are uniformly distributed in the interval (0,1)) or **"normal"**(Random numbers are normally distributed with mean 0 and variance 1).	rand(3,2, 'uniform') $\begin{bmatrix} 0.2113249 & 0.0002211 \\ 0.7560439 & 0.3303271 \\ 0.6283918 & 0.6653811 \end{bmatrix}$
diag(v, k)	This returns a square matrix of the size **n+abs(k)** with elements of the vector **v** assigned to the kth diagonal elements, where **n** is the number of elements in the vector **v**. Use **k> 0** for upper side diagonal, **k< 0** for lower side diagonal and **k=0** for the main diagonal.	diag([1 2],1) $\begin{bmatrix} 0 & 1 & 0 \\ 0 & 0 & 2 \\ 0 & 0 & 0 \end{bmatrix}$

A frank matrix is a square matrix of size **n x n** of the following structure, whose determinant is 1.

$$\begin{bmatrix} n & n-1 & n-2 & \ldots & 2 & 1 \\ n-1 & n-1 & n-2 & \ldots & 2 & 1 \\ 0 & n-2 & n-2 & \ldots & 2 & 1 \\ \vdots & 0 & n-3 & \ldots & \vdots & \vdots \\ \vdots & \vdots & \vdots & \ldots & \vdots & \vdots \\ \vdots & \vdots & \vdots & \ldots & 2 & 1 \\ 0 & 0 & 0 & \ldots & 1 & 1 \end{bmatrix}$$

The frank matrix of the size 5 x 5 as generated by the Scilab command **testmatrix ("frk", 5)** is shown as follows:

```
-->testmatrix ("frk", 5)
ans =
5.  4.  3.  2.  1.
4.  4.  3.  2.  1.
0.  3.  3.  2.  1.
0.  0.  2.  2.  1.
0.  0.  0.  1.  1.
```

A Hilbert matrix is a square matrix with the entries being the unit fractions $H_{i,j} = \frac{1}{i+j-1}$, where **i** and **j** are the row and the column indices respectively. The following is a Hilbert Matrix of the size **5x5**. The Hilbert Matrices are ill-conditioned matrices (We call a square matrix ill-conditioned if it is invertible but can become non-invertible if some of the entries are slightly changed) and pose lots of computational problems.

$$\begin{bmatrix} 1 & \frac{1}{2} & \frac{1}{3} & \frac{1}{4} & \frac{1}{5} \\ \frac{1}{2} & \frac{1}{3} & \frac{1}{4} & \frac{1}{5} & \frac{1}{6} \\ \frac{1}{3} & \frac{1}{4} & \frac{1}{5} & \frac{1}{6} & \frac{1}{7} \\ \frac{1}{4} & \frac{1}{5} & \frac{1}{6} & \frac{1}{7} & \frac{1}{8} \\ \frac{1}{5} & \frac{1}{6} & \frac{1}{7} & \frac{1}{8} & \frac{1}{9} \end{bmatrix}$$

The code, **testmatrix ("hilb", 3)** generates the inverse of the **3x3** Hilbert matrix and inverse of it generates the actual **3x3** Hilbert matrix as shown below.

-->testmatrix("hilb",3)	-->inv(testmatrix("hilb",3))
ans =	ans =
9. - 36. 30.	1. 0.5 0.3333333
- 36. 192. - 180.	0.5 0.3333333 0.25
30. - 180. 180.	0.3333333 0.25 0.2

3.11 Creating Sparse Matrices

A sparse matrix is a matrix in which most of the elements are zero and a few are non-zero. Large sparse matrices often appear in scientific and engineering applications. Storing and processing of these matrices in the standard form of matrices is not economical and optimal in terms of storage space requirements and computational efficiency. A special data structure and special algorithms have been developed for storing and processing sparse matrices.

A typical dense matrix is normally stored in a two dimensional array. Each entry in the array represents an element indexed by a row number and a column number. In contrast to this, the sparse matrix representation structure stores only the non-zero elements. This leads to substantial reduction in storage requirements. The following example illustrates creation of a sparse matrix.

$$\begin{bmatrix} 1 & 0 & 0 & 0 & 0 \\ 0 & 2 & 3 & 0 & 0 \\ 0 & 0 & 0 & 0 & 0 \\ 0 & 0 & 0 & 0 & 0 \\ 0 & 0 & 0 & 4 & 5 \end{bmatrix}$$

The **sparse ( )** command can be used to create sparse matrices in Scilab. The following syntax is used to create a sparse matrix from the non-zero values and their indices:

$$sp=sparse(ij,v\ [,mn])$$

where
ij - a two columns integer matrix storing the indices of the non-zeros entries.
v - a vector storing the non-zero elements of the sparse matrix, sequenced according to the indices stored in the vector **ij**.

mn - an integer vector with two entries storing the number of rows and number of columns in the sparse matrix. It is an optional argument. If it is not given, the size of matrix is calculated based on the indices of non-zero elements, and a compact sparse matrix of the smallest size that can just hold all the non-zero elements is created.

sp - a variable to store the sparse matrix created by the sparse command.

The following example shows commands to create a sparse matrix with the specified non-zero elements and their row and column indices.

```
-->ij=[1,1;2,2;2,3;5,4;5,5], v=[11,21,34,45,5]
 ij =
   1.   1.
   2.   2.
   2.   3.
   5.   4.
   5.   5.
 v =
   11.   21.   34.   45.   5.
-->sparse(ij,v)
 ans =
(   5,   5) sparse matrix
(   1,   1)      11.
(   2,   2)      21.
(   2,   3)      34.
(   5,   4)      45.
(   5,   5)       5.
```

The Scilab command **full (sp)** is used to convert a sparse matrix into the dense form of the matrix. The argument of the function is a sparse matrix. A matrix stored in the dense form can be converted to the sparse format by the Scilab command **sparse (dense_matrix).** The following example converts a sparse matrix into a dense matrix and then back to the sparse format.

```
-->ij=[1,1;2,2;2,3;5,4;5,5]; v=[1,2,3,4,5];
-->sp=sparse(ij, v); // Creating a sparse matrix
-->d=full(sp) // Converting the sparse matrix into a dense matrix
 d =
   1.   0.   0.   0.   0.
```

```
    0.  2.  3.  0.  0.
    0.  0.  0.  0.  0.
    0.  0.  0.  0.  0.
    0.  0.  0.  4.  5.
-->sparse(d)  // Converting the dense matrix into a sparse matrix
 ans  =
(   5,   5) sparse matrix
(   1,   1)    1.
(   2,   2)    2.
(   2,   3)    3.
(   5,   4)    4.
(   5,   5)    5.
```

3.12 Size of a Matrix

The **size** function, with the format **[nr, nc] = size (M)**, is used to query about the number of rows, **nr**, and the number columns, **nc**, in a matrix **M**. The following example shows the use of the size function.

```
-->M=ones(2,4)  //Creating a matrix of ones, with 2 rows and 4 columns
 M  =
    1.  1.  1.  1.
    1.  1.  1.  1.
-->[nr,nc]=size(M)  //Querying about the number of rows and the number of columns
 nc  =
    4.
 nr  =
    2.
```

The **size** function is one of the most widely used functions in designing Scilab programs, as most of the operations performed on matrices depend on their sizes. For example, to compute the inverse of a matrix, the matrix must be a square matrix. Similarly, users can create functions that can process a row vector only. The **size** function is used to ensure the proper implementation of such algorithms and helps in generating suitable error messages to help users to formulate their problems in the correct format. The **size** function also has another syntax **nr = size (M, sel)**, which allows to get only the number of rows or the number of columns based on the value of the additional argument **sel**. The argument **sel** takes the following values:

- **sel=1** or **sel="r"**, returns the number of rows.
- **sel=2** or **sel="c"**, returns the number of columns.
- **sel="*"**, returns the total number of elements in the argument matrix.

In the following example, the **size** function is used to calculate the number of rows, the number of columns and the total number of elements in the given matrix.

```
-->M=ones(2,5)
 M =
   1.  1.  1.  1.  1.
   1.  1.  1.  1.  1.
-->nr=size(M,'r')  // Querying for the number of rows in the matrix M
 nr =
   2.
-->nr=size(M,'c')  // Querying for the number of columns in the matrix M
 nr =
   5.
-->nr=size(M,'*')  // Querying for the total number of elements in the matrix M
 nr =
   10.
```

3.13 Accessing Matrix Elements

The following methods are used to access the elements of a matrix:
- **Accessing the whole matrix** - All the elements of a matrix can be assigned to another matrix by the assignment operator (=), with the syntax **A = B**, where all the elements of the matrix **B** are assigned to the matrix **A**.
- **Accessing individual elements** - The individual elements of a matrix can be accessed by specifying their row and column indices. The first index is the row number while the second is the column number. The element in the ith row and the jth column of a matrix **A** is written as **A (i, j)**. For example, **A (3, 5)** refers to the element located in the 3rd row and the 5th column of the matrix **A**. The Scilab statement **X=A (2, 3)** assigns the value of the element **A (2, 3)** to the variable **X**. Similarly, **A (2, 3) = 10** assigns **10** to the element **A (2, 3)**.
- **Accessing a block of elements** - The colon (:) operator is used to access a portion of a matrix. The colon operator is discussed in detail in the next section 3.14.

3.14 Creating Sub-Matrices

A sub-matrix is a portion of a matrix. Figure 3.1 shows some sub-matrices of a matrix. These sub-matrices can be extracted from the given matrix for further processing.

To extract a portion of a matrix, colon (:) operator is used. The syntax of the colon operator is **start: increment: end**. If increment is not specified, **1** is used as the default increment. For example, the Scilab command **1:4** generates the vector [1 2 3 4], the command **1:2:4** generates the vector [1 3], and the command **1:0.5:4** generates the vector [1 1.5 2 2.5 3 3.5 4]. The colon operator can use negative numbers and/or complex numbers for the start, increment and end values. For example, the command **4:-2:1** generates the vector [4 2], the command **-4:-2:-8** generates [- 4 -6 - 8], and the command **1+2i : 2+3i : 4+3i** generates the vector [1 3]. In the case of complex numbers, the vector generated uses only the real part of start, increment and end values.

For a vector to be used as matrix indices (generated by the colon operator or otherwise), the vector must contain only non-zero positive values. Scilab automatically truncates the fraction portion of the positive real values of the vector, but it generates the error message ("**!--error 21 Invalid index.**") when it contains negative numbers.

Consider Figure 3.1, to extract the sub-matrix **B** form the matrix **A**, the row index is **1** and the column indices should vary from **1** to **2**. This can be written in Scilab as **B = A (1, 1:2)**. To extract the sub-matrix **C** from the matrix **A**, the row indices should vary from **3** to **4** and the column indices from **2** to **4**. This can be written in Scilab as **C = A (3:4, 2:4)**. Similarly, the commands for the sub matrices **D** and **E** are **D = A (2:3, 2:3)** and **E = A (1:4, 4)**, respectively.

If sub-matrix indices vary from some arbitrary value to the last row or column, **$** can be used to represent the last row or column. Using this feature, the commands to extract the sub-matrix **C** and the sub-matrix **E** can also be written as **C = A (3:$, 2:$)** and **E = A (1:$,$)**, respectively. When a complete row or column is to be extracted, there is no need to specify the start and end values. Bare colon is enough for this purpose. Using this feature, command to extract the sub-matrix **E** can also be written as **E = A (: , $)**.

It is not necessary to extract elements from contiguous rows and columns of a matrix to create a new matrix. For example, the command **A (1:2:4, 1:2:4)** creates a sub matrix by picking elements from the alternate rows and columns, starting with the first row and the first column. The resultant matrix is as follows:

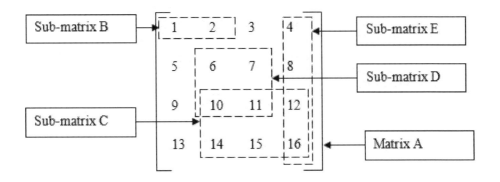

Fig. 3.1: Some sub-matrices of matrix A

```
-->A (1:2:4, 1:2:4)
 ans =
   1.   3.
   9.   11.
```

The vectors used for extracting a sub-matrix can also be created by randomly choosing the row and column indices, in any order, and the same index can be used many times. The only restriction for an index vector is that it must consist of the valid index values for the rows and columns of the given matrix. If the empty index vector is used for either row indices or column indices or both, the resultant matrix is always the empty matrix. The following example shows how to create a sub matrix by randomly selecting the rows and columns. It also shows the use of the empty index vector.

```
-->A=[1,2,3,4;5,6,7,8;9,10,11,12;13,14,15,16]
 A =
   1.   2.   3.   4.
   5.   6.   7.   8.
   9.   10.  11.  12.
   13.  14.  15.  16.
-->B=A([1,4,2],[3,2])   //Creating a sub-matrix using 1st, 4th and 2nd rows, and 3rd and 2nd columns.
 B =
```

67

```
    3.   2.
   15.  14.
    7.   6.
-->C=A([ ],[2,3])  //Use of the empty vector results into the empty matrix.
C =
   [ ]
```

3.15 Creating Multi-Dimensional Array

An array is an arrangement of data in multi-dimensional space. In Scilab, one-dimensional arrays are called vectors, and two-dimensional arrays are called matrices. Arrays of three or more dimensions are called multi-dimensional arrays. In a three dimensional array, data are arranged in rows, columns and planes. Three indices are used to locate the data elements in three dimensions. The first index refers to the first dimension, i.e. rows, the second index refers to the second dimension, i.e. columns, and the third index refers to the third dimension, i.e. planes. A book can be viewed as an example of a three dimensional array, where lines on a page refer to rows, characters position in a row refer to columns and pages refer to planes. To locate the 20th character in the 10th line of the 5th page of a book, the indices are (10, 20, 5). The indices are always arranged in the order of row number, column number, plane number and subsequent higher order dimensions. Similarly, a set of books can be viewed as a four-dimensional array. The indices to refer a character are the row, column, page and book numbers. For example, the indices (10, 20, 5, 6) refer to the character located at the 20th column in the 10th row on the 5th page of the 6th book. Similarly, books arranged in racks can be viewed as a five-dimensional array. The indices to refer a character are the row, column, page, book and rack numbers. For example, the indices (10, 20, 5, 6, 10) refer to the character located at the 20th column in the 10th row on the 5th page of the 6th book in the 10th rack.

Multi-dimensional arrays can be created in the following ways:
- Using Scilab functions
- Extending dimensions of arrays
- Using the cat function

3.15.1 Using Scilab functions

Some of the Scilab functions, such as **ones (), zeros () and rand ()**, discussed in section 3.10 of this chapter, are capable of generating multi-dimensional arrays of any dimensions. The format of the rand function is **R = rand (n1, n2, n3,…nm, 'type')**, where **n1,n2,n3, … nm** show the number of elements in the first dimension, the second dimension, the third dimension and so on up to the mth dimension, respectively. The type argument specifies the type of random number distribution. For example, if the type is equal to 'uniform', the random number generated follows a uniform random number distribution. Similarly, for generating normally distributed random numbers, the type is set to 'normal'. The following example shows the creation of a uniform random numbers matrix of three dimensions. The similar syntax is used for the other functions.

```
-->rand(3,3,3,'uniform')
 ans =
 (:,:,1)
    0.9682004   0.5283124   0.1262083
    0.6561381   0.8468926   0.7883861
    0.2445539   0.7876622   0.3453042
 (:,:,2)
    0.2659857   0.2066753   0.9152874
    0.9709819   0.8525161   0.0284860
    0.8875248   0.6744698   0.2367841
 (:,:,3)
    0.7015344   0.3161073   0.0478015
    0.1202527   0.5305191   0.8248620
    0.8287412   0.5715175   0.5798843

-->ones(2,2,2)
 ans =

 (:,:,1)

    1.   1.
    1.   1.
 (:,:,2)

    1.   1.
    1.   1.
```

3.15.2 Extending dimensions of arrays

A multi-dimensional array can be created from an existing matrix by simply extending its dimension by assigning another suitable matrix to its higher dimension. The following example shows how to convert a two dimensional matrix into a three dimensional array by inserting other two dimensional matrices of the same size in the third direction. Multidimensional matrices (arrays) are always displayed plane by plane.

```
-->a=[1,2,3;4,5,6;7,8,9]; // Creating a two dimensional matrix, a
-->b=a+9; // Creating another matrix b of size equal to the size of the matrix a
-->a(:,:,2)=b // Inserting the matrix b on the second plane of the matrix a.
 a =
 (:,:,1)    // Showing the first plane
   1.  2.  3.
   4.  5.  6.
   7.  8.  9.
 (:,:,2)   // Showing the second plane

  10.  11.  12.
  13.  14.  15.
  16.  17.  18.
```

3.15.3 Using the cat function

The **cat** function concatenates a list of arrays in a specified dimension. The syntax of **cat** function is **R=cat (dim, A1, A2, A3, …, An)**, where **A1, A2, A3,… ,An** are the matrices of the same size, **dim** is the dimension in which these matrices are inserted, and **R** is the resultant array. The following example concatenates three two dimensional matrices of size 3 x 3 to create a three dimensional matrix by using the **cat** function.

```
-->a=ones(2,3);
-->b=zeros(2,3);
-->c=eye(2,3);
-->d=cat (3, a, b, c) // Concatenating the three matrices a, b and c in the third dimension.
 d =
(:,:,1)
   1.  1.  1.
   1.  1.  1.
(:,:,2)
   0.  0.  0.
   0.  0.  0.
(:,:,3)
   1.  0.  0.
```

```
    0.   1.   0.
-->size(d)  //Size of the resultant matrix.
 ans  =
    2.   3.   3.
```

3.16 Operations on Matrices and Arrays

In Scilab, operations on matrices and arrays are classified as matrix operations and element-wise array operations. The matrix operations are only applicable to two dimensional matrices and follow the rules of linear algebra, whereas the array operations are applicable to all types of matrices and arrays and always performed element wise. The following are the various matrix operations.

3.16.1 Arithmetic matrix operations

Scilab is designed to process matrices as simple variables. Matrix variables can be directly used to write algebraic expressions, such as **C=A*B**, where **A, B** and **C** are matrices. The matrix multiplication in the previous expression is carried out similar to the normal matrix algebra as long as the operation is mathematically correct, and the matrices **A** and **B** are compatible for the operation. Table 3.3 lists the arithmetic matrix operations of Scilab. Vectors are treated as single column or single row matrices and operated upon in the same way. In addition to the normal matrix division, Scilab also has left division operator (\). This operator is normally used to solve a system equations of the form **Ax=b**. **A\B** is numerically equivalent to $A^{-1}*b$ and is computationally very fast and stable.

The matrix operations are valid even if one of the operands is a scalar. For example, let **A** be a matrix and **k** be a scalar. The expression **A+k** or **k+A** adds **k** to all the elements of **A**. Similarly, **k*A** or **A*k** multiplies all the elements of **A** by **k**, **A-k** or **–k+A** subtracts **k** from all the elements of **A** and **A/k** divides all the elements of **A** by **k**. However, **k/A** is evaluated as **k*A-¹**. Example 3.4 and Example 3.5 show various matrix operations described in this section.

Table 3.3: Matrix operations in Scilab

Operator	Operation	Example	Remark
+	Addition	A+B	Valid, if A and B are the same size matrices, or one of them is a scalar.

-	Subtraction	**A-B**	Valid, if A and B are the same size matrices, or one of them is a scalar.
*	Multiplication	**A*B**	Valid, if A's number of columns is equal to B's number of rows, or one of them is a scalar.
/	Division	**A/B**	A/B is equal to $A*B^{-1}$. It is valid if $A*B^{-1}$ is valid.
\	Left division	**A\B**	A\B is equal to $A^{-1}*B$. it is valid if $A^{-1}*B$ is valid.
^	Exponentiation	**A^n**	Valid, if A is a square matrix and n is a real or complex number.

Example 3.4: Various matrix operations

```
-->A=[1,5;3,4];
-->B=[1,2;3,4];
-->C=A+B   //Addition of two matrices
C =
  2.   7.
  6.   8.
-->C=A-B   //Subtraction of two matrices
C =
  0.   3.
  0.   0.
-->C=A*B //Matrix multiplication of two matrices
C =
  16.   22.
  15.   22.
-->C=A/B  //Right division of two matrices
C =
  5.5  - 1.5
  0.    1.
-->C=A\B  //Left division of two matrices
C =
  1.   1.0909091
  0.   0.1818182
-->C=A^2 //Square of a matrix
C =
```

16. 25.
15. 31.

Example 3.5: Matrix operations between a matrix and a scalar

```
-->A=[1,5;3,4];
-->k=2;
-->C=A+k  //Addition of a scalar and a matrix
 C =
   3.   7.
   5.   6.
-->C=A-k  //Subtraction of a scalar from a matrix
 C =
 - 1.   3.
   1.   2.
-->C=A*k  //Multiplication of a scalar and a matrix
 C =
   2.  10.
   6.   8.
-->C=A/k  //Right division of a matrix by a scalar
 C =
   0.5   2.5
   1.5   2.
-->C=A\k  //Left division of a matrix by a scalar
 C =
 - 0.7272727   0.9090909
   0.5454545 - 0.1818182
-->C=inv(A)*k  //This expression is equivalent to the left division
 C =
 - 0.7272727   0.9090909
   0.5454545 - 0.1818182
```

3.16.2 Arithmetic array operations

Array operations are carried out on element-by-element basis; hence, always require arrays (matrices) of the same dimensions. For example, let **u** and **v** are two row vectors; the element wise multiplication is a row vector whose elements are **[u_1v_1, u_2v_2, u_3v_3 ... u_nv_n]**. Table 3.4 lists element wise arithmetic operations of Scilab. For addition and subtraction, the matrix operators and the element wise operators are the same, as these two operations are performed element-wise in the matrix algebra also. The remaining other operators are preceded by dot (.) to make them element-wise. For the examples shown in Table 3.4, the inputs used are **A=[1,2,3,4], B=[2,4,6,8]** and **n=2**. The element-wise operators can be used in the similar fashion for matrices and multi-dimensional arrays. For the two same sized matrices **A** and **B**, the command **C=A.*B** produces a matrix **C** with elements $C_{ij} = A_{ij} * B_{ij}$.

Table 3.4: Matrix operations in Scilab

Operator	Operation	Example	Result	Explanation
+	Addition	A+B	[3. 6. 9. 12.]	$[a_1+b_1, a_2+b_2, …]$
-	Subtraction	A-B	[- 1. - 2. - 3. - 4.]	$[a_1-b_1, a_2-b_2, …]$
.*	Multiplication	A.*B	[2. 8. 18. 32.]	$[a_1*b_1, a_2*b_2, …]$
./	Division	A./B	[0.5 0.5 0.5 0.5]	$[a_1/b_1, a_2/b_2, …]$
		A./n	[0.5 1. 1.5 2.]	$[a_1/n, a_2/n, …]$
		n./A	[2. 1. 0.6666667 0.5]	$[n/a_1, n/a_2, …]$
.\	Left division	A.\B	[2. 2. 2. 2.]	$[b_1/a_1, b_2/a_2, …]$
		A.\n	[2. 1. 0.6666667 0.5]	$[n/a_1, n/a_2, …]$
		n.\A	[0.5 1. 1.5 2.]	$[a_1/n, a_2/n, …]$
.^	Exponentiation	A.^n	[1. 4. 9. 16.]	$[a_1^n, a_2^n, …]$
		A.^B	[1. 16. 729. 65536.]	$[a_1^{b_1}, a_2^{b_2}, …]$

Array operations are the real strength of Scilab. They help in removing many loops in Scilab programs. For example, consider computing the element-wise product of two row vectors, **P** and **Q** of **n** elements. The traditional way to compute this is given below for any conventional programming language (using its own syntax). Even the manual computation is carried out in the similar style on a piece of paper.

```
for i=1:n
        PQ(i)= P(i) *Q(i)
End
```

However, in Scilab, this computation can be carried out by just a single command **PQ = P.* Q**. To the beginners of Scilab, this may look odd, but once familiar with the array operations, Scilab can be utilised to write efficient and compact codes for the scientific and technical problems.

Now, consider the following code to compute the element wise product of two arrays **A** and **B** of two dimensions of size **m x n,** as written in most of the traditional programming languages.

```
for i=1:m
        for j=1:n
                AB(i,j)= A(i,j) *B(i,j)
        end
end
```

The previous program can be written in Scilab as a simple expression **AB=A.*B** without using any loop. It may be noted that it is not a matrix multiplication operation; it is just an element-by-element multiplication. These types of operations are termed as array operations and are always performed element-wise and require same size matrices.

Sometimes, ambiguity arises about an operator in an expression, whether it should be treated as an array operator or a matrix operator. This happens when decimal constants are directly used in expressions. For example, consider the expression **1./A** , where **A** is a square matrix. The expression can be evaluated as either **1.0/A** or **1 ./A**. The first one is evaluated as a matrix operation equivalent to **1.0 * inv(A)**, whereas, the second one is evaluated element wise, equivalent to **[1.0/$a_{1,1}$, 1.0/$a_{1,2}$, …]**. Scilab always evaluates the given expression as the first one along with the message: **Warning: "1./ ..." is interpreted as "1.0/ ...". Use "1 ./ ..." for element wise operation** as shown in Example 3.6. It is recommended that use spaces in such situations to remove the ambiguity. Example 3.7 shows matrix multiplication and array multiplication of two matrices **A** and **B**.

Example 3.6: Use of spaces to remove ambiguity in expressions

```
-->a=[1,2;3,4]
 a =
```

```
  1.   2.
  3.   4.
-->1./a
```
Warning: "1./ ..." is interpreted as "1.0/ ...". Use "1 ./ ..." for element wise operation
```
 ans  =
 - 2.   1.
   1.5  - 0.5
-->1 ./a
 ans  =
   1.         0.5
   0.3333333  0.25
```

Example 3.7: Matrix multiplication and array multiplication of two matrices

```
-->A=[1,2;3,4];
-->B=[5,6;7,8];
-->A*B  // Matrix multiplication calculated as [1*5+2*7, 1*6+2*8; 3*5+4*7,3*6+4*8]
 ans =
   19.  22.
   43.  50.
-->A.*B  // Array multiplication calculated as [1*5,2*6; 3*7, 4*8]
 ans =
   5.   12.
   21.  32.
```

3.16.3 Relational operations

There are six relational operators in Scilab, given in Table 3.5. These operators always perform operations element-by-element. The relational operations can only be performed if either both the matrices are of the same size or one of them is a scalar. If one operand is a scalar, the operations are performed with all the elements of the matrix with the scalar. The result is always a Boolean matrix. The values of the elements of the resultant matrix are **F** for false relations and **T** for true relations at the corresponding elements. Table 3.5 uses **A = [2, 5, 6], B = [3, 2, 6]** and **k = 2** to illustrate the relational operations.

Table 3.5: Relational operators

Operator	Operation	Example	Result	Example	Result
<	Less than	A < B	[T F F]	A < k	[F F F]
<=	Less than or equal to	A <= B	[T F T]	A <= k	[T F F]
>	Greater than	A > B	[F T F]	A > k	[F T T]
>=	Greater than or equal to	A >= B	[F T T]	A >= k	[T T T]
==	Equal to	A == B	[F F T]	A == k	[T F F]
~=	Not equal to	A ~= B	[T T F]	A ~= k	[F T T]

3.16.4 Boolean (logical) operations

The logical operators available in Scilab are given in Table 3.6. These operators perform element-wise logical operations on Booleans or numeric matrices. For AND and OR Boolean operations to be valid, either both the matrices should be of the same dimensions or one of them must be a single Boolean or a numeric scalar. Table 3.6 uses **A = [%t, %f, %t]**, **B = [%t, %t, %f]** and **k = %t** to illustrate the logical operations. All the numeric values except zero is considered true (T) in Scilab. For example, the numeric vector **a = [1, -2, 0, 0.5, -.5]** is equivalent to the Boolean vector **b = [%t, %t, %f, %t, %t]**, for the purpose of evaluation of logical operations. The expression **a & b** evaluates to **[T T F T T]**.

Table 3.6: Logical operators

Operator	Operation	Example	Result	Example	Result
&	Logical and	A & B	[T F F]	A & k	[T F T]
|	Logical or	A | B	[T T T]	A | k	[T T T]
~	Logical not	~A	[F T F]	~k	F

3.17 Matrix Manipulations

Matrices are dynamic objects in Scilab i.e. the shape and size of matrices can be altered as and when it is required. A matrix can be reshaped into a vector or into any other sized matrix, with the condition that the number of elements in the old matrix and the new matrix are the same. Following are the techniques to change the shape and size of matrices.

3.17.1 Reshaping a matrix (an array) as a column vector

A matrix **P** can be converted to a column vector by the command **Q = P (:)**. Example 3.8 converts a matrix into a column vector. During the conversion, the first column is stored first, and the second column is stored next, and then the third column is stored, and this process continues till the last column is appended. Example 3.9 shows conversion of a three dimensional array into a column vector. In this conversion, the first plane is taken as a two dimensional matrix and converted to a column vector as discussed above. Then the next plane is taken as a two dimensional matrix and converted to a column vector and appended at the end of the first column vector. This process is repeated, in sequence, for the remaining planes and appended to the column vector. Similar procedure is used to convert higher dimensional arrays into a column vector.

Example 3.8: Converting a matrix into a column vector

```
-->a=[1,2;3,4]
 a  =
   1.   2.
   3.   4.
-->b=a(:) //converting a two dimensional matrix into a column vector
 b  =
   1.
   3.
   2.
   4.
```

Example 3.9: Converting a three dimensional array into a column vector

```
-->a=[1,2;3,4];
-->b=[5,6;7,8];
-->a(:,:,2)=b  // Creating a three dimensional matrix by combining two two-dimensional matrices
 a  =
(:,:,1)
   1.   2.
```

```
     3.   4.
(:,:,2)
     5.   6.
     7.   8.
-->c=a(:) // Converting a three dimensional matrix into a column vector
 c  =
     1.
     3.
     2.
     4.
     5.
     7.
     6.
     8.
```

3.17.2 Reshaping a matrix as a differently sized matrix

A matrix of size **m x n** can be reshaped to another matrix of size **p x q** provided **m * n = p*q**. The command to perform reshaping of a matrix is **B=matrix (A, p, q)**, where **A** is the original matrix, and **B** is the new reshaped matrix of size **p x q**. If the specified size is not compatible to the original matrix, an error message "**!--error 60: Wrong size for argument: Incompatible dimensions**" is generated. The matrix reshaping is not limited to two dimensional matrices only, but it can be extended to an array of any dimension. The only condition for a valid matrix/array reshaping is that the number of elements in the source matrix and the resultant matrix must be the same. For reshaping, Scilab treats the input array/matrix as a column vector created by stacking columns of the source matrix one after the other, starting from the first column. The resultant matrix is always created column wise taking elements from the stacked source column vector starting from the top. Example 3.10 illustrates these concepts.

Example 3.10: Reshaping of matrices and arrays

```
-->a=1:16 //Creating a row vector of 16 elements
 a  =
        column 1 to 9
    1.   2.   3.   4.   5.   6.   7.   8.   9.
        column 10 to 16
    10.  11.  12.  13.  14.  15.  16.
-->b=matrix(a,4,4) // Reshaping the row vector into a matrix of 4x4 size
```

b =
```
   1.   5.   9.   13.
   2.   6.  10.   14.
   3.   7.  11.   15.
   4.   8.  12.   16.
```
-->b=matrix(a,2,4,2) //Reshaping the row vector into a three dimensional array of size 2 x 4 x 2
b =
(:,:,1)
```
   1.   3.   5.   7.
   2.   4.   6.   8.
```
(:,:,2)
```
   9.  11.  13.  15.
  10.  12.  14.  16.
```

-->b=matrix(a,4,5) //An invalid reshaping due to incompatibility of the matrix sizes
       !--error 60
Wrong size for argument: Incompatible dimensions.

3.17.3 Changing the size of a matrix

Scilab permits to create new elements outside the current size of the matrix. The size of the matrix is automatically changed to accommodate the new elements, and the other unspecified elements, created due to resizing, are automatically set to zeros. Scilab generates the smallest matrix that can accommodate the new elements by changing either the number of rows or columns or both. However, an attempt to read elements outside the current dimension of a matrix generates errors. Example 3.11 illustrates the above.

Example 3.11: The size adjustment of a matrix due to insertion of new elements

-->a=[1,2;3,4] // Creating a 2 x 2 matrix.
a =
```
   1.   2.
   3.   4.
```
-->a(3,2)=5 // Inserting an element outside the current size. Only the number of rows are adjusted.
a =
```
   1.   2.
```

```
     3.  4.
     0.  5.
-->a(4,5)=7 // Both the number of rows and columns are adjusted due to the new element.
 a =
   1.  2.  0.  0.  0.
   3.  4.  0.  0.  0.
   0.  5.  0.  0.  0.
   0.  0.  0.  0.  7.
-->b=a(6,5) // An attempt to read an element outside the current size of the matrix.
     !--error 21
Invalid index.
```

3.17.4 Appending a row or column to a matrix

A column can be added to a matrix using the command **A = [A, V]**, where **A** is a matrix, and **V** is a column vector. The number of elements in the column vector **V** should be equal to the number of rows in the matrix **A**. Similarly, a row can be appended to a matrix by using the command **A = [A; V]**, where **A** is a matrix, and **V** is a row vector of the compatible size. Example 3.12 shows addition of a column and a row to a matrix.

Example 3.12: Appending a column and a row to a matrix

```
-->A=[1,2,3;4,5,6]; // Creating a matrix of size 2 x 3.
-->V=[7;8]; // Creating a column vector of size 2 x 1.
-->A=[A,V] // Appending a column to the matrix A.
 A =
   1.  2.  3.  7.
   4.  5.  6.  8.
-->R=[9,10,11,12]; //Creating a row vector of size 1 x 4.
-->A=[A;R] //Appending a row to the matrix A.
 A =
   1.  2.  3.  7.
   4.  5.  6.  8.
   9.  10. 11. 12.
-->A=[A,V] //Appending a column to the matrix A failed due to inconsistent dimensions.
     !--error 5
Inconsistent column/row dimensions.
```

3.17.5 Deleting rows and columns of a matrix

Rows and columns of a matrix can be deleted by setting the corresponding rows and columns to a null vector. A null vector is a vector with no elements and represented by a pair of empty brackets. Example 3.13 shows deletion of rows and columns of a matrix. All the rows and columns of a matrix can be deleted by setting the matrix to a null matrix.

Example 3.13: Deletion of rows and columns of a matrix

```
-->A=[1,2,3;4,5,6;7,8,9]; //Creating a 3 x 3 matrix.
-->A(1,:)=[] //Deleting the first row of the matrix A.
 A =
   4.  5.  6.
   7.  8.  9.
-->A(:,2)=[] //Deleting the second column of the matrix A.
 A =
   4.  6.
   7.  9.
-->A=[] //Deleting all the rows and columns of the matrix A.
 A =
   []
-->A=[1,2,3,4;5,6,7,8];
-->A(:,2:3)=[] //Deleting a range of columns of the matrix A.
 A =
   1.  4.
   5.  8.
```

3.18 Some Useful Matrix Commands

Scilab has a number of useful built-in functions for processing matrices efficiently. Table 3.7 lists some of the matrix processing commands. The examples in Table 3.7 uses the matrix **A = [2, 3; 5, 9]** for illustration of the functions.

Table 3.7: Matrix processing functions

Function	Description	Example	Result
det(A)	Finds the determinant of a square matrix.	det(A)	3

rank(A)	Finds the rank of a rectangular matrix.	rank(A)	2
trace(A)	Calculates the sum of the diagonal elements of a rectangular matrix.	trace(A)	11
inv(A)	Calculates the inverse of a non-singular square matrix.	inv(A)	3 - 1 -1.6666667 0.6666667
norm(A)	Calculates the Euclidian norm of a rectangular matrix.	norm(A)	10.905243
A'	Returns the transpose of a rectangular matrix.	A'	2. 5. 3. 9.
spec(A)	Calculates the eigen vector values of a matrix.	spec(A)	0.2798467 10.720153
C=orth(A)	Returns an orthogonal matrix based on the given matrix. A matrix is an orthogonal matrix if its inverse and transpose are same.	orth(A)	- 0.3297667 - 0.9440625 -0.9440625 0.3297667

Summary

- The basic data unit in Scilab is matrix, which is defined by the number of rows, the number of columns and the type of data. The data types can be real, integer, complex, Boolean, string and polynomial.
- The basic strength of Scilab is its capability to apply an operation on the complete matrix simultaneously, which removes the requirement of repetition of statements in many situations.
- Matrices can be created from individual data, colon operator, or library functions, such as **ones()**, **eye()**, **zeros()**, **rand()**, etc.
- The **testmatrix** function is used to generate various test matrices, such as magic matrices, Frank matrices and Hilbert matrices.
- The **sparse** function can be used to create sparse matrices.
- Multidimensional matrix in Scilab is termed as arrays. They can be created using library functions (**ones()**, **zeros()**, etc.), by extending their dimensions or using the **cat** function.
- Scilab is designed to perform both matrix algebra operations and array operations efficiently. The array operations are performed element wise.

- Matrices can be dynamically reshaped with the help of the **matrix** function, provided the number of elements in both the matrices is the same.
- A row or a column can be added/deleted to/from a matrix, but a single element cannot be deleted from a matrix. Adding an element outside the current dimensions of a matrix automatically resizes the matrix to include the element, padding zero to the unspecified elements.
- The functions **det**, **rank**, **trace**, **inv** and **norm** are used to find the determinant, rank, sum of the diagonal elements, inverse and Euclidian norm of a matrix, respectively.

Key Terms

- arithmetic matrix operations
- array operations
- colon (:) operator
- column vector
- creating matrices
- **diag()**
- element-wise array operations
- ellipsis
- empty matrix
- Extending dimensions of arrays
- **eye()**
- **linspace()**
- logical operations
- **logspace()**
- matrix manipulations
- matrix operations
- multi dimensional array
- **ones()**
- **rand()**
- relational operations
- reshaping of matrices
- row vector
- scalar
- **size()**
- sparse matrix
- special matrices
- sub matrix
- **testmatrix()**
- **zeros()**

Exercise Problems

3.1 Create the following vectors and matrices:
- [1 2 3]

- $\begin{bmatrix} 1 \\ 2 \\ 3 \end{bmatrix}$

- $\begin{bmatrix} 1 & 2 & 3 \\ 4 & 5 & 6 \\ 7 & 8 & 9 \end{bmatrix}$

- $\begin{bmatrix} 1 & x^2 \\ e^x & \sin x \end{bmatrix}$ where x=1.5

- $\begin{bmatrix} 1 & 2+3i \\ 3-2i & i \end{bmatrix}$

3.2 Perform the following operations using the row vector A= [4 10 8] and the column vector B= $\begin{bmatrix} 5 \\ 7 \\ 9 \end{bmatrix}$:

(a) A * B
(b) B * A
(c) Transpose of the vectors A and B
(d) A' * B'
(e) Sum and average of all the elements of the vector A
(f) Count the number of elements in the vector B
(g) Arrange the elements of the vector A in ascending order
(h) Element wise sum of the elements of the vectors A and B

3.3 Create the following 4 x 4 matrices using built-in functions:
(a) Identity matrix
(b) Null matrix
(c) Matrix of uniformly distributed random numbers between 50 and 100 and round off the elements to three decimal places
(d) Matrix of normally distributed random numbers between 1 and 2
(e) Diagonal matrix with the diagonal values equal to (2,4,6,8)

3.4 Write commands to create or perform the following sub matrices or operations with the matrix A= $\begin{bmatrix} 2 & 5 & 1 & 7 \\ 2 & 1 & 4 & 3 \\ 4 & 6 & 2 & 5 \\ 9 & 8 & 8 & 7 \end{bmatrix}$:

(a) A vector containing all the elements of the first row
(b) A vector containing all the elements of the third column
(c) A sub matrix containing elements of the second and third rows and the first and second columns
(d) A vector containing the diagonal elements

(e) Delete the first row
(f) Delete the second and third columns
(g) Set values of all the elements of the third row to 8

3.5 Reshape the following matrix

$$A = \begin{bmatrix} 2 & 5 & 1 & 7 \\ 2 & 1 & 4 & 3 \\ 4 & 6 & 2 & 5 \\ 9 & 8 & 8 & 7 \end{bmatrix} \text{ as a}$$

(a) Column vector
(b) (2 x 8) matrix
(c) Row vector

3.6 Create the following matrices

with the matrix $A = \begin{bmatrix} 1 & 2 & 3 \\ 4 & 5 & 6 \\ 7 & 8 & 9 \end{bmatrix}$ and $B = \begin{bmatrix} 10 & 11 & 12 \\ 13 & 14 & 15 \\ 16 & 17 & 18 \end{bmatrix}$:

(a) $C = \begin{bmatrix} 1 & 2 & 3 & 10 & 11 & 12 \\ 4 & 5 & 6 & 13 & 14 & 15 \\ 7 & 8 & 9 & 16 & 16 & 18 \end{bmatrix}$

(b) $D = \begin{bmatrix} 1 & 2 & 3 \\ 4 & 5 & 6 \\ 7 & 8 & 9 \\ 10 & 11 & 12 \\ 13 & 14 & 15 \\ 16 & 17 & 18 \end{bmatrix}$

3.7 Find the determinant, inverse and rank of the following matrices:

(a) $\begin{bmatrix} 1 & 2 & 3 \\ 4 & 5 & 8 \\ 3 & 2 & 1 \end{bmatrix}$

(b) $\begin{bmatrix} 1 & 2 & 3 \\ 4 & 5 & 6 \\ 3 & 2 & 1 \end{bmatrix}$

3.8 Generate a 4 x 5 matrix of uniformly distributed random numbers between 0 and 100 and then set all the elements of the matrix to 0 whose value is less than 50.

3.9 With the matrix $A = \begin{bmatrix} 1 & -2 \\ 3 & 4 \end{bmatrix}$, calculate A^2, A^3 and A^4.

3.10 Solve the following system of equations using the left division Scilab operator:

$$x + 2y + z = 4$$

3.1 Create the following sparse matrix:
$$\begin{bmatrix} 2 & 0 & 1 & 0 \\ 0 & 1 & 0 & 0 \\ 0 & 0 & 0 & 2 \\ 1 & 1 & 0 & 0 \end{bmatrix}$$

3.12 Find the eigen values and eigen vectors of the following matrix:
$$\begin{bmatrix} 5 & 0 & 1 \\ 0 & -2 & 0 \\ 1 & 0 & 5 \end{bmatrix}$$

3.13 Perform the following relational and logical operations on the vectors A=[1 0 3] and B=[2 3 1]:
   a. A>B
   b. A≠B
   c. A & B
   d. A | B

3.14 With A=[1 2 3] and B=[4 5 6], perform the following array operations:
   a. A+B
   b. A*B
   c. A/B
   d. A-B
   e. A^2

Chapter 4
Polynomials

Learning Objectives

- Representation and creation of polynomials
- Finding roots of a polynomial
- Evaluation of a polynomial at given data
- Operations on polynomials
- Integration and differentiation of polynomials
- Polynomial curve fitting

4.1 Introduction

A polynomial is a mathematical expression consisting of a sum of terms, each term consists of one or more variables raised to positive whole numbers, and multiplied by a coefficient. For example, $3x^2y^2 + 2xy + 5$. The simplest and most widely used polynomials have one variable. The general form of a single variable polynomial is as follows:

$$a_n x^n + a_{n-1} x^{n-1} + \cdots + a_1 x + a_0$$

Where the a's represent coefficients, x represents the variable, and n represents the order (also called degree) of the polynomial.

The Scilab software has built-in functions to perform standard operations on polynomials, such as creation, evaluation, arithmetic operations (addition, subtraction, multiplication, and division) and finding roots of polynomials.

4.2 Polynomial Creation

In Scilab, a single variable polynomial is represented by a row vector which stores the coefficients of various terms arranged in descending order of its powers. For the missing terms, the coefficients are assigned zero values and stored at the proper positions in the row vector. The size of the coefficients vector is always equal to the order of the polynomial plus one. Table 4.1 shows some polynomials along with the corresponding coefficient vectors. Polynomials can be assigned symbolic names which can be used like variables in Scilab expressions.

Polynomials can be created either from its coefficients vector or from its roots using the **poly** function. The syntax of the **poly** function is given as below:

polynomial_name = poly (row_vector, "variable_name", ["Flag"])

The value of the optional parameter **Flag** can be set either **"roots"** or **"coeff"**, in short **"r"** or **"c"**, respectively. By default, the value of the **Flag** is **"roots"**, and polynomials are created from the roots. In this case, the **row_vector** is treated as the roots of the polynomial. If the value of the flag is set to **"coeff"**, the polynomial is created from the coefficients, and the **row_vector** is treated as the coefficients of the polynomial. The parameter **variable_name** is a character, such as 'x','s', used as a symbol for the polynomial variable. The parameter **polynomial_name** is a variable holding the defined polynomial. If the **polynomial_name** is not specified, the default name **"ans"** is used. The **poly** function can be used to create polynomials from the real as well as complex roots and coefficients. Table 4.2 shows some examples of polynomial creations.

We can also define a polynomial by writing the polynomial directly as a mathematical expression, using a polynomial seed. A polynomial seed is a symbol used to write a polynomial. For example, x is a polynomial seed in the polynomial $3x^3 + 2x^2 + 5x + 1$. A polynomial seed can be created by calling the **poly** function with zero as the first argument and variable name (as a string) as the second argument. For example, **s = poly (0, "x")** creates a polynomial seed, **"x"** and name it **s**. Now, the polynomial $3x^3 + 2x^2 + 5x + 1$ can be created by writing the expression **3*s^3+2*s^2+5*s+1**.

Table 4.1: Polynomials and their corresponding coefficient vectors

Polynomial	Coefficients Vector
$3x^3 + 2x^2 + 4x + 1$	[3, 2, 4, 1]
$3x^3 + 4x + 1$	[3, 0, 4, 1]
$3x^3 + 1$	[3, 0, 0, 1]

Table 4.2: Examples of polynomial creation

Row Vector	Command	Output
a=[2,3]	poly(a, "x", "roots") or poly(a, "x")	$6 - 5x + x^2$
b=[2,3]	poly(b, "x", "coeff")	$2 + 3x$

c=[3, 0, 0, 1]	poly(b, "s", "coeff")	$1 + 3s^3$
d= [1. + 2.i, 1. - 2.i]	poly(d, "x", "roots")	$5 - 2x + x^2$
e= [1. + 2.i, 1. - 2.i, 3]	poly(e, "x", "roots")	$-15 + 11x - 5x^2 + x^3$

4.3 Polynomial Evaluation

A polynomial can be evaluated for given values of the polynomial variable by using the **horner** function, which has the following syntax:

   y=horner (P, x)

where **P** is a polynomial; **x** and **y** are vectors of numbers.
   Polynomials can be evaluated for real values as well as for complex values. Example 4.1 illustrates the evaluation of a polynomial.

Example 4.1 : Evaluation of polynomials

```
-->x=[1,2,3];

-->P=poly(x,"x","roots")
 P  =
              2    3
 - 6 + 11x - 6x + x

-->x1=[1.5,2,4]
-->y=horner(P,x1)    //Evaluation at real values
 y  =

   0.375    0.    6.

-->x2=x1+%i*3
 x2 =

   1.5 + 3.i    2. + 3.i    4. + 3.i

-->y=horner(P,x2)    //Evaluation at complex values
```

```
y  =

   13.875 - 27.75i   - 30.i   - 48. + 6.i
```

4.4 Roots of a Polynomial

The roots of a polynomial can be found by using the **roots** function, which has the following syntax:

    r=roots (P)

where **P** is a polynomial, and **r** is a vector, which consists of the roots of the polynomial **P**.

Example 4.2 shows the application of the **roots** function to evaluate the roots of the polynomials $x^2 - x - 2$ and $x^2 + 2x + 3$.

Example 4.2 : Finding the roots of polynomials

```
-->c=[-2 -1 1];

-->P=poly(c,"x","c")
 P  =

            2
  - 2 - x + x

-->r=roots(P)
 r  =

    2.
  - 1.

-->c=[3 2 1];

-->P=poly(c,"x","c")
 P  =
```

```
            2
 3 + 2x + x

-->r=roots(P)
 r  =

  - 1. + 1.4142136i
  - 1. - 1.4142136i
```

4.5 Polynomial Arithmetic Operations

Arithmetic operations – addition, subtraction, multiplication, division, etc. – can be used to process polynomials. Two or more polynomials can be added by using plus operator ('+'). For example, $(x^3 + 2x^2 + x) + (3x^2 + 5x + 1)$ results into $x^3 + 5x^2 + 6x + 1$. Similarly, minus operator ('-') can be used for subtracting one polynomial form the other. For example, $(x^3 + 2x^2 + x) - (3x^2 + 5x + 1)$ results into $x^3 - x^2 - 4x - 1$ Table 4.2 lists some commonly used arithmetic operations used for processing polynomials. The **pdiv**, polynomial division function, returns quotient (q) and reminder (r). The Polynomials used for the illustrations are P1 = $(6x^2 + 19x + 20)$ and P2 = $(2x + 3)$.

Table 4.3: Arithmetic operations for polynomials

Operation	Operator	Example	Output
Addition	+	P1+P2	$6x^2 + 21x + 23$
Subtraction	-	P1-P2	$6x^2 + 17x + 17$
Multiplication	*	P1*P2	$12x^3 + 56x^2 + 97x + 60$
Division	pdiv()	[r,q]=pdiv(P1,P2)	$q = 3x + 5, r = 5$
Power	^	P2^2	$4x^2 + 12x + 9$

4.6 Polynomial Differentiation and Integration

The derivative of a polynomial can be computed by using the function **derivat**, which has the following syntax:

Pd = derivat (P)

where **P** is a polynomial and **Pd** is its derivative with respect to the polynomial seed variable. Use of the **derivat** function is shown in Example 4.3.

There is no direct function available in Scilab for the analytical integration of a polynomial, but it can be easily performed as illustrated in Example 4.4. The basis of the integration calculation is to multiply each term of the given polynomial by the seed variable and then divide the coefficients by the new power of the corresponding terms and finally add a constant term.

Example 4.3 : Finding derivative of a polynomial

```
-->c=[1,2,3,4,5];  //Coefficient row vector
-->p=poly(c,"x","c")  //Create the polynomial p with the coefficient row vector c
 p  =

                  2     3     4
    1 + 2x + 3x + 4x + 5x

-->pd=derivat(p)  // Find the derivative of the polynomial p w.r.t. x
 pd  =

                  2     3
    2 + 6x + 12x + 20x
```

Example 4.4 : Integration of a polynomial

```
-->c=[1,2,0,8,10];

-->p=poly(c,"x","c")  // Create a polynomial
 p  =

                3     4
    1 + 2x + 8x + 10x

-->c1=coeff(p)  //Extract the coefficients of the polynomial p
```

```
c1  =

   1.   2.   0.   8.   10.

-->n=1:length(c1);

-->c2=c1./n   //Create new coefficients
c2  =

   1.   1.   0.   2.   2.

-->c3=[2,c2]  //Add a constant term ( any value can be taken; here, 2 is used)
c3  =

   2.   1.   1.   0.   2.   2.

-->pi=poly(c3,"x","c")  // Create the integrated polynomial
pi  =

              2     4    5
   2 + x + x + 2x + 2x
```

4.7 Polynomial Curve Fitting

For a given set of data points (x, y), the **polyfit** function can be used to find the best fit polynomial passing through the data. The syntax of the function is as given below:

$$p = \text{polyfit}(x, y, n)$$

where **n** is the order of the polynomial to fit, **x** and **y** are vectors containing the data points, and **p** is the polynomial returned by the function. The function uses the least-square method for fitting. The **polyfit ( )** returns the polynomial coefficients **p**. The function **polyval (p, x)** can be used to find values of the polynomial **p** at the values specified by the vector **x**. Example 4.5 illustrates the polynomial curve fitting using the function **polyfit** . The original data points and the estimated data points are plotted in Figure 4.1.

Example 4.5 : Polynomial curve fitting

```
-->x = linspace(0,%pi,10); // Create 10 equal-spaced data points between 0 and π

-->y = sin(x);

-->p = polyfit(x,y,3) // Find the best polynomial of order three for (x, y) data points
 p =

  - 1.900D-16  - 0.4038881   1.2688517  - 0.0234222

-->f = polyval(p, x); // Find the values of the polynomial p at specified x values

-->scf(); // Create a Scilab graphics window

-->plot(x, y, "r.-") // Plot the original data points

-->plot(x, f, "b+-") // Plot the estimated data points

-->legend(["Sin","Polynomial"],"in_lower_left");

-->xtitle("Degree 3 least squares polynomial","X","F(x)")
```

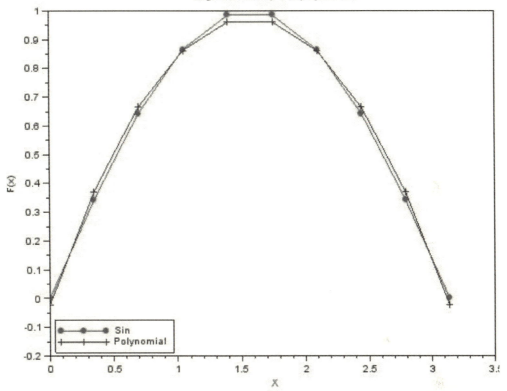

Fig. 4.1: Polynomial curve fitting

Summary

- A polynomial is a mathematical expression consisting of a sum of terms, each term consists of one or more variables raised to positive whole numbers, and multiplied by a coefficient. For example, $3x^2y^2 + 2xy + 5$.
- The simplest and most widely used polynomials have one variable, with the general form as follows: $a_n x^n + a_{n-1} x^{n-1} + \cdots + a_1 x + a_0$.
- In Scilab, a single variable polynomial is represented by a row vector, which stores the coefficients of various terms arranged in descending order of its powers. The values of the coefficients of the missing terms are zero.
- The **poly** function is used to create a polynomial either from the coefficients or roots of the polynomial.
- The **horner** function is used to find the values of a polynomial at the specified points.

- The **root** function is used to find the roots of a polynomial.
- The arithmetic operations that can be performed on polynomials are addition, subtraction, multiplication, division and power.
- The **derivat** function is used to find the derivative of a polynomial.
- The **polyfit** function is used to find the best fit polynomial from a given set of data.

Key Terms

- coefficient vector
- **derivate()**
- derivative of a polynomial
- differentiation of a polynomial
- **horner()**
- integration of a polynomial
- **pdiv()**
- **poly()**
- **polyfit()**
- polynomial arithmetic operations
- polynomial creation
- polynomial curve fitting
- polynomial evaluation
- **roots()**

Exercise Problems

4.1 Create the polynomials with the following roots:
    (a) $r_1=3$, $r_2=2$
    (b) $r_1=-3$, $r_2=2$
    (c) $r_1=1$, $r_2=2$, $r_3=3$
    (d) $r_1=1+2i$, $r_2=1-2i$
    (e) $r_1=1+2i$, $r_2=1+3i$

4.2 Create the following polynomials and find their roots and evaluate them at $x=2$, -4 and $2+3i$:
    (a) $p(x) = 2x^2 + 3x + 1$
    (b) $p(x) = 2x^2 - 3x + 3$
    (c) $p(x) = 4x^3 - 2x^2 + 3x + 1$

4.3 With the polynomials $P_1(x) = 4x^3 - 2x^2 + 3x + 1$ and $P_2(x) = 2x^2 + 3x + 1$, perform the following operations:
    (a) $P_1 + P_2$
    (b) $P_1 - P_2$
    (c) $P_1 * P_2$
    (d) P_1 / P_2

4.4 For the following data, find the best fit polynomial of the order of 3 and plot the data and the polynomial on a line plot.

1	2	3	4	5	6	7
- 28	0	10	8	0	- 8	- 10

4.5 Obtain the derivatives and integrals of the following polynomials:
 (a) $p(x) = 2x^2 + 3x + 1$
 (b) $p(x) = 2x^2 - 3x + 3$
 (c) $p(x) = 4x^3 - 2x^2 + 3x + 1$

Take the constant terms for all the above polynomials equal to 2.

Chapter 5
Scilab Graphics

Learning Objectives

- Creating two dimensional plots
- Adding title, legends, grid, etc. to a plot
- Editing the appearance of plots
- Creating sub-plots
- Creating logarithmic scale plots
- Creating three dimensional plots

5.1 Introduction

Scilab provides a rich set of tools for two-dimensional (2D) and three-dimensional (3D) plots. Vector data can be visualised by plotting the data as line, area, bar, pie charts, histograms, scatter and many other 2D plots. The matrix data can be visualised as surface plots, images and many other 3D plots. These plots can be rotated in three dimensions and can be viewed from any specified view point. These tools have easy and interactive user interfaces and have capabilities to export the results in a variety of formats, such as GPEG, PNG and the other popular formats. The plot area can be customised — such as changing the background colour, line colour, line type, text colour, etc. of plots — as per the requirements of users. Users can also control the quality of plots.

5.2 Two Dimensional Plots

To create a 2D plot, the **plot (x, y)** command, in its most basic form, is used, where **x** and **y** are two vectors containing the x-coordinates and y-coordinates of the data points, respectively. When executed, the plot command, by default, creates a new graphics window if there is no graphics window open else it erases the previous content of the currently active graphics window and re-plots it with the new data. However, this default behaviour can be changed by calling the function **set(gca(),"auto_clear","off")**, which sets clearing of the previous plot to off. Now, the new data is plotted over the previous contents of the graphics window. Example 5.1 shows the use of the **plot** function to plot the function **y=sin(x)** in the range **–π to π**; the result is shown in Figure 5.1.

The plot function can be used only with one argument, such as **plot(y)**. In this case, the **x** values are generated linearly between zero and the number of data in the **y** vector. Thereafter, the plot is drawn between the generated **x** values and **y** data. Example 5.2 illustrates the above and the result is shown in Figure 5.2.

Example 5.1: Use of the plot function

// To plot a sine curve
x=-%pi:.2:%pi;   // Generate x-coordinates
y=sin(x);   // Calculate y-coordinates
plot(x, y)   // Plot the data

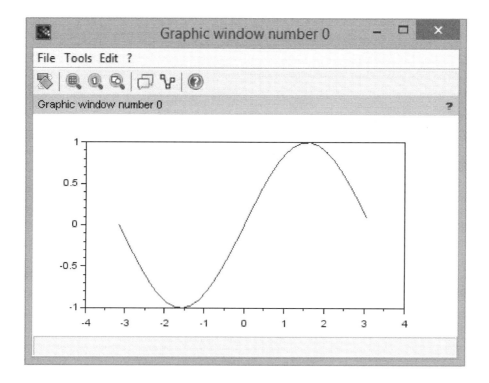

Fig. 5.1: Plot of sine curve

By default, there is no labelling of axes and no markers are placed in the plot. Further, by default, the line style is set to solid and the line colour to blue. These can be changed as explained below.

5.2.1 Adding labels and title

The commands **xlabel** ("x-label") and **ylabel ("y-label")** are used to add labels to x-axis and y-axis, respectively. The command **title ("Plot Title")** is used to add a title to the plot. The strings **"x-label", "y-label"** and **"Plot Title"** can be any string as per the requirements of users. Example 5.2 illustrates the use of these commands and Figure 5.2 shows the result.

Example 5.2 : Adding Labels to axes and Title to a plot

```
// To plot a sine curve and add Labels and Title
x=-%pi:.2:%pi; // Generate x-coordinates
y=sin(x);       // Calculate y-coordinates
plot(x, y)      // Plot the data
xlabel("x")            //Add a label to the x-axis
ylabel("sin(x)")       //Add a label to the y-axis
title("Plot of sin(x)") //Add a title to the plot
```

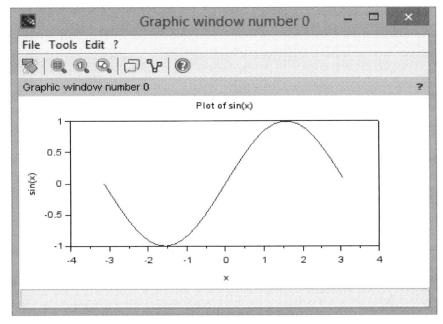

Fig. 5.2: Plot of a sine curve with a title, x-axis label and y-axis label

5.2.2 Activating and deactivating grid

A grid is a set of horizontal and vertical lines added on a plot for the better visibility of the co-ordinates. The grid can be added by the command **xgrid (color_id)**, and it can be removed by the command **xgrid (-1)**. The **color_id** is an integer corresponding to a specific colour. It can be obtained by the **color_id= color ("color_name")** function. For example, **color ("red")** returns **5**, which is **color_ id** for the red color in Scilab. By default, Scilab generates plots without a grid. For the complete list of colours and its id, please see Scilab help. Example 5.3 shows use of the **xgrid** command, and Figure 5.3 shows the results.

Example 5.3 : Adding and removing a grid to a plot

```
//To add and remove a grid to the plot.
x=-%pi:.2:%pi;
y=sin(x); plot2d(x,y);
xgrid(5)    // Adds a grid
xgrid(-1)  // Removes the grid
```

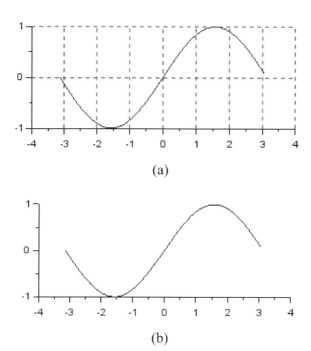

(a)

(b)

Fig. 5.3: Plots of a sine curve (a) with a grid and (b) without a grid

5.2.3 Adding texts to a plot

Sometimes, it is required to add some additional text to a plot, for giving more information in the plot. This can be done by the command **xstring (x, y, text, angle, box).** Where, **x** and **y** are the co-ordinates of the lower left corner of a box in which the text is drawn, **text** is the string to be drawn, **angle** is the amount of rotation in degree (a positive value rotates in clockwise direction) of the bounding box. The **box** argument draws a box around the drawn string if angle is zero degree. The text can be formatted using Latex. For more details about Latex, refer any good book on Latex.   Example 5.4 shows the use of the **xstring** function to write additional text to a plot, and Figure 5.4 shows the result.

Example 5.4 : Adding texts to a plot

```
//To add texts to the plot

x=-%pi:.2:%pi;
y=4*sin(x);
plot2d(x,y)
xstring(1,1,"plot of sine curve",0,1) // draws a string at zero degree with a box
xstring(.5,.5,"plot of sine curve",90,1) // draws a string at 90°
xstring(-.5,-.5,"plot of sine curve",-45,1) // draws a string  at -45°
xstring(1,2,'$\LARGE{sum_{n=1}^{+\infty}\frac1{n^2}=\frac{\pi^2}{6}}$')    // draws a Latex string
```

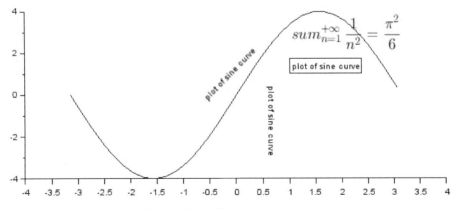

Fig. 5.4: Adding text to a plot

5.2.4 Plotting multiple curves

The generic syntax of the **plot** command is as given below:

plot(x1,y1,<LineSpec1>,x2,y2,<LineSpec2>,...xN,yN,<LineSpecN>,<GlobalProperty1>,<GlobalProperty2>,..<GlobalPropertyM>)

This syntax can be used to plot multiple series of data in a graph. Various data series are specified by pairs of vectors **x** and **y**. Each pair must be of the same size. The **LineSpec** parameter, which controls the plot appearance, consists of three components: line style, line color and data point marker. The various line styles available are shown in Table 5.1, along with the corresponding specifiers. The various curve colors available along with the corresponding specifiers are shown in Table 5.2. The various data point markers available along with the corresponding specifiers are shown in Table 5.3. The **LineSpec** parameter can combine its three components in any order. Example 5.5 shows the use of the generic format of the plot function to plot a graph with multiple data series, with different line specifications for the different data series.

Table 5.1: Various line style

Specifier	Line Style
-	Solid line (default)
--	Dashed line
:	Dotted line
-.	Dash-dotted line

Table 5.2: Line colors

Specifier	Line color
R	Red
G	Green
B	Blue
C	Cyan
M	Magenta
Y	Yellow
K	Black
W	White

Table 5.3: Various Markers

Specifier	Line color
+	Plus sign
o	Circle
*	Asterisk
.	Point
x	Cross
'square' or 's'	Square
'diamond' or 'd'	Diamond
^	Upward-pointing triangle
v	Downward-pointing triangle
>	Right-pointing triangle
<	Left-pointing triangle
'pentagram' or 'p'	Five-pointed star (pentagram)
	No marker (default)
+	Plus sign

The **GlobalProperty** parameters are used to apply common appearance to all the curves drawn on a plot. The appearance specified by the **LineSpec** parameters for the individual curves are overwritten by it. Global parameters are specified as a pair of strings, where the first string in each pair is the name of a property, and the second string is the value to be assigned to the property. For example, in the commands, **t=0:%pi/20:2*%pi; plot(t, sin(t),'ro-.', t, cos(t),'cya+', t, abs(sin(t)),'--mo', 'markstyl', 'diam')**, **'markstyl', 'diam'** is a global property pair, which specifies the marker style used for the various data series. It overwrites all the previous marker styles specified in the commands. Figure 5.6 shows the result of the previous commands. The markers of each curve are changed to diamond style.

Example 5.5: A Multiple data series plot

```
// To plot two curves in a plot using the plot function
x=-%pi:.2:2*%pi;
y1=sin(x);
y2=cos(x);
plot(x,y1,"-rx",x,y2,":gO")
```

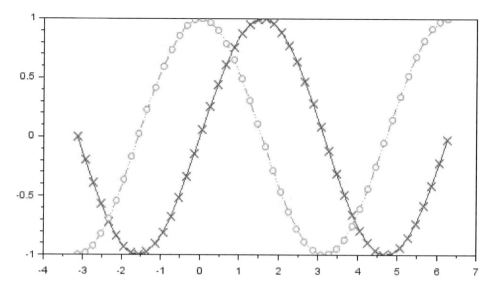

Fig. 5.5: Multiple plots

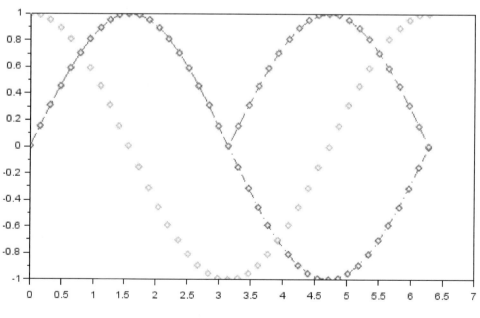

Fig. 5.6: Use of a global property

The plot function can also be used in the following formats:

i. If **y** is a vector, **plot(y)** plots vector **y** versus vector 1: size(y,'*').
ii. If **y** is a matrix, **plot(y)** plots each column of **y** versus vector 1: size (y, 1).
iii. If **x** and **y** are vectors, **plot (x, y)** plots vector **y** versus vector **x**. **x** and **y** vectors should have the same number of entries.
iv. If **x** is a vector and **y** is a matrix, **plot (x, y)** plots each column of **y** versus the vector **x** if their sizes are compatible. Otherwise, it tries to plot each rows of **y** versus the vector **x** if they are compatible. If both attempts fail, it generates error that sizes are not compatible.
v. If **x** and **y** are matrices, **plot (x, y)** plots each column of y versus the corresponding column of **x**. In this case, the **x** and **y** should be of the same size.
vi. Finally, **y** can also be a function defined as a macro or a primitive. In this case, **x** data must be given (as a vector or matrix), and the corresponding computation y(x) is done implicitly.

5.2.5 Adding legends

When a plot consists of more than one graph, legends are added to the plot for its easy comprehension. The legend command in its simplest format, **legend (string1, string2, ...)**, can be used to add legends to the current plot. The **string1** is assigned to the first curve; the **string2** is assigned to the second curve and so on. The curves are numbered in the sequence of their creation. By default, legends are placed at the right top corner of the plot. However, their position and other properties can be controlled by using the following syntax of the command:

legend (string1, string2, ... [, pos] [, boxed])

The optional **pos** parameter specifies where to draw the legend. This parameter may be assigned any one of the values given in Table 5.4, to select the legend location. Figure 5.7 shows the various positions listed in Table 5.4. The optional parameter **boxed** can be set to **true (%t)** or **false (%f)**. If it is set to true, a rectangle is drawn around the legend, and if it is set to false, no rectangle is drawn. Its default value is true. Example 5.6 shows the uses of the **legend** command; the results are shown in Figure 5.8.

Table 5.4: Various locations of legends

Value of pos parameter	Location of legends in a plot
1 or "in_upper_right"	upper right-hand corner (default)
2 or "in_upper_left"	upper left-hand corner
3 or "in_lower_left"	lower left-hand corner
4 or "in_lower_right"	lower right-hand corner
5 or "by_coordinates"	interactive placement with the mouse
-1 or "out_upper_right"	right of the upper right-hand corner

-2 or "out_upper_left"	left of the upper left-hand corner
-3 or "out_lower_left"	left of the lower left-hand corner
-4 or "out_lower_right"	right of the lower right-hand corner
-5 or "upper_caption"	above the upper left-hand corner
-6 or "lower_caption"	below the lower left-hand corner

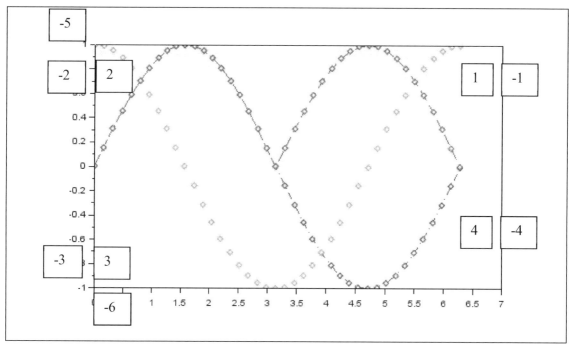

Fig. 5.7: Various locations of legends

Example 5.6: Uses of the legend command

```
//To plot curves using the plot function and add legend to the curve
x=-%pi:.2:2*%pi; y1=sin(x); y2=cos(x);
plot (x, y1,"-rx", x, y2,":gO")
legend ("Sine curve", "Cosine Curve",1,%t);  // Output in Fig. 5.8a
legend ("Sine curve", "Cosine Curve",3,%f);  //Output in Fig. 5.8b
```

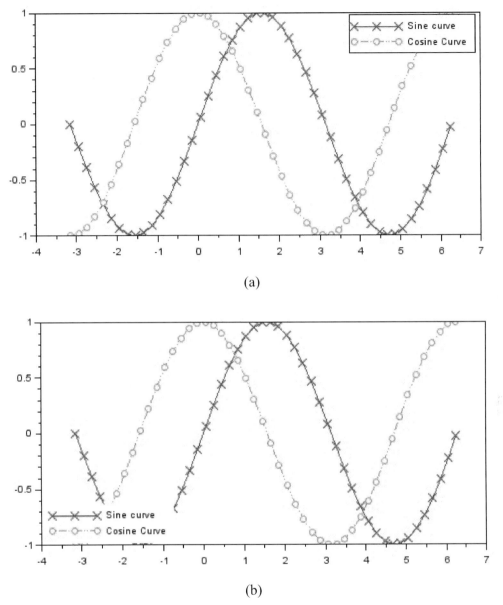

Fig. 5.8: Plots with legends

5.2.6 Interactively editing a figure

Sometimes, it is more convenient to customise the appearance of a plot interactively, using a graphical user interface (GUI). Scilab has an excellent GUI facility to interactively customise and enhance the appearance of graphics generated by various plotting functions. This is possible as plots created by any function consist of various identifiable objects (axes, legends, polylines, texts, etc) that can be individually changed. The various objects of a plot are arranged in a hierarchical structure with the Figure object at the top, as shown in the left portion of Figure 5.9. In the right portion of Figure 5.9, the properties of the selected object are shown. The object model tree shown in Figure 5.9 is for the plot shown in Figure 5.5. The number of objects in a model object tree varies with the content of plots. The window shown in Figure 5.9 is known as Figure Editor, and it consists of an Object Browser pane and an Object Properties pane. It is launched through the current graphics window's Edit->Figure Properties command.

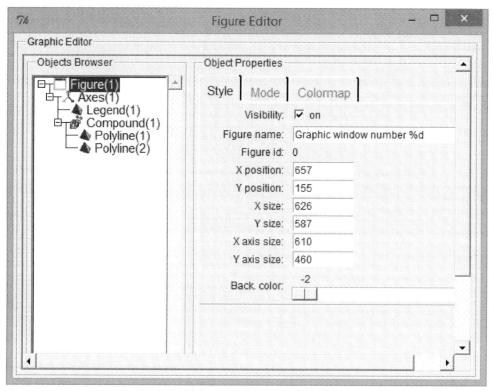

Fig. 5.9: Object model of a plot window

Once figure editor is active, various objects and their corresponding properties can be accessed by just selecting the object of interest. The properties pane shows the properties of the object selected in the object browser pane. The effects of the changes made in the properties pane are immediately updated in the figure window. The readers are encouraged to experiment with the various properties of various objects and observe their effects. Further, it can be noticed that properties of an object are arranged in various tabs, based on the subcomponents of the object. For example, through the axes object, we can customize all the axes (x, y and z), title, style, aspect and view point of the plot.

5.2.7 Editing a plot through the console window

It is also possible to edit a plot by changing the properties of various objects of a plot in the console window. The axes class is one of the most important classes of the Scilab Graphics and is most widely used to customise a plot. The handle of the axes object of the current plot is obtained by calling the **h = gca** function, where h is the handle of the axes object of the current plot, through which every property of the plot can be changed. Table 5.5 shows the properties associated with the axes object as generated by the **gca** command. The handle of the parent object, i.e. the current figure, can be obtained by the command **p= h.parent**, where the variables **h** and **p** represent the handles of the axes and figure objects, respectively. Similarly, the handle of a particular child object (e.g. a curve in a plot) can be obtained by the command **c= h.children.children(n)**, where, the variables **h** and **c** represent the handles of the axes object and the child object, respectively. The variable **n** is the child number. The children of the axes object are numbered in order of their creation in the object model tree. Table 5.6 and Table 5.7 show the properties of the parent class and the child class, respectively. For the details of the individual objects and their properties, see the help of Scilab. Once the handle of an object is obtained, the current value of a property of the underlying object can be shown by the command **h.property_name**, and the property can be changed by the command **h.property_name = new_value_of_the_property**. Through this process, we can change the appearance of a plot through the Console Window. Example 5.7 shows how the grid of a plot can be activated and how the color of a curve can be changed, using the properties of the various objects in the Console Window. The output of the changes is shown in Figure 5.10. The object-oriented editing of a plot is more suitable through programming to gain consistency of plot style.

Table 5.5: Properties of an axes object

```
//To get the properties of an axes object
h=gca()
h =
 Handle of type "Axes" with properties:
========================================
parent: Figure
children: "Compound"

visible = "on"
axes_visible = ["on","on","on"]
axes_reverse = ["off","off","off"]
grid = [-1,-1]
```

```
grid_position = "background"
x_location = "bottom"
y_location = "left"
title: "Label"
x_label: "Label"
y_label: "Label"
z_label: "Label"
auto_ticks = ["on","on","on"]
x_ticks.locations = matrix 15x1
y_ticks.locations = matrix 11x1
z_ticks.locations = []
x_ticks.labels = matrix 15x1
y_ticks.labels = matrix 11x1
z_ticks.labels = []
box = "on"
filled = "on"
sub_ticks = [0,1]
font_style = 6
font_size = 1
font_color = -1
fractional_font = "off"
 isoview = "off"
cube_scaling = "off"
view = "2d"
rotation_angles = [0,270]
log_flags = "nnn"
tight_limits = "off"
data_bounds = [0,-0.9999233;6.2,0.9995736]
zoom_box = []
margins = [0.125,0.125,0.125,0.125]
axes_bounds = [0,0,1,1]

auto_clear = "off"
auto_scale = "on"

hidden_axis_color = 4
hiddencolor = 4
line_mode = "on"
```

line_style = 1
thickness = 1
mark_mode = "off"
mark_style = 0
mark_size_unit = "tabulated"
mark_size = 0
mark_foreground = -1
mark_background = -2
foreground = -1
background = -2
arc_drawing_method = "lines"
clip_state = "clipgrf"
clip_box = []
user_data = []
tag =

Table 5.6: Properties of the parent object

//To get the properties of the parent object
a.parent
 ans =
Handle of type "Figure" with properties:
==

children: "Axes"
figure_position = [200,200]
figure_size = [626,586]
axes_size = [610,460]
auto_resize = "on"
viewport = [0,0]
figure_name = "Graphic window number %d"
figure_id = 0
info_message = ""
color_map = matrix 32x3
pixmap = "off"
pixel_drawing_mode = "copy"
anti_aliasing = "off"
immediate_drawing = "on"
background = 3

```
visible = "on"
rotation_style = "unary"
event_handler = ""
event_handler_enable = "off"
user_data = []
resizefcn = ""
closerequestfcn = ""
tag = ""
```

Table 5.7: Properties of a child object

```
//To get the properties of a child object
a.children.children(1)
 ans =
Handle of type "Polyline" with properties:
==========================================
parent: Compound
children: []
visible = "on"
data = matrix 48x2
closed = "off"
line_mode = "on"
fill_mode = "off"
line_style = 5
thickness = 1
arrow_size_factor = 1
polyline_style = 1
foreground = 2
background = -2
interp_color_vector = []
interp_color_mode = "off"
mark_mode = "on"
mark_style = 9
mark_size_unit = "point"
mark_size = 6
mark_foreground = 3
mark_background = -2
x_shift = []
y_shift = []
```

```
z_shift = []
bar_width = 0
clip_state = "clipgrf"
clip_box = []
user_data = []
```

Example 5.7: Editing of a plot through the Console Window

```
// To change the color of a curve using the properties of various objects
x=-%pi:.2:2*%pi; y1=sin(x); y2=cos(x); plot(x,y1,"-rx",x,y2,":gO");
a=gca();
a.grid
 ans  =
 - 1.  - 1.
a.grid=[1,1];
p=a.parent;
p.background
 ans  =
 - 2.
p.background=3;
c=a.children(1).children(1);
c.foreground
 ans  =
   3.
c.foreground=2;
```

5.3 Sub-Plots

With the help of the **subplot** command, a graphics window is divided into a matrix of sub-plots. Each plot can be selected individually and can have different graphs. The **subplot (m, n, p)** command (It can be also written as **subplot (mnp)**, where **mnp** is an integer consisting of digits **m**, **n** and **p**, in sequence. For example, subplot (2, 3, 2) can be written as **subplot (232)**) breaks the graphics window into an **m-by-n** matrix of sub-windows and selects the pth sub-window for drawing the current plot. The number of a sub-window into the matrices is counted row by row, i.e. the sub-window corresponding to element **(i, j)** of the matrix has number **(i-1)*n + j**. The properties of a sub-plot can be controlled individually. Example 5.8 shows the use of this command to create four sub-plots and shows four different graphs in the sub-plots. The result is shown in Figure 5.11.

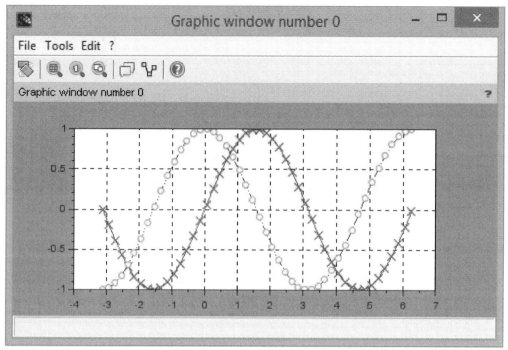

Fig. 5.10: The result of Example 5.7

Example 5.8: Uses of subplot commands

```
//To plot multiple graphs in a graphics window using the subplot command
x=0:.1:5;
subplot (2,2,1); plot (x, sin(x));
xtitle ("Plot of x vs sin(x)");
subplot (2,2,2);
plot (x, cos(x));
xtitle ("Plot of x vs cos(x)");
subplot (2,2,3); plot (x, x.^2)
xtitle ("Plot of x vs x^2");
subplot (2,2,4); plot (x, sin(-x), x, cos(x))
xtitle ("Plot of x vs sin(-x) and x vs cos(x)");
```

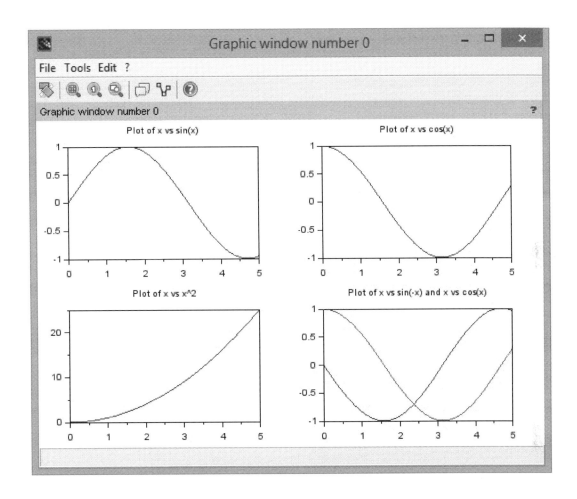

Fig. 5.11: Multiple graphs using subplot commands

5.4 Creating Commonly Used 2D Plots

Scilab has a number of functions for creating various types of plots, such as logarithmic plots, polar plots, area plots, bar charts, histograms, pie charts and many more. Some of the commonly used plots are described in the following sections.

5.4.1 Logarithmic plots

Logarithmic plots can be of three types, based on the types of scale used for the various axes: **semilogx**, **semilogy** and **loglog**. In **semilogx**, the x–axis uses the logarithmic scale while y-axis uses the normal scale. In **semilogy**, the y-axis uses the logarithmic scale while x-axis uses the normal scale. In **loglog**, both the axes (x and y) use the logarithmic scale.

To plot the various types of logarithmic plots, the **plot2d** function is used with a flag to decide the type of plot. The syntax of the function is **plot2d ("logflag", x, y)**, where **logflag** is a string that sets the scale (linear or logarithmic) along the axes. The possible values are: **"nn"**, **"nl"**, **"ln"** and **"ll"**, where **"l"** stands for the logarithmic scale and **"n"** stands for the normal scale. For example, the command **plot2d ("ln", x, y)** creates a **semilogx** plot for the data series (**x** and **y**). Similarly, the command **plot2d ("nl", x, y)** creates a **semilogy** plot, and the command **plot2d ("ll", x, y)** creates a **loglog** plot. If the **logflag** is omitted in the command, the plot uses the normal scale for both axes. Example 5.9 illustrates the use of various forms of the **plot2d** command and Figure 5.12 shows the results.

Example 5.9 : Examples of subplot commands

```
// To plot various types of logarithmic plots
a=1:.01:3;
x=a.^2;
y=exp (-x);
subplot (2,2,1); plot2d(x,y)
xtitle ("(a) Nornal plot");
subplot (2,2,2); plot2d("nl",x,y);
xtitle ("(b) y-axis in logarithmic scale");
subplot (2,2,3); plot2d("ll",x,y);
xtitle ("(c) Both axes in logarithmic scale");
subplot (2,2,4); plot2d("ln",x,y);
xtitle ("(d) x-axis in logarithmic scale");
```

5.4.2 Polar plots

The **polarplot** command is used to create polar plots. The syntax of the command is **polarplot (theta, r)**, where **theta** is an angle vector and **r** the corresponding radius vector. Example 5.10 illustrates the use of the **polarplot** command to plot the **sin (4θ)** curve in the range $-\pi$ to π. The result is shown in Figure 5.13.

5.4.3 Area plots

Area plots are similar to line plots except that the areas between curves are filled with different colours. There is no direct function to create an area plot in Scilab, but the **plot2d** and **plot** functions can be used to create it by setting the **polyline_style** property of the curve to **5**, which fills the area between the curve and the x-axis. Before setting the **polyline_style** property to fill mode, it must be ensured that the curve and x-axis form a closed loop. For this, sometimes, we have to add a few extra data points to extend the curve, on both sides, up to the x-axis so as to create a closed loop. Example 5.11(a) illustrates the process of creation of an area plot for the function **y=1+abs (sin(x))** in the range **0** to **5**. The result is shown in Figure 5.14. The fill color of the area plot can be changed by changing the **foreground** property of the curves.

For plotting an area plot with more than one curve, the new area is stacked up on the previously drawn areas. Further, it must be ensured that all the curves must be extended up to the x-axis. Example 5.11(b) illustrates the creation of a multi-area plot and the result is shown in Figure 5.15.

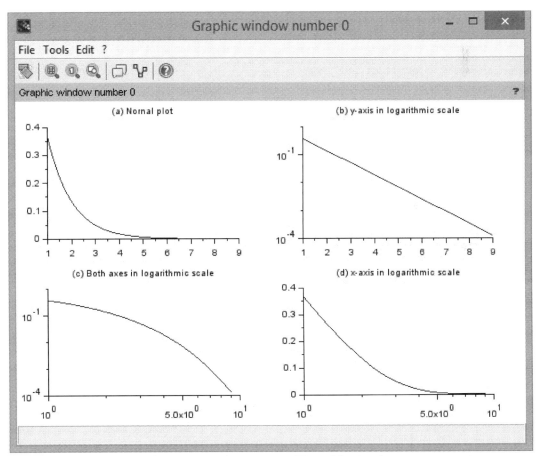

Fig. 5.12: Various types of logarithmic plots

Example 5.10: A polar plot

```
//To plot a polar plot
t=-%pi:.1: %pi;
subplot (1,2,1); polarplot(t, sin(2*t));
```

```
xtitle ("Polar plot of sin(2t)","t", "sin(2t)");
subplot (1,2,2); plot2d(t,sin(2*t));
xtitle ("Normal plot of sin(2t)","t", "sin(2t)");
```

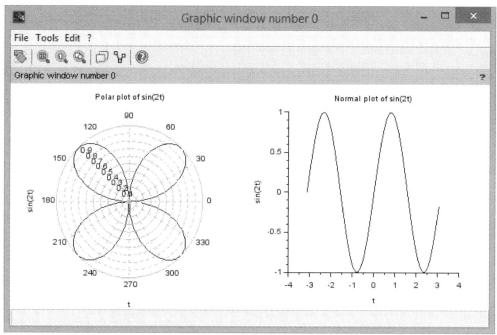

Fig. 5.13: A polar plot

Example 5.11(a): An Area Plot

```
// To plot an area plot
x=0:.1:5;
y=1+abs(sin(x));
m=min(y);   // Finding the minimum value of y data points, where x-axis is placed.
x= [0, x, 5];   //Extending the x data points
y=[m,y,m];   //Extending the y data points
plot(x,y);
e=gce ();   // Getting the handle of the plotted curve
e.children(1).polyline_style=5;   // Setting the fill style of the curve to convert it into an area plot
xtitle ("Area plot","x","1+abs(sin(x))");
```

Example 5.11(b) : A Multi-Area Plot

```
//To plot a multi- area plot
y = [1 5 3; 3 2 7; 3 5 3; 2 6 1];
 [nL, nC] = size(y);   //Get the size of the data
 x=[ 1 ,1:nL, nL];      // Generating x axis data, with two extra points at the end to extend the curve
base = min(y)-1;     // Finding the base level of y data up to which all the curves is extended
bottom = ones(1,nC)*base;      // Proper bottom closure
y= flipdim (cumsum (y, "c"),2) ;    //Stacking y data one by one
y=[ bottom ; y;bottom];      // Extending y data for proper closure
plot2d(x, y)       // Plotting the extended curves
e = gce();    //Getting the entity handle of the current plot
c=e.children;     // Getting the handles of the plotted curves
c(:).polyline_style=5;     // Changing the polyline_style Property to filled mode
```

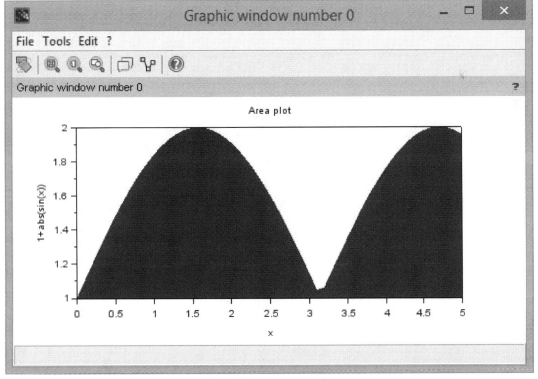

Fig. 5.14 : An area plot

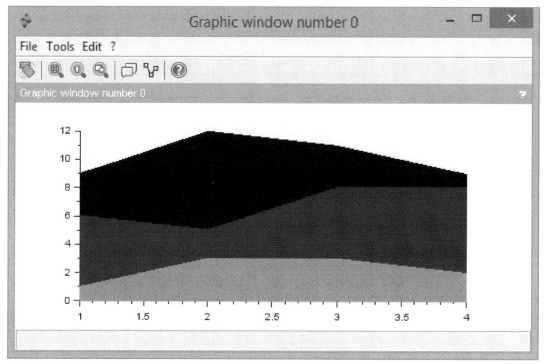

Fig. 5.15: A multi-area plot

5.4.4 Bar charts

The **bar** command is used to plot vertical bar charts. The following are the various syntaxes of this command:

    bar(y)
    bar (x, y)
    bar (x, y [, width [, color [, style]]])

The command **bar(x, y)** plots a vertical bar chart, where **x** must be a vector and **y** can be a vector or a matrix of appropriate size. If **y** is a matrix, the number of rows must be equal to the number of elements in **x**. If **y** is a vector, the values of **y** (negative values are also allowed, the bars are flipped downward) are used as the heights of the bars and the bars are placed along x-axis according to the values in the vector **x**. On the other hand, if **y** is a matrix, a grouped bar chart is plotted. The number of groups is equal to the number of rows in the matrix **y**, and the number of bars in a group is equal to the number of columns in the matrix **y**. The grouped bars are placed according to the vector **x**. The grouped bars can be placed either side by side (this is the default setting) or stacked vertically (by specifying stacked style in the bar command). If **x** is not specified and y is a matrix, i.e. **bar(y)**, the default **x = 1: size(y, "r")** is used. For a vector **y**, the **default x=1: length(y)** is used. Example 5.12 illustrates the creation of various types of bar charts and the results are shown in Figure 5.16.

In a more advanced form, we can control the width, colour and style of bars using the last syntax of the bar command as given above. For more details, see the Scilab help.

The **barh** command, with identical syntax as of **bar** command, is used to create horizontal bar charts. Example 5.13 illustrates the creation of horizontal bar charts, and the results are shown in Figure 5.17.

Example 5.12: Vertical Bar Charts

```
// To plot various types of vertical bar charts in a graphics window
x=3:5;
y=1:3;
x1= [1,4,5];
y1=5*rand (3,3);
y2= [1, -2,3];
subplot (2,3,1), bar(y);
subplot (2,3,2), bar(x, y);
subplot (2,3,3), bar (x, y1);
subplot (2,3,4), bar (x, y1,"stacked");
subplot (2,3,5), bar (x, y2);
subplot (2,3,6), bar (x, y1,.2,"green");
```

Example 5.13: Horizontal Bar Charts

```
//To plot various types of horizontal bar charts
x=3:5;
y=1:3;
x1= [1,4,5];
y1=5*rand (3,3);
y2= [1, -2,3];
subplot (2,3,1), barh(y);
subplot (2,3,2), barh (x, y);
subplot (2,3,3), barh (x, y1);
subplot (2,3,4), barh (x, y1,"stacked");
subplot (2,3,5), barh (x, y2);
subplot (2,3,6), barh (x, y1,.2,"green");
```

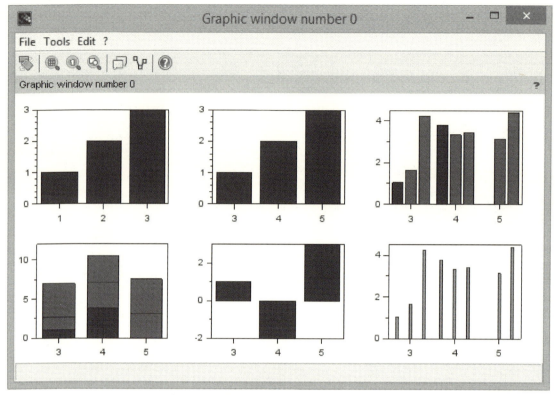

Fig. 5.16: Different types of bar charts

5.4.5 Histogram plots

Histograms can be plotted by using the **histplot** command, which has the following syntaxes:

    histplot (n, data, <opt_args>)
    histplot (x, data, <opt_args>)

The **histplot** command plots a histogram of a `data` vector. The class intervals can be explicitly specified by an increasing vector (**x**), which must have at least two components. Alternatively, if the number of classes (**n**) is provided instead of the vector **x**, then the classes are equally spaced and $x(1) = min(data) < x(2) = x(1) + dx < ... < x(n+1) = max(data)$ with $dx = (x(n+1)-x(1))/n$.

By default, the **histplot** command plots a normalised histogram. The regular histogram can be plotted by setting the normalization option to false, such as **histplot (n, data, normalization=%f).** Similarly, other optional arguments can be used to change the appearance of the plot. For example, the command **histplot (n, data, style=5)** plots the histogram in red color. For other optional arguments, see the Scilab help.

Example 5.14 illustrates the use of the **histplot** command for plotting the histogram of Gaussian random sample, both normalised and regular plot. The results are shown in Figure 5.18.

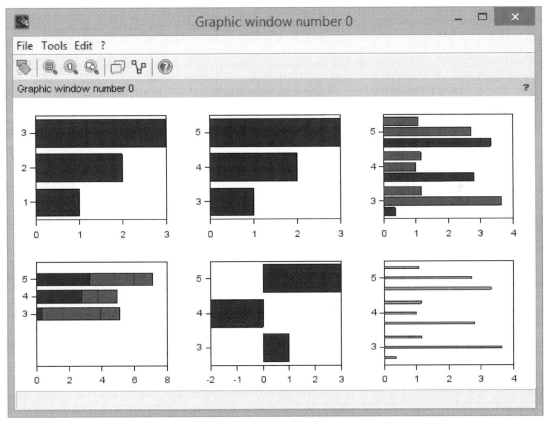

Fig. 5.17 : Different types of horizontal bar charts

Example 5.14: Histogram Charts

//To plot different types of histograms in a graphics window
d=rand(1,10000,'normal');   // the Gaussian random sample
subplot (2,2,1); histplot (20, d); xtitle ("Normalised Histogram");
subplot (2,2,2); histplot (20, d, normalization=%f); xtitle ("Regular Histogram");
subplot (2,2,3); histplot (20, d, style=5); xtitle ("Color Changed");
c=0:4;
subplot (2,2,4); histplot (c, d, style=3); xtitle ("Portion of Normalised Histogram");

5.4.6 Pie charts

The command **pie** draws a pie plot, which has the following syntaxes:

pie(x)
pie (x [, sp [, txt]])

where **x** is a scalar or a vector of positive real numbers, **sp** is a vector of real numbers, and **txt**, optional, is a cell or a vector of strings.

The number of pieces in the pie chart is equal to the number of elements in **x**, and the sizes of pieces are in proportion to the values of the elements of **x**. The pieces of the pie chart are drawn in counter clockwise and are, by default, drawn together, but they can be drawn separately with the help of the **sp** vector, which is of size **x**. The non-zero entry in **sp** separates the corresponding pie piece. By default, each piece is labeled with the percentage contribution of that piece. The optional parameter **txt**, a vector of strings of size **x**, can be used to write specific labels. Example 5.15 illustrates the use of the **pie** command, and the results are shown in Figure 5.19. The color of the individual pieces of a pie chart can be changed interactively or through axes objects, as discussed earlier, a common editing procedure for every type of charts created in Scilab.

Example 5.15: Pie Charts
// To plot different types of pie charts in a graphics window
x= [10,20,15,25];
subplot (2,2,1), pie(x); xtitle ("Simple Pie Chart");
sp= [1,1,1,1];
subplot (2,2,2), pie (x, sp); xtitle ("Separated Pie Chart");
txt= ["Red", "Green", "Blue", "Yellow"];
subplot (2,2,3), pie (x, txt); xtitle ("Labelled Pie Chart");
sp= [0,1,0,0];
subplot (2,2,4), pie (x, sp, txt); xtitle ("Separated (Individual pieces) Pie Chart");

5.4.7 Stair-step plot (this function is not available in Scilab 6.01)

The **stairs** command can be used to plot stair-step plots, which has the following syntaxes:

stairs(y)
stairs(x, y)

where **x** is a vector, and **y** can be a vector or a matrix of numbers. When the vector **x** is not specified in the command **stairs(y)**, the **x** vector is calculated as: if **y** is a **vector, x=1: length(y)** is used, and if **y** is a matrix, **x=1: size (y,"r")** is used. If **y** is a matrix, one stair plot corresponding to each column is plotted. Example 5.16 illustrates the use of stairs command, and the results are shown in Figure 5.20.

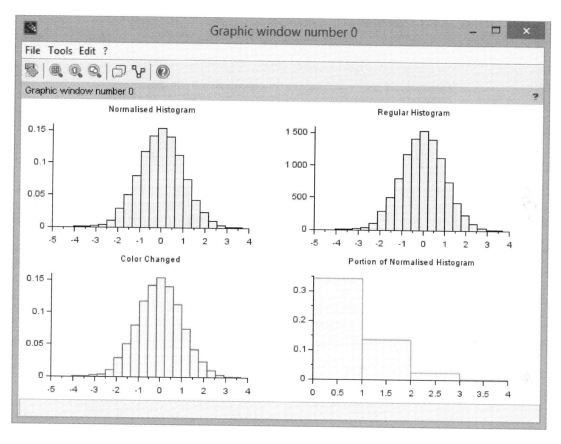

Fig. 5.18: Different types of histograms

Example 5.16 : Stair-step Plots

```
// To plot different types of Stair-step plots in a graphics window
x=1:10;
y=rand(1,10)*10;
y1=(rand(3,10)*10)';
subplot(1,2,1), stairs(y);xtitle("Single stair-step plot");
subplot(1,2,2), stairs(x,y1);xtitle("Multiple stair-step plot");
```

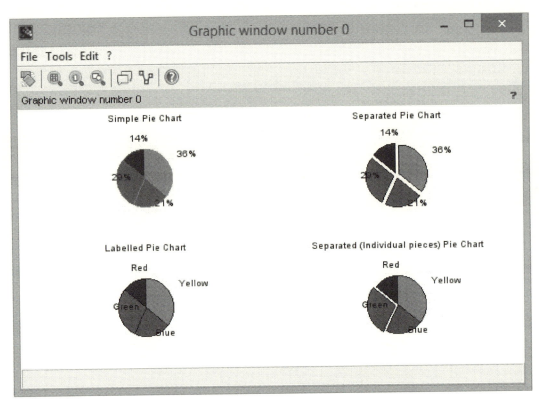

Fig. 5.19: Different types of pie charts

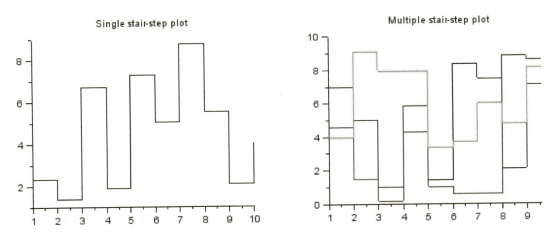

Fig. 5.20 : Different types of stair-step plots

5.4.8 2D contour plot

The **contour2d** command is used to plot two dimensional contour plots. The syntaxes of the **contour2d** command are given as below:

contour2d(x, y, z, nz, [style, strf, leg, rect, nax])
contour2d(x, y, z, nz, <opt_args>)

where **x** and **y** are vectors of numbers, used to form the grid for the plot; **z** is a matrix of numbers of the **size (length(x), length(y))**, which contains values of the function at the grid points; **nz** is an integer, which controls the number of levels in the plot; the other parameters, which are optional, are the standard parameters for every plot and control the appearance of the plot. See Scilab help for more details about these parameters.

Example 5.17 illustrates the use of the **contour2d** command, and Figure 5.21 shows the result. By default, contour plots draw the level values on the plotted curves. However, this behaviour can be changed by using the **xset("fpf","")** command, which controls the display of labels in a contour plot. If the parameter **"fpf"**, which stands for floating point format, is set to " ", i.e. set to a space, then the labels are not plotted. The default behaviour can be restored by setting it to null string **("")**.

Example 5.17 : 2D Contour Plots

// To plot 2D contour plots with labels and without labels.
x=0:.1:3*%pi;y=x;z = cos(x')*cos(x); xset("fpf","");subplot(2,1,1);
contour2d(x,y,z,7, rect=[0,0,3*%pi,3*%pi]);
xtitle("Contour curves of the function cos(x)cos(y) with legends on the curves");
xset("fpf"," ")   // This command stops the display of levels on the curve.
subplot(2,1,2); l=contour2d(x,y,z,7,frameflag=3,rect=[0,0,3*%pi,2*%pi]);
legends(string(round(l*100)/100),1:7,"lr"); xtitle("Contour curves of the function cos(x)cos(y)");

5.5 Three-Dimensional Plots

In many science and engineering problems, there are frequent requirements of data visualisation in three dimensions, for example, the motion of a particle through the space and the variation of ground elevation across a region of Earth's surface. These data can be plotted in the form of 3D curves, surfaces, meshes, shapes or contours. 3D plots can be created as parametric curves, parametric surfaces or faceted surfaces. Parametric curve plots are typically used to plot the trajectory of a particle in space at various point of time. Here, the independent variable time does not form an axis of the plot. A parametric surface is defined by an equation of the form **z=f(x, y)**, where **x** and **y** are independent variables, and **z** is the function value at a given **x, y** pair. On the other hand, a faceted surface is defined by a set of polygonal facets (patches) whose co-ordinates are given. Each facet of a faceted surface can have different colours and other attributes. This makes it more versatile in controlling the appearance of a surface.

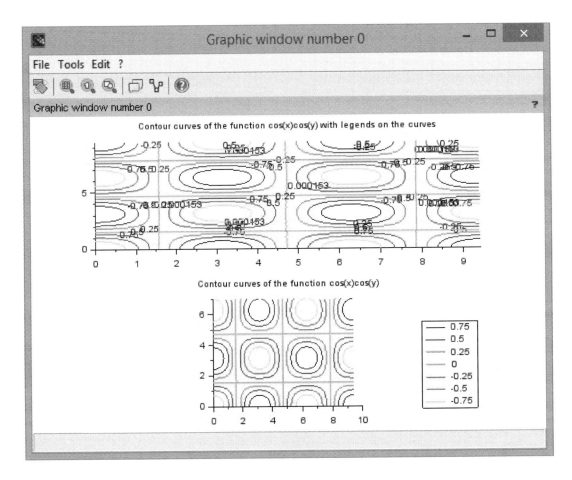

Fig. 5.21: 2D Contour plots

Scilab has a number of functions to draw various types of 3D plots. Most of the 3D plot functions are extension of their 2D counterparts and share the similar syntaxes. This section describes the most commonly used 3D plots. Table 5.8 shows a list of commonly used functions for three dimensional plots.

Table 5.8: Commonly used functions for three dimensional plots

Command	Description
plot3d	A generic function to create both parametric and faceted 3D plots of a surface.
param3d	It creates 3D parametric curves.
mesh	It creates a 3D mesh plot of a surface.
surf	It creates a 3D surface plot of a surface.
contour	It creates level curves on a 3D surface.
scatter3	It creates a 3D scatter plot from data points.
hist3d	It creates a 3D histogram of data.
fplot3d	It creates a 3D plot of a surface directly from the function.
eval3dp	It is a support function to compute the facets data of a 3D parametric surface directly from the function.
genfac3d	It is also a support function to compute the facets data of a 3D surface from raw data.

5.5.1 3D plots

The **plot3d** function is the most widely used and versatile function to create 3D plots. It can be used to create both parametric surfaces and faceted surfaces. Parametric surfaces can be created using anyone of the following syntaxes of the plot3d command:

    plot3d (x, y, z, [theta, alpha, leg, flag, ebox])
    plot3d (x, y, z, <opt_args>)

Faceted surfaces can be created using anyone of the following syntaxes:
    plot3d (xf, yf, zf, [theta, alpha, leg, flag, ebox])
    plot3d (xf, yf, zf, <opt_args>)

    plot3d (xf, yf, list (zf, colors), [theta, alpha, leg, flag, ebox])
    plot3d (xf, yf, list (zf, colors), <opt_args>)

The descriptions of the various parameters of the **plot3d** function are given in Table 5.9. Example 5.18 shows some illustrative examples to use **plot3d** using various options.

Table 5.9: Meaning of 3D plot parameters

x, y	Numeric vectors of sizes n1 and n2. The vectors x and y are used by the plot3d function to automatically generate rectangular mesh grid for creating the parametric surface plot.
z	A matrix of size (n1, n2) that holds the function values of the parametric surface at various grid points.
xf, yf, zf	Matrices of size (nf, n) that store data for creating faceted surfaces. Here, the surface is broken into n facets and each facet is defined by a polygon with nf points. The x-axis, y-axis and z-axis coordinates of the points of the ith facet are given by xf(:,i), yf(:,i) and zf(:,i).
colors	It can be either a vector of size n for storing colors of facets or a matrix of size (nf, n) for storing colors at various points of facets. In the case of matrix, the color of a facet is interpolated from the colors of the vertex points of the polygon. This facilitates gradual change of color of a facet.
theta, alpha	Numeric values. They are used to set the 3D orientation of the view point, in the spherical coordinate system, for the plotted surface. By default, alpha=35° (polar angle) and theta=45° (azimuthal angle) are used. The values are specified in degrees.
leg	A string. It is used to define the labels for each axis with @ as a field separator. For example, the string "A@B@C" displays A, B and C on x, y and z axis, respectively. By default, the axes have no labels.
flag	A real vector of size three (flag = [mode, type, box]) which is used to control the appearance of the plot. The default value of flag is set to [2, 6, 4]. The first element, i.e. mode, is an integer which controls the color and mesh of the plotted surfaces as given below: <table><tr><th>mode</th><th>Appearance of the surface</th></tr><tr><td>> 0</td><td>The surface is painted with the color value equal to mode if the colors for the facets are not explicitly given along with the zf values, and the boundary of the facet is drawn with current line style and color.</td></tr><tr><td>= 0</td><td>The surface is plotted as a mesh without color even if the colors are explicitly given for the facets, and the boundaries of the facets are drawn with the current line color.</td></tr><tr><td>< 0</td><td>The surface is painted with the color value equal to mode if the colors for the facets are not explicitly given along with the zf values, and the boundary of the facet and the boundaries of the facets are not drawn.</td></tr></table> The second element of flag, i.e. type, controls the scaling of the plotted surface as per the following scheme:

	type	Effect on the plot
	0	The plot is created using the current 3D scaling which is set by a previous call to `param3d`, `plot3d`, `contour` or `plot3d1`.
	1	The plot is rescaled automatically with the extreme aspect ratio (i.e. 16:9) to fit into a 3D box specified by the value of the optional argument `ebox`.
	2	The plot is rescaled automatically to fit into a 3D box, the bounds of the box computed using the given surface data, with extreme aspect ratios.
	3	A 3D plot with isometric scale is created with the box bounds given by the optional `ebox`. It is similar to `type=1`.
	4	A 3D plot with isometric scale is created with the bounds derived from the data. It is similar to `type=2`.
	5	A 3D expanded plot with isometric scale is created with box bounds given by optional `ebox`. It is similar to `type=1`.
	6	A 3D expanded plot with isometric scale is created with bounds derived from the surface data. It is similar to `type=2`.
	The third element, i.e. box, controls how borders around the plot are drawn	
	box	Effect on the plot
	0	No border is drawn around the plot.
	1	It is unimplemented, and the plot is similar to box=0.
	2	Only the borders behind the surface are drawn.
	3	A box surrounding the surface is drawn and captions are added.
	4	A box surrounding the surface is drawn, captions and axes are added.
ebox	It specifies the boundaries of the plot as the vector `[xmin, xmax, ymin, ymax, zmin, zmax]`. This argument is used only if the value of the `type` in `flag` is set to 1, 3 or 5. For the other values of type, `ebox` is ignored.	
<opt_args>	The optional arguments to control the appearance of a plot can also be specified in the form of argument_name=value pairs. For example, plot3d (x_data, y_data, z_data, flag = [2, 2, 3], leg = 'X@Y@Z'). This approach is more convenient if only a few parameters are to be specified and others are to be kept at their default values. The arguments can be given in any order.	

Scilab has many support functions that can be used to prepare data for the **plot3d** function. The most widely used support functions are **genfac3d** and **eval3dp** functions. The

genfac3d function computes four sides (i.e. rectangular) facets of a 3D surface and has the following syntax:

    [xx, yy, zz] =genfac3d (x, y, z, [mask])

where **x** and **y** are real vectors, **z, xx, yy, zz** are real matrices, and **mask** is a Boolean matrix. The vectors **x** and **y** are used for generating the rectangular grid points for the facets. The matrix **z** stores the surface data at various grid points, hence its size must be compatible with the sizes of **x** and **y**; the **mask** matrix is used to select the **z** values where facets are to be generated. By default, the facets for all the **z** values are generated. The matrices **xx, yy,** and **zz** store the facets data.

The **eval3dp** function generates the rectangular facets for the parametric surface directly from its function definition using the specified grid points. The syntax of the function is as given below:

    [xf, yf, zf]=eval3dp (fun, x, y)

where **fun** is the function handle, **x** and **y** are vectors storing the grid point data, and **xf, yf** and **zf** are matrices for storing the facets data.

Example 5.18 – Illustrative examples of plot3D

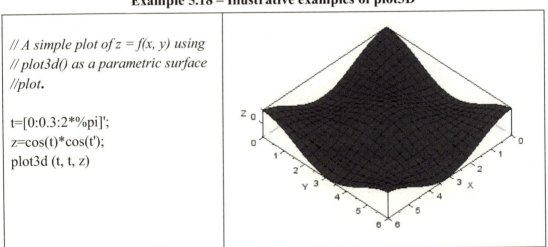

```
// A simple plot of z = f(x, y) using
// plot3d() as a parametric surface
//plot.

t=[0:0.3:2*%pi]';
z=cos(t)*cos(t');
plot3d (t, t, z)
```

`// The same plot using facets`
`//computed by eval3dp function.`
`t1=[0:0.3:2*%pi]; t2=t1;`
`// deff is a library function to`
`define an inline function.`
`deff ("[x, y, z] =fun (t1, t2)",`
`["x=t1"; "y=t2"; "z=cos(t1).*`
`cos(t2)"]);`
`[xx, yy, zz] =eval3dp (fun, t1, t2);`
`plot3d(xx, yy, zz);`
`// by default, in plots generated using`
`// eval3dp function, surfaces are`
`//shown in hidden color.`
	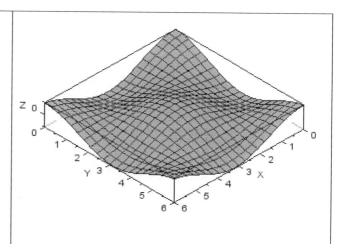

`// Multiple plots using colors`
`t=[0:0.3:2*%pi]';`
`z=cos(t)*cos(t');`
`[xx, yy, zz] =genfac3d (t, t, z);`
`// Color values- 3 for Green and 5`
`//for Red color.`
`plot3d([xx xx],[yy yy],list([zz`
`zz+4],[5*ones(1,400)`
`3*ones(1,400)]))`
	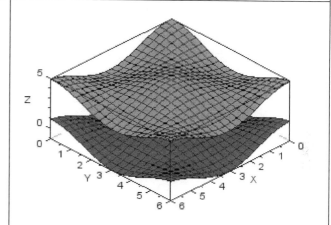

`// A plot() with more parameters`
`t=[0:0.3:2*%pi]';`
`z=cos(t)*cos(t');`
`[xx, yy, zz] =genfac3d (t, t, z);`
`//flag=[5,2,3] where, 5 is for red`
`//color,2 is the type value and 3 is`
`//the box value`
`plot3d (xx, yy, zz, alpha=60,`
`theta=45, flag= [5,2,3])`
	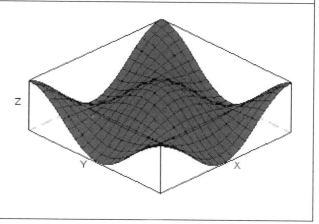

5.5.2 3D Parametric curves

A 3D parametric curve, such as the trajectory of a particle moving in a 3D space with respect to time and a 3D curve passing through a given set of 3D points, is created using the **param3d** function. Here, the independent variable time is used as a parameter to calculate the locations of the particle at various point of time and is not plotted on any axis. The syntax of the function is given below:

param3d (x, y, z, [theta, alpha, leg, flag, ebox])

where **x, y, z** are vectors of the same size storing the co-ordinates of points. Other arguments have identical meaning to their corresponding arguments in the **plot3d** function except for the **flag**. Here, **flag** has only two elements: **type** and **box**. The **type** and **box** have identical meaning to their counterparts in the **plot3d** function. Example 5.19 shows the use to the **param3d** function to plot a particle moving on a spiral path.

Example 5.19: Use of the plot3d function to draw a spiral curve

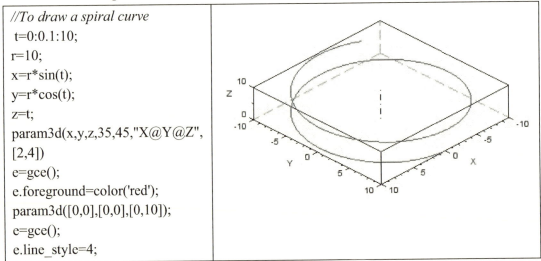

```
//To draw a spiral curve
t=0:0.1:10;
r=10;
x=r*sin(t);
y=r*cos(t);
z=t;
param3d(x,y,z,35,45,"X@Y@Z",[2,4])
e=gce();
e.foreground=color('red');
param3d([0,0],[0,0],[0,10]);
e=gce();
e.line_style=4;
```

5.5.3 3D mesh and surf plots

The **mesh** function is used to create a plot having the appearance of a wire mesh, and the **surf** function is used to create a surface plot. Both the functions have the similar syntaxes and plot a surface using rectangular grids. The **z** values for each grid point is generated either using **z=f (x, y)** or explicitly given for each grid point **(x, y)**. If **x** and **y** coordinates are not specified, the grid is determined using the dimensions of the **z** matrix. 3D mesh and surf plots take multiple optional arguments and are created using anyone of the following syntaxes:

mesh(z)	**surf(z)**
mesh(x, y, z)	**surf(x, y, z)**
mesh(x, y, z, <GlobalProperty>)	**surf(x, y, z, <GlobalProperty>)**
mesh(x,y,z, color > ,	**surf(x, y, z, <color>,**
<GlobalProperty>)	**<GlobalProperty>)**
mesh (x, y, z, <axes_handle>...)	**surf (x, y, z, <axes_handle> ...)**

The arguments of the **mesh** and **surf** functions are described in table 5.10. Example 5.20 and Example 5.21 show some illustrations of the mesh and surf commands, respectively.

Table 5.10: Meaning of 3D Mesh and Surf plot parameters

x, y	x and y are either vectors or matrices of numbers. For vectors, Scilab internally generates a meshgrid using the vectors. For matrices, the matrices are used as the meshgrid for the plot.
z	z is a matrix that stores the value of the function f (x, y) at various grid points. In case x and y are not explicitly given, the mesh function uses the vectors 1: size(z,1) and 1: size(z,2) to generate the meshgrid.
Color	color, applicable for surface plots only, is a matrix of the size of the meshgrid and specifies the color of each grid point. Depending upon the value of color_flag of the current entity, the color of a facet can either be a single color or a shade interpolated from the colors of the grid points. For more details, see the Scilab help. The color of the mesh lines are controlled by the surface_property foreground.
GlobalProperty	The appearance of mesh plot can further be customized using the GlobalProperty option. It is a key value pair, like {PropertyName, PropertyValue}, that defines the global properties of the plot and is applied to all the curves/surfaces created by a plot function. The PropertyName must be a string defining the property to be set, and the PropertyValue can be a real, integer or string (scalar or matrix) depending on the type of property used. For example, to change the color of the mesh lines of a mesh plot, the command is mesh (x, y, z, "foreground", "red"). For more details on GlobalProperty options, please refer Scilab help.
axes_handle	axes_handle is an optional argument that forces the plot to appear inside the selected axes given by axes_handle, rather than the current axes.

Example 5.20: Some mesh plots

//To draw a mesh plot
 	
[X,Y]=meshgrid(1:10,1:10);
Z=X.^2+Y.^2;
// $\huge is a latex command
xtitle('$\huge z=x^2+y^2$');
mesh(X,Y,Z);
	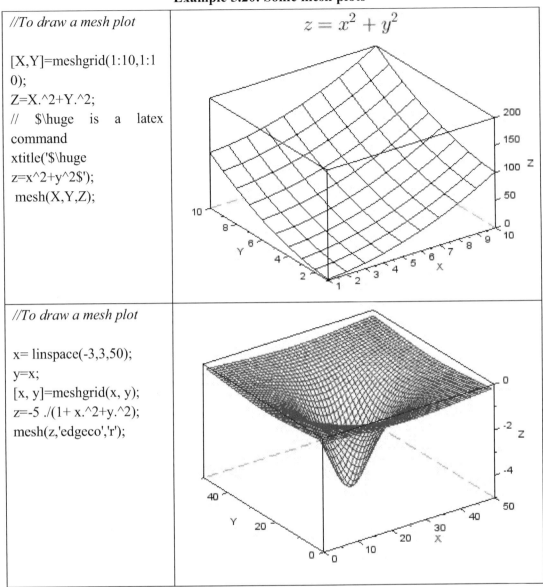

//To draw a mesh plot
 	
x= linspace(-3,3,50);
y=x;
[x, y]=meshgrid(x, y);
z=-5 ./(1+ x.^2+y.^2);
mesh(z,'edgeco','r');	

Example 5.21: Some surface plots

```
//To draw a surface plot using
//the surf command

x= linspace (-%pi/2, %pi/2, 30);
y=x;
[x, y] =meshgrid (x, y);
z=sin(x.^2) + sin(y.^2);
surf(z);
```

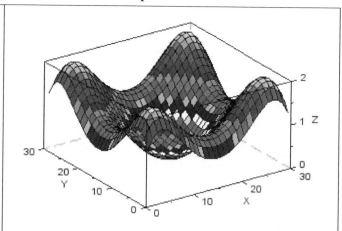

```
//To draw a surface plot using
//the surf command

x= linspace (-%pi/2, %pi/2,30);
y=x;
[x, y] = meshgrid (x, y);
z=sin(x.^2) +sin(y.^2);
surf (z, 'facecol', 'blu', 'edgecol',
'red');
```

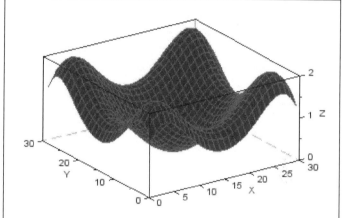

```
//To draw a surface plot
// The gdf function gets the handle
of the default figure and
jetcolormap returns a set of
predefines color codes.
f=gdf ();
f.color_map=jetcolormap();
x=1:3; y=x;
[xx, yy] =meshgrid (x, y);
z= [1,1,1;2,2,2;3,3,3];
col= [1,2;3,4];
surf (x, y, z, col);
```

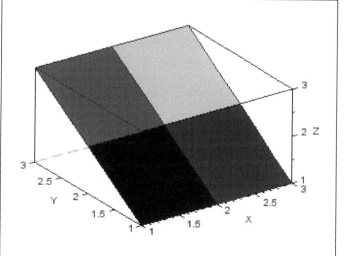

5.5.4 3D contour plot

The **contour** function plots level curves, a level curve has the same **z** value, for a 3D surface. Level curves may be plotted on the surface or on a plane. The function has the following syntaxes:

    contour (x, y, z, nz, [theta, alpha, leg, flag, ebox, zlev])
    contour (x, y, z, nz, <opt_args>)

The meanings of the various arguments of the function are identical to the corresponding arguments used in the **plot3d** function except for **nz**, **flag** and **zlev**. The argument **nz** can be either a real number representing the number of equally spaced level curves to be plotted between **min (z)** and **max (z)**, excluding both extreme points or a vector of real numbers storing various **z** values for which level curves are to be plotted. The argument flag also carries similar meaning to the corresponding flag of the **plot3d** function except for its mode component. The mode in the **contour** function is interpreted as: for **mode=0**, the level curves are drawn on the surface defined by **(x, y, z)**; for **mode=1**, the level curves are drawn as a 3D plot on a plane defined by the equation **z=zlev** (if **zlev** is not specified, it is assumed zero), and for **mode=2**, the level curves are drawn as a 2D plot on the xy plane. The last argument **zlev**, a real number, is only meaningful for **mode=2** as described above. For the other mode values, it is ignored. Example 5.22 shows some uses of contour plots.

Example 5.22 : Examples of contour plots

```
//To plot level curves
x= linspace (-3,3,50);
[xx,yy]=meshgrid(x, x);
z=-5 ./(1+ xx.^2+yy.^2);
// the parameters of the flag are
[mode, type, box]
// mode=0 means the level curves
are drawn on the surface defined by
(x, y, z).
// type=2, rescales automatically 3d
boxes with extreme aspect ratios.
// box =3 means a box surrounding
the surface is drawn and captions are
added.
contour (x, x, z, 10, flag= [0 2 3]);
```

```
//To plot level curves


x= linspace (-3,3,50);
[xx,yy]=meshgrid(x ,x);
z=sin(xx.^2)+sin(yy.^2);
contour (x, x, z, 5, flag= [0 2 3]);
```

5.5.5 3D scatter plot

The **scatter3** function (introduced in Scilab 6.0) is used to create a 3D scatter plot. The scatter plot is created with markers of various types, sizes and colors, at the locations specified by the user. The default type of the marker is circle, the default color is blue, and the default marker size is 36. The 3D scatter plot is created using anyone of the following syntaxes:

scatter3(x, y, z, msizes, mcolors, "fill", marker, <marker_property, value>)
scatter3(axes_handle, x, y, z, msizes, mcolors, "fill", marker, <marker_property, value>)

where the meanings of the parameters are given in Table 5.11; Example 5.23 shows the use of the **scatter3** function.

Table 5.11: Meaning of scatter3 parameters

x, y, z	x, y and z (column or row vectors of n real numbers) are the data points where the centres of the markers are drawn.
msizes	msizes controls the sizes of the markers. To plot each marker of the same size, specify msizes as a scalar, and to plot each marker with a different size, specify msizes as a vector of size x.
mcolors	Specifies the colors of the markers. The markers can be of the same color or each marker can be of a different color. To plot each marker with a different color, specify mcolors as a vector with n elements.
fill	The markers are filled with colors. By default, the filling colors of markers are the same as the edge color of the shape. However, both colors can be set independently.
marker	Specifies the type of a marker that is used for all the specified points.

marker_property, value	A sequence of property value pairs to specify type, color and line width of the markers.
axes_handle	The scatter plot is plotted inside the specified axes given by axes_handle.

Example 5.23 : An example of a 3D Scatter Plot

```
//To plot a scatter plot
t=linspace(0,6*%pi,50);
x=t; y=t.*sin(t);
z=exp(t./5);
col (1:50) =t;
clf ();
// size of the markers=25
//color of the markers are
defined by // the col vector
//fill- Markers are to be filled
//s – Marker type is square
//markerEdgeColor is set black
scatter3(x,y,z,25,col,"fill","s",
"markerEdgeColor", "black");
```

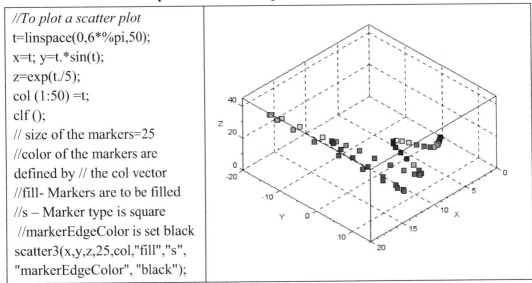

Summary

- Scilab provides a rich set of tools for two-dimensional (2D) and three-dimensional (3D) plots. Vector data can be visualised by plotting the data as line, area, bar, pie charts, histograms, scatter and many other 2D plots. The matrix data can be visualised as surface plots, images and many other 3D plots.
- The **plot** function is the most basic function to create a general 2D plot. More than one set of data can be plotted on a plot, with different line styles, colors and markers.
- The **set** function is used to control the behaviour of a graphics window for all the plotting functions.
- The functions **xlabel**, **ylabel** and **title** are used to add axis labels and title to a plot, respectively.
- The **xgrid** function is used to activate and deactivate grids in a plot.
- The **xstring** function is used to add plain and Latex texts at specified locations in a plot.
- The **legend** function adds legends in a plot.
- Scilab allows interactive editing of a plot, through a GUI or the console window, using the graphics handle.

- The **subplot** function divides the graphics window into multiple plotting areas.
- The functions **semilogx**, **semilogy** and **loglog** are used to plot using log scales.
- Polar plots are created using the **polarplot** function.
- The functions **bar** and **barh** are used to create vertical and horizontal bar charts, respectively.
- Histograms can be plotted using the **histplot** function.
- The command **pie** draws a pie plot.
- The **stairs** command can be used to plot stair-step plots.
- The **contour2d** command is used to plot two-dimensional contour plots.
- The **plot3d** function is the basic command to create 3D plots.
- A 3D parametric curve is created using the **param3d** function.
- The **mesh** and **surf** functions are used to create mesh and surface plots, respectively.
- The **contour** function plots level curves, a level curve has the same **z** value, for a 3D surface.
- The **scatter3** function is used to create 3D scatter plots.

Key Terms

- 2d contour plot
- 3d contour plot
- 3d mesh plot
- 3d parametric curves
- 3d plots
- 3d scatter plot
- 3d surf plot
- 3d surface
- area plots
- axes
- bar charts
- child object
- faceted surface
- figure editor

- **legend()**
- level curves
- logarithmic plots
- matrix data
- multiple curves
- multiple data series
- multiple stair-step plot
- object browser pane
- object properties pane
- parametric curve
- parametric surface
- parent object
- pie chart
- **plot ()**

- figure objects
- graphical user interface
- graphics window
- grid
- handle of the axes
- histograms
- labels
- Latex
- polar plot
- stair-step plot
- sub-plot
- sub-window
- three-dimensional plots
- **title()**
- two-dimensional plots
- vector data

Exercise Problems

5.1 Plot the equation $y = 3x^3 - x^2 + 4x + 4$, where x varies from -5 to 5. Write the equation on the plot and add a title to it.

5.2 Plot the equation $y = \cos(x) + 2 * \sin(x)$, x varies between $(0, 2\pi)$. Label the plot and show gridlines.

5.3 Plot the equations $y = \sin(x), y = \cos(x)$, where x varies between $(2\pi, 5\pi)$, in green and red color, respectively, on the same plot with legends, axis tick marks and a title.

5.4 Plot the equations $y = \sin^2(x),\ y = \cos^2(x), y = \log(x),\ y = e^x$, where x varies between $(1, 2\pi)$, in four sub-plots. Add a title to each.

5.6 Create a polar plot of $y = \sin(3x)$, for x between 0 and 2π.

5.7 The numbers of fish in a lake is given as below:

Fish type	Frequency
Perch	100
Bream	230
Carp	390

Draw a pie chart, histogram, a bar chart, a horizontal bar chart to show this information, in four different sub plots.

5.8 Plot the normal, semilogx, semiology and loglog plots for the equation $y = e^x$, for x=1 to 10.

5.9 Draw the mesh and surface plots for the following equations:
   a. $z = x^2 + y^2$ for x= -2 to 2 and y=-2 to 2
   b. $z = x^2 - y^2$ for x= -2 to 2 and y=-2 to 2

5.10 Draw the trajectory of an object thrown from the top of a building of height h at an angle θ with a velocity v till it reaches the ground.

5.11 Draw a scatter plot of the motion of a particle moving in the space as per the following parametric equations for the first 10 seconds:
$x = t, y = t\sin(t) \text{ and } z = e^{0.5t}$

5.12 Draw contour plots for the following equations for 10 equally spaced contours.
    a. $z = x^2 + y^2$ for x= -2 to 2 and y=-2 to 2
    b. $z = x^2 - y^2$ for x= -2 to 2 and y=-2 to 2

Chapter 6
Programming in Scilab

Learning Objectives

- Keywords and predefined constants
- Reading and writing data from/to the console
- Interactive input of data
- Looping and branching constructs
- File handling
- Importing and exporting data
- Writing user defined functions
- Inline and recursive functions
- Error handling
- Program debugging

6.1 Introduction

Scilab is a high-level programming language. The basic data types of Scilab are arrays and matrices, and the language is designed to process them efficiently. It has all the programming constructs and features, such as input/output, flow control, looping, data structures, user defined functions, and object oriented features, like other popular computer programming languages. Further, Scilab has its own integrated editor for writing, editing, and debugging programs. The language has many libraries of technical functions, written using the state of the art algorithms, for efficiently solving engineering and scientific problems. Libraries are expanding rapidly to incorporate new functions from different engineering disciplines.

6.2 Scilab Programs

Similar to conventional programming languages, such as C++, Java, etc., a Scilab program is also an ASCII text file (with extensions .sci or .sce) consisting of Scilab commands and other programming constructs. These commands and constructs can be directly entered at the command prompt, but this way of writing a program is very inconvenient and cumbersome as it does not lend itself for easy editing and modifications. Hence, programs are normally created using a plain text editor, such as notepad. Scilab has a built-in editor of its own, called SciNotes. Based on the structure of programs, Scilab programs are of two types: scripts and functions. Both types of programs consist of Scilab commands and various programming constructs but have the following major differences:

- In a script program, all the variables of the current workspace are visible to a script program. Further, a variable created in a script program is automatically available in the workspace at the end of the script execution. Hence, there is no need to pass any workspace variable to the script, and there is no need to return any script variable back to the workspace. On the other hand, in a function program, the current workspace variables are visible but a local variable created inside a function is not visible to the workspace, and the variable is killed at the end of the function execution. Hence, any local variable (created in the function) whose value is required in the current workspace after the end of the function execution has to be returned to the workspace, explicitly. Fortunately, any number of variables can be passed to a function, and any number of variables can be returned by a function.

- In a function program, the same name can be used to name a variable in a function as well as in the workspace, as Scilab uses separate memory spaces for the two. However, this is not possible in the case of a script program as the same memory space is used by the script program and the workspace. Due to this, a long script program may create clutter of variables in the workspace. Hence, it is not recommended to write a long program in the form of a script program. It should be written in the form of a function program. This promotes reusability of a program. More details about functions are discussed later in the chapter in the scripts and functions section.

6.3 Scilab Editor

Scilab has a very powerful integrated development editor (IDE), called SciNotes, for creating, debugging and running various types of programs. The IDE has many features, which make programming easier and reduce the occurrence of syntax errors: automatic indenting and indentation correction; highlighting (using different colours) to indicate special parts of the program, such as keywords, test strings, and comments; auto-completion; changing double quote strings to single quote strings; removing trailing spaces; commenting/uncommenting a block of code; run complete program or run up to the caret (cursor) for debugging programs. At present, debugging facilities of the editor are not very powerful; however, it is expected that, in the next version, it will be enhanced.

The IDE can be started in the following three ways: the edit command, the SciNotes command and the File menu option.

- **edit** command - The edit command is mainly used to create function type programs. The syntax used for this option is **edit <filename>**, where filename is an optional argument. If a filename is given, and a file with the same name exists in the search path of Scilab, the file is loaded and opened in the SciNotes window for editing. If such a file does not exist, a new function program file is created with a function name same as the name of the file specified. This function will work as the main function. By default, the edit command creates files with .sci extension. If the filename argument is not specified, a function program is created with the name untitled.sci. Figure 6.1 shows a function program to convert the temperature given in Fahrenheit (°F) to Celsius (°C). The user defined function has to be loaded into memory using the **exec** command before use. The basic syntax of the exec command is **exec('program file name along with its extension and', mode),** where mode is an integer which controls the execution mode. For example, the command exec ('C:\Users\Arvind\FahrenheitToCelsius.sci', -1) loads the function FahrenheitToCelsius into the memory to run silently. Various execution modes are discussed in the section scripts and functions. Once loaded into the memory, the function can be used like any built in function by its name. A function can be run like a script program by calling it without its arguments, but in this case, all argument variables must be predefined in the current workspace.

- **SciNotes** command -The SciNotes command is mainly used to create script type programs. The syntax used for this option is **SciNotes<filename>**, where filename is an optional argument. Again, similar to the edit command, if a filename is given and a file with the same name exists in the search path of Scilab, the file is loaded in the SciNotes window for editing. If such a file does not exist, a new script program file is created with the same name as the filename argument. By default, the SciNotes command creates files with .sce extension. The filename is used to run the script, using the **exec** command, form the work space or from other programs. Figure 6.2 shows a script program to plot a sine curve.

- **File menu** option - The File menu option of the main Scilab window can be used to open any text file—may be Scilab programs or other text files—in the SciNotes window for editing. If the SciNotes window is open, its File menu option can also be used to create a new file or to open an existing file.

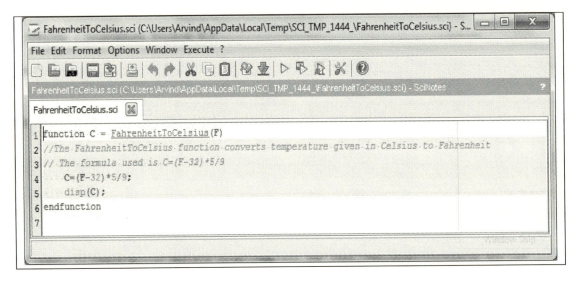

Fig. 6.1: An example of a Scilab function program

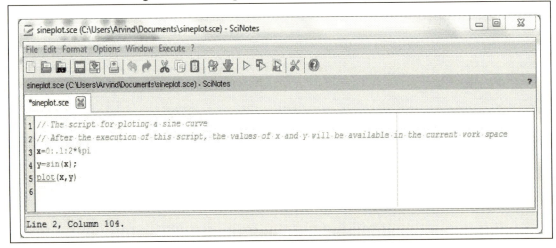

Fig. 6.2: An example of a Scilab script program

6.4 Scilab Keywords

Like all other programming languages, the Scilab programming environment has a set of reserved words, or keywords, with special meaning in programs. These words should not be used for any other purpose to avoid ambiguity in programs. Table 6.1 lists some of the commonly used Scilab keywords with their brief descriptions.

Table 6.1: List of commonly used keywords

Keyword	Description
ans	To store the result of the last expression evaluated if the result is not assigned to any variable.
else	Used in if-then-else and select-case-then-else constructions.
elseif	Used in if-then-elseif-then-else.
end	Used for marking end of some constructions, such as for loop.
global	To define global variables.
catch	To begin a catch block in try-catch control instruction.
abort	To interrupt the evaluation of a program.
break	Used to interrupt loops.
case	Used in select statement.
continue	Used to pass control to the next iteration of a loop.
do	Used in do loops.
for	Used in for loops.
if	Used for conditional execution.
pause	Used to enter into the pause mode during execution of a program.
resume	Used to resume execution of a paused program.
return	Same as the resume keyword.
select	Used in select-case statement.
then	Used in control flow statements, such as 'if' and 'select'.
while	Used in while loop.

6.5 Predefined Variables

For the consistency and accuracy of a program developed in Scilab, Scilab has a set of predefined variables, as shown in Table 6.2. It is recommended that these variables should not be redefined and used for any other purpose.

Table 6.2: Predefined Variables

Variables	Description
%e	Euler number.
%f or %F	Boolean false.
%t or %T	Boolean true.
%eps	Floating point calculations performed by Scilab are not exact but performed for a given precision. Scilab uses the IEEE 754 standard for

	evaluating the floating-point expression. The %eps is a predefined variable with the value equal to 2^(-52) and used for floating-point relative accuracy.
%i	It represents the imaginary unit (%i=√-1) to be used in complex numbers.
%inf	It represents the positive infinity value as per the IEEE standard.
%nan	It returns the IEEE double representation for Not-a-Number (NaN).
%pi	It returns the floating-point number nearest the value of π, which is the ratio of circle's circumference to its diameter.

6.6 Constants, Variables and Expressions

Since the programming environment of Scilab is tightly integrated with the workspace of Scilab, both (the workspace and the program) have the same character set and the identical types of constants, variables and expressions. The same rules, as described for the workspace in chapter 2, are applied for naming variables and evaluating expressions. Also, the same set of operators and library functions are available in the programming environment.

6.7 Input and Output Statements

Scilab has a rich set of input commands through which raw data are fed to the program, either directly through key board or files. Similarly, there are a number of commands through which the processed information is displayed on the display device or stored into a file. In this section, simple input and output commands are discussed and the file handling is discussed in a separate section, later in this chapter. There are three common ways to input data in Scilab:

- Assign data directly to variables using assignment operators.
- Interactive input through input command.
- Read data from a data file.

6.7.1. Assignment statements

A value can be assigned to a variable using the assignment operator '=' with the following syntax:

Variable name = value to be assigned;

For example,
```
x=10;        // Assigning a constant. The constant can be integer, real number or complex
r=10.56      // Assigning a real constant
```

```
f=10D-3           //Assigning a real constant in scientific notation.
                  //It can also be written as 10E-3, 10e-3,10d-3, or 10*10^-3
c=10+%i*20        // Assigning a complex value to a variable
y=x;              // Assigning the value of a variable to another variable
z=x+1;            // Assigning the value of an expression to a variable
s= 'abc' ;        // Assigning a string value of a variable
m= [1, 2, 3; 4, 5, 6]   //Assigning a matrix data to a variable
n= 1:2:10         // Assigning a series to a variable
```

The semicolon at the end of a statement is optional. If a semicolon is added at the end of a statement, Scilab suppresses the display of the assigned value at the prompt of the current workspace else the assigned value will be displayed at the command prompt during the program execution.

In Scilab, no separate statement is required to declare the type of a variable before assigning a value to it. The data type of a variable is decided by the data type last assigned to it. For example, the assignment statement **x=10** will create a variable **x** with the type constant (real or complex), and the statement **x='abc'** will create a variable **x** with the type string. The type of a variable is enquired by the command **typeof**. For example, the statement **typeof(x)** will return string if the last value assigned to the variable **x** is a string.

6.7.2. Interactive input

Scilab has a number of functions which are used to input data in a program interactively. Table 6.3 shows some of the commonly used functions along with a brief description of each. The functions are either prompt based, such as input function, or GUI based, such as **x_dialog** function. Each GUI based input function is prefixed with 'x_' and creates a popup window to input data. The popup window can be either modal (i.e. user is not allowed to do any other operation without closing the popup window) or non-modal (i.e. users can perform other operations without closing the popup window).

Table 6.3: Interactive input functions

Function	Description
input	It prompts for user input for various types of data, such as integer, real, string, complex, matrix, etc.
x_choices	It pops up a window with toggle buttons to select choices and returns the sequence number of the selected button.
x_choose	It pops up a window with a list of choices to select from and returns the sequence number of the selected item.

x_dialog	It pops up a window with a multi-line input text box and returns the entered value as a string.
x_matrix	It pops up a window for editing a matrix of real numbers and returns the edited matrix.
x_mdialog	It pops up a window for interactive input of a vector or a matrix in the form of strings.

i. input function

The input function is used for entering data, any type of value, through a command prompt. It has the following syntax:

x = input (message [, "string"])

where **message** is a character string which is used as the prompt for data entry and an optional parameter **"string"** (may be abbreviated as "s"), which is used if the user wants that the input function should return the entered numeric data as a string. By default, this function returns the entered numeric data as a number and the string data as a string. For string data entry, the string data should be enclosed between either a pair of single quote (' ') or double quote (" "), for example, 'String Value' and "String Value". For complex number, the format is **Real_Part + %i * Imaginary_Part**, for example, **10+%i*25**. The variable **x** stores the returned value. Example 6.1 shows a script program that uses the input function to find the area of a circle.

Example 6.1: Use of input function

// Calculates the area of a Circle. Prompts for the radius and the unit of the radius.

radius=input ('Enter the radius of the circle: ');
unit=input ('Enter the unit of the entered radius (as a string): ');
area=%pi*radius^2;
s=msprintf ("\r%s:%f %s %s", 'The Area of the circle is ',area, 'square', unit);
disp(s);

Output:

```
Scilab 5.4.1 Console
File Edit Control Applications ? Toolboxes

-->exec('C:\Users\Arvind\Documents\area_circle', -1)
Enter the radius of the circle: 10
Enter the unit of the entered radius (as a string): 'mm'

 The Area of the circle is :314.159265 square mm

-->
```

ii. x_choices function

The **x_choices** function is a GUI based interactive input function for getting choices from users through toggle buttons. Users indicate their choices by selecting an appropriate button from a set of buttons. The syntax of the x_choices function is as given below:

rep=x_choices (title, items)

where **title** is a vector of strings that works as the title for the choices popup window, and **items** is a list of items showing choice groups. The choice groups are created by using the list function of Scilab, which has the following syntax: **items=list (item1,...,itemn)**, where each item is also a list of the following type : **item=list('label', default_choice, choices)**, where the first entry in the list is the label of the choice group, the second entry is the default_choice (an integer, which shows the position of the button that is selected by default when popup window appears) for the group and the last entry is a row vector of strings that gives the labels to the buttons of the possible choices. On click of the OK button on the dialog, the return values are stored in rep, an integer vector, which stores, for each item group, the sequence number of the selected button in the group. If user exits dialog with the "cancel" button, rep is set to []. Example 6.2 shows use of the **x_choices** function along with the output.

Example 6.2: Use of x_choices function

```
// Use of the x_choices function.
list1=list ('choice 1',1, ['A','B','C']);
list2=list ('choice 2',2, ['X','Y','X']);
list3=list ('choice 3',3, ['1','2','3','4']);
```

rep=x_choices ('Toggle Menu', list(list1, list2,list3));

Output: 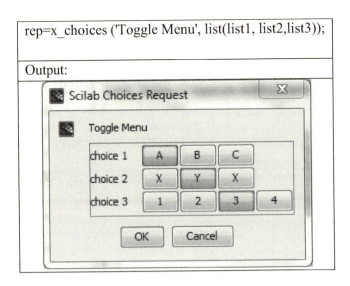

iii. x_choose function

The **x_choose** is another GUI based function to choose an option from a given list of options. The options are listed in a list box in the popup dialog window, and the desired option is selected by double clicking the item of choice. In addition to the option list, there is a button at the bottom to cancel the selection process i.e. returning without choosing any item. The syntax of the function is as given below:

[num]=x_choose (item_list, title [, button])

where **item_list** is a column vector of strings (showing items to choose from), **title** is a column vector of strings used as the title of the dialog, **button** (an optional argument) is a string used to label the button (the default label is 'Cancel'), and **num** is the returned value by the function and is an integer. The value of **num** is the sequence number of the selected item or zero if "Cancel" button is clicked. Be careful, the button is always a cancel button irrespective of its label. Example 6.2 shows a script program that uses the **x_choose** function to select a colour from a given list of colours.

Example 6.3: Use of x_choose function

//Use of the x_choose function.
n=x_choose(['Red'; 'Green'; 'Blue'],['Choose a color by double clicking'],'Return without selection')

Output:

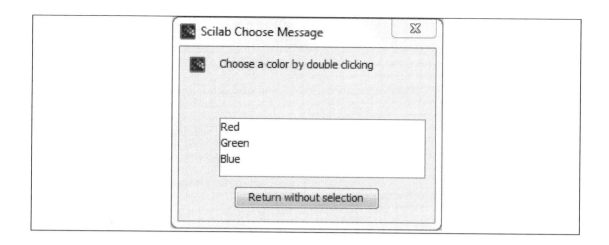

iv. x_dialog function

The **x_dialog** function is a general purpose GUI input function to interactively accept multi-lines input. The syntax of the function is as given below:

result=x_dialog (labels, default_value)

where **labels** is a column vector of strings that is used as the label of the input text box, and **default_value** is a column vector of strings used as the initial values, and **result** is a column vector of strings that stores the returned values.

The function creates a dialog box with a multi-line text box (with a vertical scroll and a horizontal scroll to facilitate entry of long strings) and two buttons: "Ok" and "Cancel". If the user selects the "Ok" button, the texts entered in the text box is returned as a column vector of strings (each line in the text box is a separate entry in the returned vector); otherwise, it returns null string ([]) if the "Cancel" button is clicked. Example 6.4 shows the use of the **x_dialog** function to input a multi-line text along with its output. It should be noted that the returned strings may require additional processing to extract useful information.

Example 6.4: Use of x_dialog function

// A program showing a use of the x-dialog function.
result=x_dialog (['Enter Sales of the Last Quarter'],['Jan:10','Feb:20','March: 15']);

Output:

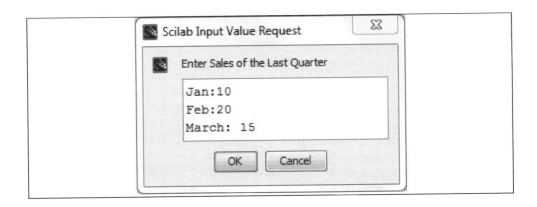

v. **x_mdialog function**

The **x_mdialog** function is basically an extended version of the **x_dialog** function to show a matrix, or a vector, of input text boxes for data entry in place of a single text box as provided in the **x_dialog** function. The data entered in the text boxes are returned in the form of a matrix, or a vector, of strings. The following two syntaxes are used to call the function:

result = x_mdialog (title, labels, default_inputs_vector)
result = x_mdialog (title, labelsv, labelsh, default_input_matrix)

where **title** is a column vector of strings used as the title of the dialog window, **labels** is a column vector of strings used as the labels of the input text boxes (i.e. **labels (i)** is the label of the ith text box), **default_inputs_vector** is a column vector of strings (to be used as the default values for the text boxes, i.e. **default_inputs_vector (i)** is the initial value of the ith text box) of the same size of the labels argument, and **result** is a vector of strings of entered values in the text boxes if returned with the "Ok" button or null vector ([]) if returned with the "Cancel" button.

For the second format of the function, **title** is a column vector of strings used as the title of the dialog window, **labelsv** is a vector (size n) of strings used as the labels for the rows of the text boxes matrix (i.e. **labelsv (i)** is the label of the ith line of the matrix), **labelsh** is a vector(size m) of strings for labelling the columns of the text boxes matrix (i.e. **labelsh(j)** is the label of the jth column of the matrix), **default_input_matrix** is a matrix (size n x m) of strings used as the default values of the text boxes matrix (i.e. **default_input_matrix(i, j)** is the initial value of the text box (i, j)) , and result is a matrix (size n x m) of strings of entered values in the text boxes if returned with the "Ok" button or null matrix ([]) if returned with the "Cancel" button. Example 6.5 shows the use of the **x_mdialog** function in its both formats along with the output generated.

Example 6.5: Use of x_mdialog function

```
//Use of the x_mdialog function.
labels=['magnitude'; 'frequency'; 'phase'];
//The first format
sig=x_mdialog ('enter sine signal', labels, ['1';'10';'0'])
labelsh= ['magnitude'; frequency'; 'phase'];
labelsv= ['sine wave'; 'cosine wave';];
title=['Enter details for both signals'];
//The Second format
rep=x_mdialog (title, labelsv, labelsh, ['1','10','0';'1','10','0']);
```

Output:

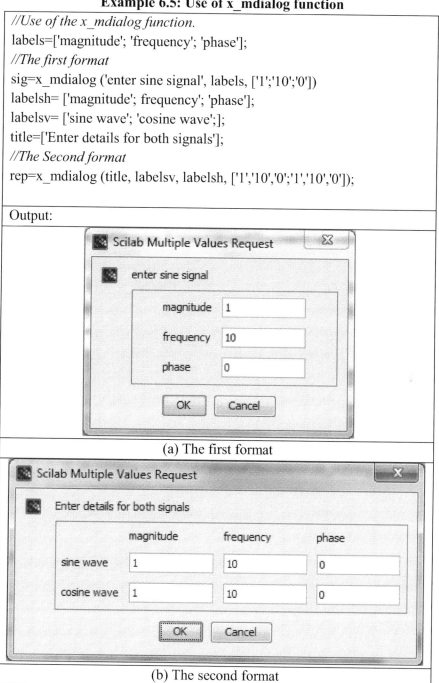

(a) The first format

(b) The second format

vi.   x_matrix function

The **x_matrix** function provides GUI for data entry and editing in the form of matrix. The function is mainly designed for entry of a number matrix; however, the data can be integers, real numbers, complex numbers or strings. The complex number should be entered in the form of **Real_Part + Imaginary_Part * %i** and the string data should be enclosed between either a pair of double quote or a pair of single quote. The syntax of the function is as given below:

[result]=x_matrix (label, matrix_initial)

where **label** is a string to name the matrix, **matrix_initial** is a number matrix used as the initial values of the matrix (the string data matrix is not allowed), and **result** is a matrix of entered values. The function returns a string matrix if user changes all the entry in the entered matrix to string type manually.

The function displays the initial matrix (which can be edited by the user manually) in the row and column style and provides horizontal and/or vertical sliders if required. Example 6.6 shows the use of the **x_matrix** function along with the output.

Example 6.6: Use of x_matrix function

| //Use of the x_matrix function. |
| m=x_matrix ('enter a 3x3 matrix ', [1,2,3;4,5,6;7,8,9]) |

Output:

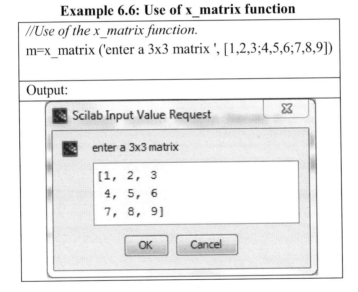

6.7.3. Output functions

Output functions are used to print the computed data either on the screen or in files. In this section, the functions used for showing text data on the screen, either in the console window or in a graphics window, are discussed. The file handling is discussed separately.

By default, Scilab shows the computed results, at the end of evaluation, in the console window if the statement is not followed by a semi colon. The function **disp** and **mprintf** are used to display the results in the console window. The function **xstring** is used to show the textual information in a graphics window.

i. disp function

The **disp** function displays the values of variables and constants in the current console window. The syntax of the function is as given below:

disp (x1, [x2, ..., xn])

where **x1, x2, ..., xn** are variables (or constants) to be displayed. The variables could be any arbitrary objects, such as matrices of constants, strings, functions, lists.

The function **disp** uses LIFO (last in first out) queue discipline to display the arguments, i.e. the last argument is printed first and the first argument is printed last. For example, **disp (10, 20, and 30)** displays **30, 20,** and **10** (in separate lines, **30** in the first line and **10** in the last line) in the console window. The matrix data is printed in the matrix format. If there is more than one matrix, each matrix is separated by a blank line. For large matrices that cannot be accommodated in the display area of the console window, the matrices are broken column-wise and printed one after the other. The display area of the console window can be customized by the function **lines (nl, nc)**, where **nl** is the number of lines and **nc** is the number of columns of the console window. If **nc** and **nl** are larger than the physical size of the console window, scroll bars are added for proper display.

If a function call is used as an argument in the **disp** function, the returned values are printed. If a function's name is used as an argument in the **disp** function, the header of the function definition are printed. Example 6.7 shows the use of the **disp** function along with the output.

Example 6.7: Use of disp function

```
//Use of the disp function.
clc
disp (10,20,30);
disp ([12],3);
disp("a",1,"c");
```

```
a=ones (2,2);
b=rand(3,3,"normal")
disp (a, b);
deff('[x]=myplus (y, z)','x=y + z')
//deff defines inline functions. For detail, see scripts and functions.
disp (myplus (10,20))
disp(myplus) // Displays the header of the function.
```

Output:
30.
20.
10.
 3.
12.
c
 1.
a
 - 0.8498895 - 0.6834217   0.3240162
   0.2546697 - 0.7209534 - 0.1884803
 - 1.5417209   0.8145126   0.4241610

   1.   1.
   1.   1.

   30.
[x]=myplus(y,z)

ii. mprintf function

The **mprintf** function converts, formats, and writes data to the main Scilab window. It is equivalent to the **printf** function of C programming language. The syntax of this function is given below:

mprintf (format, a1, a2, ..., an);

where **format**, called control string, is a Scilab string containing control characters, such as %d, %c, and escape sequence characters, such as \n, \t, along with normal characters are used to format the display of the values of the remaining operands (for more details about the format string, refer section 6.12.2, later in the chapter); **a1, a2, ..., an** are variables. The number of control characters in the format string must be less than or equal to the total number of columns of all the variables. The **mprintf** function is designed to automatically print all the rows of a matrix variable with the same format string. In the case of more than one matrix in the variable list, the matrix variable with the lowest number of rows decides the number of rows to be printed. If there is a scalar in the variable list, only one row of matrix variables is printed. To print all the columns of a matrix, the format string must contain the number of control characters equal to the number of columns in the matrix. Example 6.8 shows the use of this function.

Example 6.8: Use of mprintf function

// use of the mprintf function.
clc
for i=1:1:4
mprintf ('\nIteration %i, %f', i, i*i);
end
r=rand (1,4);
mprintf ("\nRandom numbers are: %8.4f,%8.4f,%8.4f,%8.4f",r);
a=[1,2;3,4;5,6];
b=[7,8;9,10];
mprintf("\n%3d,%3d,%3d,%3d",a,b)
Output:
Iteration 1, 1.000000
Iteration 2, 4.000000
Iteration 3, 9.000000
Iteration 4, 16.000000
Random numbers are: 0.6654, 0.6284, 0.8497, 0.6857
1, 2, 7, 8
3, 4, 9, 10

iii. **xstring function**

The **xstring** function is used to draw strings in the current graphics window. The syntax of the function is as given below:

xstring(x, y, str, [angle,[box]])

where, **x** and **y** are real vectors or scalars that species the location of the lower-left point of the strings in the graphics window on a scale of 0 to 1(for example, the coordinate (.5,.5) represents the midpoint, the coordinate (0,0) represents he lower left corner, the coordinate (1,1) represents the upper right corner, the coordinate (0,1) represents the upper left corner, and the coordinate (1,0) represents the lower right corner of the graphics window, irrespective of its current size), **str** is a matrix of strings to be drawn, **angle** is a real vector or scalar used to specify the inclination angle (in degree) of the drawn string from the horizontal axis (clockwise angle is positive degree; default is 0), **box** is an integer vector or scalar used to draw a rectangle around the drawn text if angle is zero else ignored(None zero value means draw a rectangle and zero means do not draw a rectangle; the default is 0). The last two parameters are optional.

If **x** and **y** are vectors of the same size (different sizes of x and y is an error) and **str** is a scalar string or a vector of different size than **x** (the various elements of str will be concatenated, with space between elements, to form a single string), the text, **str**, is repeated at points **(x(i), y(i))**. On the other hand, if **x**, **y**, and **str** are vectors of the same size, the text **str (i)** will be drawn at point **(x (i), y (i))**.

Starting from Scilab 5.2, it is possible to write the **str** parameter using LaTeX or MathML expressions for the formatting of the drawn text (for LaTeX or MathML formatting style, many standard books are available). The font, colour, size and other attributes of the drawn text can be controlled through **xset** ('attribute', 'attribute value') function. Example 6.9 shows use of the **xstring** function for various style of graphical text output.

Example 6.9: Use of xstring function

```
//Use of the xstring function.

str=['lower left', 'upper left', 'centre','lower right', 'upper right'];
xstring([0,0,.5,1,1],[0,1,.5,0,1],str)// Strings at various locations
xstring(.1,.1,str);// Strings concatenated together
xstring(.2,.2,'at angle',30)// String drawn at an angle
xstring(.3,.3,'In the box',0,1)// String drawn in a box
xset("font",0,3)// change size font
xstring(.6,.6,'Larger font')
xstring(.7,.8,'Latext Style')// Latex strings
xstring(.7,.7,'$\textstyle\sum_{n=1}^{+\infty}\frac1{n^2}=\frac{\pi^2}{6}$')
xstring(.1,.8,'Different font (Roman)');
xset("font",1,10);
xstring(0.1,0.6,"abc")//Different font
```

Output:

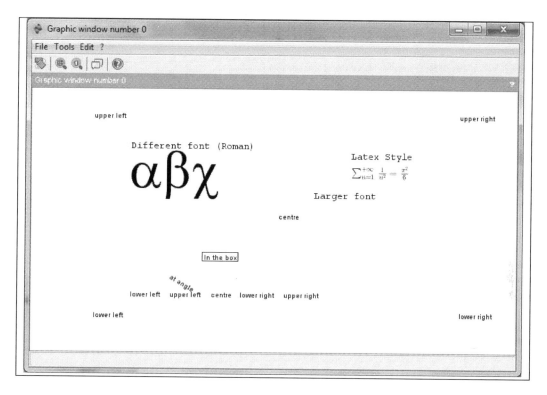

6.8 Control Structures

The execution of a program, by default, follows the water fall model, i.e. instructions in a program are executed in the sequence they are written in the program. However, many times, the solution of a problem requires repeated execution of certain set of instructions a number of times or executes only some part of the program based on some specific conditions. Control structures are the basic facilities in a programming language to solve such problems. Like other programming languages, Scilab has a rich set of control structures for various situations. The control structures are broadly divided into two groups: looping structures and branching structures. Looping structures are used to repeat the execution of a specific group of instructions either for a fixed number of times or until specified conditions are satisfied. The most commonly used looping structures are **for** and **while**. Branching structures are used for the conditional execution of a portion of a program if certain specified conditions exist. The commonly used branching structures are **if**, **if-else** and **switch**.

6.9 Looping

Loops are used to repeat the execution of a certain portion of a program. Based on the manner in which the execution of instructions is controlled, either a **for** loop or a **while** loop can be used.

When the number of repetition is known in advance, a **for** loop is generally used. On the other hand, when the number of repetition is unknown and is decided by some conditions, a **while** loop is generally used.

6.9.1 for loop

Generally, the **for** loop control structure is used for unconditional looping in which a group of statements are executed for a fixed number of times. The looping process is controlled by an index variable and it is recommended that the variable should not be modified inside the loop. The **for** loop has two parts: a loop header and a loop body. The loop header consists of an initial value, an increment value and a termination value of the loop index variable in one statement. This makes it easier to read the loop. The body of a loop consists of all the statements written between the header and the corresponding end statement. For better readability, the body of the loop should be properly indented. The **for** loop in Scilab is used in the following two syntaxes, depending on the requirement of problems:

Syntax 1:
    for index =initial_value: increment: last_value
        Statement 1
        Statement 2
        .
        .
        .
        Statement n
    end
    Statement (n+1)

where **index** is a variable, and **initial_value**, **increment** and **last_value** could be scalars (integers, real numbers and complex numbers), variables or expressions returning scalars. For complex numbers, only the real part is used to control the loop. The variable index is known as loop index variable whose value is set equal to **initial_value** at the start of the loop. Before starting the execution of the loop body, Scilab ensures that **index** will reach to the termination condition in finite number of steps. If it is not possible to reach the termination condition, the loop terminates without executing the body of the loop, called null loop. At the end of each iteration, **index** is incremented by a value equal to **increment** and if the new value of **index** is within the limit specified by **last_value**, the next iteration of the loop begins. This process is continued until the limit set by **last_value** is violated by the current value of index. Once the loop terminates, the statement written next to the loop is executed. Based on the value of the

increment, loops can be of increment type (positive value), decrement type (negative value), or null type (unreachable termination value).

Syntax 2:
    for index=expression
        Statement 1
        Statement 2
        .
        .
        .
        Statement n
    end
    Statement (n+1)

where **index** is a variable or an expression that can be a vector or a matrix (only two dimensional) or an expression returning a vector or a matrix. The body of the loop is executed, in sequence, for each entry in the vector/matrix, starting from the first entry. In case of a matrix, the sequence of execution of the loop is column-wise, i.e. the loop body is executed first for the first column then the second column and so on. This type of for loops is called a vector or matrix for loop.

A loop can be written inside the body of another loop, called nested loops, with the condition that an inner loop must completely lie inside its immediate outer loop. The syntax of nesting is given as below:

    for index =initial_value: increment: last_value
        statements
        for index =initial_value: increment: last_value
            statements
        end
    end

Example 6.10 shows some uses of for loops in various formats.

Example 6.10: for loops

```
// for loop syntax 1
// Increment for loop
clear all;
for i=1:1:5
   a(i)=i;
end
```

```
disp(a);
//Decrement for loop
for i=5:-1:1
    a(5-i+1)=i;
end
disp(a);

//Null for loop
for i=5:1:1
    disp(i);
end
// for loop syntax 2
a=[2,3,1,4]
for i=a
    disp(i);
end

// Loop nesting
for i=1:1:4
    for j=1:1:3
        b(i, j)=i*j;
    end
end
disp(b);

//loop on matrix columns
for e=eye (3,3), e, end
//loop on list entries
for l=list(1,2,'example');l, end
```

Output
1. 2. 3. 4. 5.
5. 4. 3. 2. 1.
2.
3.
1.
4.
1. 2. 3.
2. 4. 6.

```
    3.    6.    9.
    4.    8.   12.
e  =

    1.
    0.
    0.
e  =

    0.
    1.
    0.
e  =

    0.
    0.
    1.
l  =

    1.
l  =

    2.
l  =
example
```

6.9.2 while loop

Another looping construct in Scilab is **while** loop, which uses a test expression to control the loop. The initialization of the loop control variables must precede the loop definition, and their update must be done in the body of the loop. At the beginning of an iteration of a loop, the test expression is evaluated, and if the result is true, the loop continues, else it terminates. The while loop uses any of the following syntaxes:

(i)   while expr
            Statements
        end
(ii)   while expr do
            statements
        end
(iii)   while expr then
            Statements
        end

The keywords **then** and **do** are optional. However, if used, they must be written on the same line where the **while** keyword is written. They can be replaced by a carriage return or a comma. Example 6.11 shows some uses of while loops in various formats.

Example 6.11: while loop

```
// A program to generate a series.
i = 0; // Initialization of the loop control variable
s='Series:';
while i<5
    s=s+' '+string(i*i);
    i = i + 1; //Update the loop control variable
end
disp(s);

//To extract digits of a number and calculate their sum
n=789;
s=0;
d=sprintf ("The digits of %d are:",n);
while (n>0)
    r=pmodulo(n,10); //pmodulo is a library function to calculate reminder
    d=d+' '+ string(r);
    s=s + r;
    n=int(n/10);
end
s='The sum of the digits is:'+string(s);
disp (s, d);
```

Output
Series: 0 1 4 9 16
The digits of 789 are: 9 8 7
The sum of the digits is:24

6.9.3 break and continue statements

The **break** statement is used to unconditionally terminate the execution of a loop (both **for** and **while**), even if the test condition specified for the loop is true. If loops are nested then **break** terminates only the innermost loop. It is typically used for looping problems where multiple termination conditions exist or used to terminate an infinite loop.

The **continue** statement unconditionally skips execution of the portion of a loop written after it and starts the next iteration of the loop. Examples 6.12 shows use of **break** and **continue** keywords.

Example 6.12- The break and continue keywords

```
//An example to print the number of iterations required to find the first occurrence of 5
by the rand function.
i=0;
while %t do //infinite loop
   i=i+1;
   n=round (10*rand (1,1))
   if(n==5)
      printf ("5 is found after %d iterations", i)
      break;
   end
end

//An example to display odd integers
s="Odd Numbers: "
for x=1:10
   if(pmodulo(x,2)==0)
      continue;
   end
   s=s+" " +string(x);
end
disp(s);
```

Output

5 is found after 13 iterations
Odd Numbers: 1 3 5 7 9

6.10 Branching Control Structures

The default flow of execution of statements in a program is from top to bottom. However, in many problems, there are requirements to selectively execute some portions of a program for certain conditions and other portions for the other conditions. Scilab has many constructs to handle these types of situations. The most widely used branching constructs are: **if-elseif-else** and **select-case-else statements.**

6.10.1 if-elseif-else statements

The syntax of **if-elseif-else** is as given below:

>**if expr then**
>   **statements**
>**elseif expr 1 then**
>   **statements**
>**elseif expr 2 then**
>   **statements**
>   ....
>**else**
>   **statements**
>**end**

The **expr**, **expr1**, **expr2**... are expressions, scalar or vector/matrix, that evaluate to either numeric or Boolean values. For a scalar expression, all real numerical values other than zero are treated as true and zero as false. All the complex values are treated as false. For a vector/matrix expression, if every entry in the expression is true then the expression is treated as true else it is treated as false, for example, **x= [1,2,3,4]** is true, whereas **x= [0,1,2,3]** is false.

The **elseif** and **else** portions of the structure are optional and are used for multiple branching based on different conditions. Every **if** statement must be terminated by a corresponding **end** statement. The keyword **then** in an **if** or **elseif** statement can be replaced by either a comma, semicolon, space or carriage return. Whenever **then** is used in an **if** or **elseif** statement, it must be written in the same line. Example 6.13 shows some uses of **if** statements. Note the way vectors are handled in the test expressions of **if** statements.

Scilab supports multiple level of nesting of branching constructs. A nested branching construct must completely lie inside the single block of its immediate outer branching construct. Example 6.14 illustrates the concept of nesting for finding the largest of three given numbers.

Example 6.13- if-elseif-else keywords

```
//Simple if-else-end
flag=input ("Enter the value of flag:");
if flag then
   disp("True");
else
   disp("False");
end

//Ladder if-elseif-else-end example
```

```
a=input ("Enter marks:")
if a >=75 then
    disp("Honors");
elseif a>=60, //then replaced by a comma
    disp ("First division");
elseif a>=45 // then replaced by a space
    disp ("Second division");
elseif a>=35; // then replaced by a semicolon
    disp ("Third division");
else
    disp("Fail");
end
```

Output

//Scalar Inputs
Enter the value of flag:10
 True
Enter marks:76
 Honors
Enter the value of flag:0
 False
Enter marks:34
 Fail
Enter the value of flag: -10
 True
Enter marks:63
 First division
//Vector Input
 Enter the value of flag: [1,2,3,4] // All the entries of flag are non-zero, hence true.
 True
Enter marks: [60,78] // all the entries satisfy the first division criteria, hence output First Division.
 First division
 Enter the value of flag: [1,2,3,0,5] //One entry of flag is zero, hence false;
 False
Enter marks: [40,50,60,80]
 Third division // all the entries satisfy the Third division criteria, hence output Third division.

Example 6.14: Nested if statements

```
// A program to find the largest of three given numbers.
x=input ("Enter a vector of three numbers:");
s="The largest number is ";
if x (1)>x (2) then
   if x (1)>x (3) then
      s=s + string (x (1));
   else
      s=s + string (x (2));
   end
else
   if x (2)>x (3) then
      s=s + string (x (2));
   else
      s=s + string (x (3));
   end
end
disp(s);
```

Output

Enter a vector of three numbers: [3,6,2]
 The largest number is 6

6.11 select-case-else Statements

The **select-case-else** statement is used for selectively executing different portions of a program based on the fixed values, called cases, of a test expression. If the value of the test expression does not match with any specified cases, the default statements written in the else block are executed. Case values can be scalars or vectors, of integer, real number, complex number and string types. Case values can also be predefined variables with valid values. In case of duplicate case values, the block corresponding to the first matching case value is executed. The general syntax of a **select-case-else** statement is as given below:

       select expr
        case value1 then
               statements
        case value2 then
               statements

```
    ...
    case valuen then
        statements
[else statements]
end
```

where **expr** is an expression and **value1**, **value2**, …, **valuen** are case values. The **select** keyword evaluates the expression **expr** and hands over the control to the first matching case to execute that block. If no matching case is found, **else** block is executed. Example 6.15 shows the use of **select** keyword.

Example 6.15- Select-case-else statements

```
// A program to select a color from the given colors, using GUI.
n=x_choose (['Red'; 'Green'; 'Blue'], ['Select a color'])
select n
  case 1
    disp ('You chose- Red')
  case 2
    disp ('You chose - Green')
  case 3
    disp ('You chose - Blue')
  else
    disp ('Sorry, you canceled the color selection!');
end
```

6.12 File Handling

Scilab supports many file reading and writing functions for both binary and ASCII text files. Syntaxes and flags used in these functions are similar to 'C' language file handling functions. However, Scilab file handling functions are capable of handling both scalar and vector data. Table 6.5 lists commonly used functions along with brief descriptions. These functions are generally categorised as:

1. File opening and closing functions
2. Formatted input and output functions
3. Importing data from Excel
4. Reading/writing CSV files

Table 6.5- Some file related I/O functions

Command	Description
mopen	Opens a file in Scilab.
mclose	Closes an opened file.
meof	Checks if end of file has been reached.
mfprintf	Converts, formats, and writes data to a file.
mfscanf	Reads, converts and formats data from a file.
mgetl	Reads lines from a text file. Lines read are stored as a vector of strings.
mputl	Writes strings in a text file.
fprintfMat	Writes a matrix in a file.
fscanfMat	Reads a matrix from a text file.
xls_open	Opens an Excel file for reading.
xls_read	Reads a sheet in an Excel file.
csvRead	Reads a comma separated file.
csvWrite	Generates a CSV file.
mget	Reads byte or word in a given binary format from a file and converts to a double type.
mput	Writes byte or word in a given binary format.
mgetstr	Reads a character string from a file.
mputstr	Writes a character string in a file.
mseek	Sets current position in a binary file.
mtell	Returns the offset of the current byte relative to the beginning of a file.
mdelete	Deletes file(s).

6.12.1 File opening and closing functions

Most of file reading and writing functions require an active file handle to perform any activity on a file. In Scilab, a file handle, basically an integer, is created by the **mopen** function. The **mopen** function has the following syntax:

   [fd, err] = mopen (file [, mode, swap])

where **file** is a character string containing the path of the file to open, **mode** is a character string specifying the access mode requested for the file, **swap** is a scalar to cater for file data coding, **err** is a scalar for error reporting and **fd** is a scalar used as a file handle.

The file string contains either absolute address, such as **"C:\myfiles\xyz.txt"**, or relative address with reference to predefined addresses, such as **SCI**, **SCIHOME** or **TMPDIR**, of the file to be opened. The **SCI** variable contains the value of the root path of Scilab; **SCIHOME** contains the path to preferences and history files of the current Scilab session; **TMPDIR** contains the temporary directory path. An example of relative address is **SCI + "\myfiles\xyz.txt"**. If the file string contains only the file name, the file is opened from the current working directory. The address of the current working directory is obtained by the commands **cd** or **pwd**.

The **mode** parameter determines the access type requested for the file to be opened. Table 6.6 shows the possible values for the mode parameter along with a brief description.

Table 6.6 - Various modes of file input/output operations

Mode value	Description
r	Opens a file for reading (default). The file must exist, otherwise it fails.
w	Opens a file for writing. If the file exists, its contents are destroyed and the new contents are written in it.
a	Opens a file for appending. It creates the file if it does not exist. The new contents are added at the end of the existing contents.
r+	Opens a file for both reading and writing. The file must exist, otherwise it fails. The contents can be read/written from anywhere in the file with the help of positioning command **mseek**.
w+	Opens a file for both reading and writing. If the file exists, its contents are destroyed. Reading and writing is allowed anywhere with the help of file positioning commands.
a+	Opens a file for both reading and appending. It creates the file if it does not exist. Reading of the file is allowed from anywhere in the file, but the writing is allowed only after the end of the original contents of the file. The original contents of the file cannot be overwritten.
t	It is added to the above values of modes to process a text file. For example, the mode value 'rt' opens a text file for reading.
b	It is added to the above values of mode to process a binary file. For example, the mode value 'rb' opens a binary file for reading. The value 'rb' is the default setting of the mopen function.

The **swap** parameter is used to process files coded in either the little-endian IEEE format or the big-endian IEEE format. In the big-endian IEEE format, the most significant byte of a word is written at the smallest address; whereas, in the little-endian IEEE format, the most significant byte of a word is written at the largest address. For example, consider a four-byte word with a value $90AB12CD_{16}$, it's binary value is written in the sequence 90, AB,12, CD in the big-endian IEEE format, whereas CD,12, AB,90 in the little-endian IEEE format in a file. The value **swap=0**, or missing **swap** parameter, processes the file assuming the little-endian IEEE format and the value **swap=1** as the big-endian IEEE format.

The **err** parameter records the error code generated by the system due to an error during the file opening process. There are various causes for the failure of the file opening process, such as faulty drive, lack of memory, etc. Unique codes are assigned to various causes of errors so that proper action is taken to resolve it. Table 6.7 describes various error values returned by the **mopen** function.

Table 6.7- File opening error codes

Error value	Description
0	No error. It indicates that there is no error during the file opening process and the file is ready for further actions.
-1	No more logical units. It indicates that the maximum number of files that can be opened simultaneously is exhausted. Currently, Scilab allows to open 19 files simultaneously. For this reason, it is recommended that a file should be immediately closed if its processing is over.
-2	Cannot open file. The reasons for this code could be: the file does not exist or no permission to read/write the file.
-3	No more memory. This error code is generated if there is insufficient memory to store the file data.
-4	Invalid name. This error code is generated if the file name is invalid as per the operating system requirements.
-5	Invalid status. This error code is generated if the drives are not ready for the file operations.

The files opened by the **mopen** command should be closed by the **mclose** command to free the resources so that new files can be opened. The syntax of the **mclose** command is as given below:

err = mclose([fd])

where **fd** is the file handle returned by a previous **mopen** command and **err** is a scalar returned by the command to report any error during file closing, such as invalid file handle. The zero value of **err** indicates successful file closing.

If the **mclose** command is called without a file handle, it closes the last opened file. If the command is called with **fd = 'all'**, it closes all the opened files, including the opened script files. Be careful with this use of **mclose** because when it is used inside a Scilab script file, it also closes the script and Scilab will not execute commands written after **mclose ('all')**. Example 6.16 illustrates the basic file handling operations.

Example 6.16- Basic file handling program

```
// A program to write and read y=4*sin(x) values to/from the file named sine_table.txt.
fd = mopen('sine_table.txt', "w")      //creates a file in write mode
mfprintf(fd,"Sin curve values\n");     // writes the table header
mfprintf(fd,"----------------\n");
x=(-%pi:.5:%pi)';
mfprintf(fd,"%6.3f %6.3f\n",x,4*sin(x))    // writing values to the file
mclose(fd);                            //closing the file pointer

//read the same file line by line
fd = mopen('sine_table.txt', "r")
txt=mgetl(fd,-1)        //reads lines from the text file, -1 means read all lines
mclose(fd)
```

6.12.2 Formatted input/output functions

There are many functions for reading and writing formatted data. The most common are: **mfprintf, mfscanf, mgetl, mputl, fprintfMat** and **fscanfMat**.

6.12.2.1 mfprintf function

The **mfprintf** function writes data in a file in a desired format. The general syntax of this function is as given below:

mfprintf (fd, format, a1, a2, ..., an)

where **fd** is a scalar holding a file-handle created by a **mopen** command, **format** is a string controlling the format of the output and **a1, a2, an** are variables.

The similar functions, **mprintf** and **msprintf**, are used to write data in the console window (standard output) and in a string, respectively. These functions use the following syntaxes; the symbols have the identical meaning as for **mfprintf** function:

mprintf (format, a1, ..., an)

str=msprintf (format, a1, ..., an)

where **str** is a string variable that stores the output of the function.

The format string consists of three types of texts: static text, special character sequences and escape sequences. The static texts are displayed as it is. A special character sequence describes the format, such as field width, number of significant digits, alignment and padding, to be used for the data. The special characters are replaced by the values of the variables in the desired formats. The general format of a special character sequence is as given below:

%fw.de

where '**%**' indicates the start of a special character sequence, '**f**' specifies a flag to control the alignment (valid values are shown in Table 6.8) and padding to the output, '**w**' specifies the field width, '**d**' specifies the number of digits after the decimal point and '**e**' , known as format conversion character, specifies the desired data format type (common values are shown in Table 6.9). For a numeric value, the width (**w**) specified is overruled if the integer portion of the number cannot be accommodated in it.

The different escape sequence characters used in **mfprintf** are listed in Table 6.10. Example 6.17 shows a simple example to illustrate the various formats used in formatted output using the **mfprintf** function, **mprintf** and **msprintf** functions.

Table 6.8- Valid values of alignment and padding flag

flag	Description
-	The output is left-justified in the specified field width.
+	By default, a positive number is displayed without any sign. With this flag, the + sign is displayed before a positive number.
0	The output is padded with leading zeros instead of spaces (the default padding character).

Table 6.9- Format conversion characters in formatted output

Conversion character	Description
%c	Displays the first character of a string data.
%d	Displays the integer portion of a numeric value in the signed decimal integer notation.
%e	Displays a numeric value in the exponential notation with lower case e as the exponent symbol.
%E	Displays a numeric value in the exponential notation with upper case E as the exponent symbol.
%f	Displays a numeric value in the standard fixed point notation without using exponential notation even for large number values.
%g	Displays a numeric value in a more compact form out of %e and %f forms. The lower case e is used as the exponent symbol for the exponential form.
%G	The same as %g, except the upper case E is used as the exponent symbol.

%o	Displays the integer portion of a numeric value in the unsigned octal integer notation.
%s	Displays a string of characters.
%u	Displays the integer portion of a numeric value in the unsigned decimal integer notation.
%x	Displays the integer portion of a numeric value in the unsigned hexadecimal integer notation, using lower case letters (a, b, c, d, e, f).
%X	Displays the integer portion of a numeric value in the unsigned hexadecimal integer notation, using upper case letters (A, B, C, D, E, F).

Table 6.10- Escape characters in formatted output

Escape sequence character	Description
\n	Sends the subsequent output to the next line.
\t	Inserts a horizontal tab before the subsequent output. Equivalent to the tab key.
\b	Repositions the cursor one character backward. Equivalent to the backspace key.
\r	Returns the carriage to the first start position of the same line.
\\	Displays the backslash character (\) in the output.
\'	Displays the apostrophe character (') in the output.
%%	Displays the percentage character (%) in the output.

Example 6.17- Formatted output

```
// A program to illustrate the formatted output using mfprintf function in a file.

x=[0:45:180]';
y=sin(x);
fd=mopen("sine.dat","w");
mfprintf (fd, "Default format\n");
mfprintf (fd, "%d,%f\n", x, y);
mfprintf (fd, "Width specified format\n");
mfprintf (fd,"%4d,%8.3f\n", x, y);
mfprintf (fd, "Hex decimal format for integers\n");
mfprintf (fd,"%4X,%8.3f\n", x, y);
mfprintf (fd, "Exponential format\n");
```

```
mfprintf (fd,"%12.3e,%12.3e\n", x, y);
mclose(fd);
```

Output (Contents of the output file sine.dat)

Default format
0,0.000000
45,0.850904
90,0.893997
135,0.088369
180,-0.801153

Width specified format
  0,   0.000
 45,   0.851
 90,   0.894
135,   0.088
180, -0.801

Hex decimal format for integers
  0,   0.000
 2D,   0.851
 5A,   0.894
 87,   0.088
 B4, -0.801

Exponential format
   0.000e+00,   0.000e+00
   4.500e+01,   8.509e-01
   9.000e+01,   8.940e-01
   1.350e+02,   8.837e-02
   1.800e+02, -8.012e-01

```
// A program to illustrate the uses of mprintf function.

mprintf('There are %d students in %s with weight less than %8.2f kg.',20,"the class", 52.5);
mprintf('\n%e ', [1; 2; 3]);// printing a vector
mprintf('\n%d %d\n', [1, 2; 3, 4]);// printing a matrix

// Uses of msprintf function
```

```
str1= msprintf('There are %d students in %s with weight less than %f.',20,"the class",
52.5);
str2= msprintf('%e ', [1; 2; 3]);// printing a vector
str3= msprintf('%d %d\n', [1, 2; 3, 4]);// printing a matrix
disp(str1);
disp(str2);
disp(str3);
```

Output
There are 20 students in the class with weight less than   52.50 kg. 1.000000e+00 2.000000e+00 3.000000e+00 1 2 3 4 There are 20 students in the class with weight less than 52.500000. 1.000000e+00 2.000000e+00 3.000000e+00 !1 2 ! !   ! !3 4 !

6.12.2.2 mfscanf function

The **mfscanf** function reads formatted data from a file. It has the following syntaxes:

> [n, v1, ..., vm] = mfscanf([niter,] fd, format)
> L = mfscanf([niter,] fd, format)

where **format** is a Scilab string describing the format to be used to read the file data and convert them to appropriate types and then assign them to the variables **v1, v2, …, vm**; **fd** is a file handle; **niter** is an integer that determines the number of times the format to be used; **n** is an integer that stores the number of data successfully read; and **L** is either a vector (matrix) or a list.

The functions, **mscanf** and **msscanf**, are used to read formatted data from standard input and strings, respectively. The syntaxes for these functions are:

    [n, v1, ..., vm] = mscanf([niter,] format)
    L = mscanf([niter,] format)

    [n, v1, ..., vm] = msscanf([niter,]str, format)
    L = msscanf([niter,] str, format)

where **str** is a vector of strings and all other symbols have the identical meaning to the corresponding symbols of the **mfscanf** function.

The **format** string consists of format conversion characters listed above in table 6.9 along with normal characters. This is a powerful mechanism to extract useful data from a string and convert them into desired data type. For example, from the text "**Name:ABC,Age:20,Weight:50.32**", the name, age and weight can be extracted using the format **"Name:%3s,Age:%d,Weight:%f"**. Please note, while reading a string, specify the exact number of characters to be read. The normal characters in the **format** string must be identical in case with the text data otherwise reading fails. The spaces in the format string are ignored. If the data in the file does not match with the specified format in an **mfscanf** statement, the function **mfscanf** stops immediately. However, the data successfully read up to the mismatch are returned in the appropriate variables and the subsequent variables are assigned null values.

The list of variables on the left stores the data returned by the function. If the argument **niter** is given, the same format is used to read the data **niter** times. If **niter = -1**, the same format is used to read the data till the end of data is reached. If more than one set of data are read, the data are stored as vectors in the output arguments.

In the second format of these functions, if all data are homogeneous (i.e. all integers, all floats, or all strings), they are returned as a vector, otherwise they are returned as a mlist.

Example 6.18 illustrates some uses of the **mfscanf** function to read data from the files sine.dat and test.dat. The contents of these files are given in Table 6.11. Example 6.19 illustrates some uses of **mscanf** and **msscanf** functions. It is important to note that during reading from strings, exactly the same number of characters must be given in the input data as specified in the format string; otherwise, reading fails. To match the size, the input string can be padded with spaces or with any other characters.

Table 6.11: The contents of the files for Example 6.18

sine.dat
Default format
0,0.000000
45,0.850904
90,0.893997

135,0.088369 180,-0.801153
test.dat
Name:ABC,Age:20,Weight:50.32 Name:XYZ,Age:30,Weight:75.32 Name:PRQ,Age:60,Weight:100

Example 6.18- Formatted input from a file

```
//A program to read formatted data from files.

fd=mopen("sine.dat","r");
s=mfscanf (fd, "%s %s"); // Reads two words. The %s reads up to the first white space.
[n, x1, y1] =mfscanf (4, fd, "%d,%f"); // Reads the next four data set.
mclose(fd)
disp (y1, x1, n, s);

//Reading embedded data

fd=mopen("test.dat","r");
A=mfscanf(-1,fd,"Name:%3s,Age:%d,Weight:%f\n");
mclose(fd)
disp("The data from the test.dat file")
disp(A);
```

Output

!Default format !

  2.

  0.
  45.
  90.
  135.

  0.
  0.8509040
  0.8939970

> 0.0883690
>
> The data from the test.dat file
>
> ABC 20 50.32
> XYZ 30 75.32
> PRQ 60 100

Example 6.19- Formatted input from a string

// A program to read data from a string.
mprintf("\nEnter a string in the format Name:ABC,ID:01,Age:20,Weight:50.35kg");
s=mscanf("%s");
[n,Name,ID,Age,Weight]=msscanf(s,"Name:%3s,ID:%d,Age:%d,Weight:%fkg");
disp(Weight,Age,ID,n);
A=msscanf(s,"Name:%3s,ID:%d,Age:%d,Weight:%fkg");
disp(A);

Output

Enter a string in the format Name:ABC,ID:01,Age:20,Weight:50.35kg
-->Name:ABC,ID:01,Age:20,Weight:50.35kg
 	
   4.
 	
   1.
 	
   20.
 	
   50.349998
 	
ABC 1 20 50.349998

6.12.2.3 mgetl and mputl functions

The **mgetl** function reads lines from a text file. The syntax of the function is as given below:

txt = mgetl (file_desc [, m])

where **file_desc** is a character string giving the file name or a file handle returned by **mopen**, **m** is an integer scalar that controls the number of lines to be read (default value is -1 which means read till the end of the file) and **txt** is a column vector of strings.

If **file_desc** contains the file address directly, the file is automatically opened in the read mode and after reading it is closed automatically. No explicit action is required for file opening and closing. For reading a file in multiple steps, **file_desc** is assigned a valid file handle generated by **mopen** function in the read mode. After reading, the file should be closed.

If **m** is given, the **mgetl** function tries to read exactly **m** lines. However, if the end of file (EOF) occurs before **m** lines are read, the lines read up to this point are returned and end-of-file error flag is set which can be tested by the **meof** function. Example 6.20 illustrates the use of **mgetl** function.

Example 6.20- mgetl function

```
// A program to read the specified number of lines from a file.
txt=mgetl("sine.dat",4) // Opens and reads the first four lines of the sine.dat file and closes the file.
fd=mopen("sine.dat","r"); // Reopens the sine.dat file for reading.
t1=mgetl(fd,4) // Reads the first four lines again from the beginning.
t2=mgetl(fd,4) // Try to read the next four lines, but returns only two lines as there were only six lines in the file.
mclose(fd);
```

Output

txt =

!Default format !
!   !
!0,0.000000   !
!   !
!45,0.850904   !
t1 =

!Default format !
!   !
!0,0.000000   !
!   !
!45,0.850904   !
t2 =

!90,0.893997   !
!   !
!135,0.088369 !

The **mputl** function writes a vector of strings in a text file, sequentially. The syntax of the function is as given below:

    r = mputl (txt, file_desc)

where **file_desc** is a character string giving the name of the file or a file handle returned by the **mopen** function in write/append mode, **txt** is a vector of strings that is to be written in the file and **r** is a Boolean variable. If the file operation is successful, **r** is set to **%t**, else **%f**. Example 6.21 illustrates a use of **mputl** function.

Example 6.21- mputl function

//A program to write strings in a file.
x=[1:3]';
y=x.^2;
s=msprintf("%4d%4d\n",x,y);
mputl(s,"out.dat");

Output (the contents of **out.dat**)

1   1
  2   4
  3   9

6.12.2.4 fprintfMat and fscanfMat functions

The functions **fprintfMat** and **fscanfMat** are specifically designed to write and read a matrix in/from a file. They use the following syntaxes:

    printfMat (file, M [, format, text])

    M = fscanfMat (filename [, format])
    [M, text] = fscanfMat (filename [, format])

where **file** is the filename along with the address where matrix is written/read from, **M** is a matrix. The optional parameter **format** specifies the format (such as **%d, %8.3f, %gl**) used to write/read the matrix data and text is comment lines written/read before the matrix data. The default format for reading and writing is double floating number (**%lg**), however the data can be read/written as decimal integer (**%d, %i**), octal(**%o**), hexadecimal (**%x**), floating number (**%f, %f, %g, %lg**), characters (**%c**) and strings(**%s**). Example 6.22 shows basic matrix file handling operations.

Example 6.22: Basic matrix file handling operations

// A program to directly writing and reading a matrix to/from a file.   A = rand (4,3);   fprintfMat ("MatrixA.txt", A, "%lg");   B = fscanfMat ("MatrixA.txt", "%lg");   disp(B);
Output
0.726351   0.231224   0.307609   0.198514   0.216463   0.932962   0.544257   0.883389   0.214601   0.232075   0.652513   0.312642

6.12.3 Importing data from Excel files

Frequently, there are requirements to import data stored in Excel workbooks. Scilab has two functions, **xls-open** and **xls_read**, to facilitate import of data. The **xls_open** function opens an Excel file for reading and has the following syntax:

[fd, SST, Sheetnames, Sheetpos] = xls_open(file_path)

where **file_path** is a character string which stores the path of the Excel file, **fd** is a file handle which is used in the **xls_read** function for data reading, **SST** is a vector of all character strings which appear in the Excel sheets, **Sheetnames** is a vector of strings storing the sheet names and **Sheetpos** is a vector of numbers storing the position of the beginning of sheets in the Excel stream.

This function analyses the data structure of the Excel file and internally creates a temporary Excel stream to read data from the sheets. The **fd** is the logical unit points to this temporary file. Then the first sheet in this stream is read to get the global information like number of sheets, sheet names (returned as **Sheetnames**), sheet addresses within the stream (returned as **Sheetpos**). The function also creates indexed list of all the text data contained in various sheets and return them as a row vector of strings (the variable **SST**).

The actual data of various sheets are read by the **xls_read** function. The syntax of the function is as given below:

[Value, TextInd] = xls_read (fd, Sheetpos)

where **fd** is a file handle returned by a previous call of the **xls_open** function, **Sheetpos** is the address of a sheet in the Excel stream returned by the **xls_open** function, **Value** is a matrix of the numerical data found in the sheet (non-numerical data are represented by **NaN** values), and

TextInd is a matrix of indices of non-numeric data (stored in **SST** returned by the **xls_open** function) of the sheet and has the same size as **Value**.

The zero indices in **TextInd** indicates that no string exists in the corresponding Excel cell and a positive index **i** points to the string **SST(i)** returned by the corresponding **xls_open** function. Using **SST**, **Value** and **TextInd**, the numeric data and text data in an Excel file are segregated for further processing.

Example 6.23 illustrates the process of importing data from an Excel file and then segregating the numeric and textual data.

Example 6.23: Importing data from an Excel spreadsheet

```
//This program reads the following Excel sheet data, segregates the numeric and
string data and //calculates BMI from the data.

// Name         Age     Weight   Height
// Ramesh       20      55       160
// Shyam        30      65       172
// Ram          25      72       180

[fd, SST, Sheetnames, Sheetpos] = xls_open("e:\test\book1.xls");
s= ['The number of sheets are:', string(size(Sheetnames,2)), ' and their names are:',
Sheetnames];
disp(s);
[Value, TextInd] = xls_read (fd, Sheetpos (1));
mclose(fd);
a=Value(TextInd(:)==0); // Extracting the numeric values
s= ['The numeric values in the Excel sheet are:', string(a')];
disp (s);
disp (['The strings in the sheet are:', SST]);
age=Value(2:$,2); // Extracting the second column's numeric data
Weight=Value(2:$,3); // Extracting the third column's numeric data
Height=Value(2:$,4); // Extracting the fourth column's numeric data
Name=[SST(TextInd(2:$,1))]'; // Extracting names from the first column
BMI=10000*Weight./(Height.^2);
str=msprintf ("%-10s%5.2f\n", Name, BMI);
s=msprintf ("%-10s%s\n", "Name", "BMI");
s1= [s; str];
```

disp(s1);
Output
!The number of sheets are: 2   and their names are: Sheet1 Sheet2 !   !The numeric values in the Excel sheet are: 20 30 25 55 65 72 160 172 180 !   !The strings in the sheet are: Name Age Weight Height Ramesh Shyam Ram !   !Name   BMI !   !   !   !Ramesh 21.48 !   !   !   !Shyam 21.97 !   !   !   !Ram 22.22 !

6.12.4 Reading/writing CSV files

The comma separated value (CSV) format of data is one of the most convenient forms to exchange data among various applications, as this does not require the proprietary details of the native format. Scilab has two functions, **csvWrite** and **csvRead**, to write and read CSV files. In their simplest format, the following syntaxes are commonly used for the functions:

    csvWrite (M, filename, separator, [decimal], [precision])
    M = csvRead (filename, separator, [decimal], [conversion])

where **filename** is a string holding the file address, **M** is a matrix of data, **separator** is a character holding the column separator mark (the tab character, ASCII code 9, is commonly used), **decimal** is a character matrix for holding the symbol used for the decimal point in numeric data (valid values are "." or ",", the default is the dot), **precision** is string for holing the format string used to write the data (for example, "%8.3f" for writing numbers in fixed format) and **conversion** is a string controlling the type of the output **M** (Available values are "string" or "double" (by default) for importing data as a string or double, respectively).

    Example 6.24 illustrates writing and reading of a CSV data file, where a matrix of random numbers is first written in a CSV file and then the same is read back and displayed.

Example 6.24: Writing and reading CSV data files

```
// A program to save a matrix of random numbers as a CSV data file.
M = rand(3,3);
filename = "data.csv";
// Use tabs as the separator
csvWrite(M, filename,ascii(9),[],'%.3g');
disp('Read as numeric values');
//Read a CSV file
M1=csvRead(filename,ascii(9),[],"double");
disp(M1);
disp('Read as string values');
M2=csvRead(filename,ascii(9),[],"string");
disp(M2);
```

Output

Read as numeric values

```
   0.387   0.344   0.262
   0.922   0.376   0.499
   0.949   0.734   0.264
```

Read as string values

```
!0.387  0.344  0.262  !
!                     !
!0.922  0.376  0.499  !
!                     !
!0.949  0.734  0.264  !
```

6.13 Scripts and Functions

In Scilab, commands are executed either by typing interactively in the console window or first writing a set of commands (called a program) in a text file and then executing it. For complicated algorithms, the first approach is not suitable as it does not lend itself for easy editing and corrections. Hence, for such situations, the second approach to implement algorithms is more suitable and desirable. There are two approaches to write programs in Scilab: scripts and functions. Script programs, similar to Linux shell programs or windows batch programs, are more suitable for the automation of processing for different set of data whereas function programs are more suitable for building reusable and modular codes in the form of library to extend the capabilities of Scilab.

Scilab programs are written using any ASCII text editor. Scilab has its own built-in text editor for creating programs, which can be launched with the **edit** or **SciNotes** commands. By default, the **edit** command opens the editor for creating a function file with .sci extension and **SciNotes** for creating a script file with .sce extension. In both the modes, there are facilities for executing and debugging programs.

6.13.1 Script programs

Script programs are text files, with either .sce or .sci extensions, which contain valid Scilab commands and user defined functions. They are typically used when one needs to run a group of Scilab commands many times for different sets of data or to solve complex and long problems. A script program mostly contains executable statements along with some functions, i.e. a file with a main program and some functions. If a script file contains function definitions, the definitions must appear before the use of the functions in the main program. A function definition may appear anywhere in the main program, but its use must be after its definition.

The distinctive feature of a script program is that all the variables used in the main program are available in the current workspace, i.e. they are global in scope and life (i.e. they are not killed at the end of the script execution). In other words, the current workspace variables are available in the script files directly and the results produced by a script file are also available in the current workspace. Example 6.25 shows a simple script program to calculate distance between two points and area of a right-angle triangle. To run a program, use execute menu of the Scilab editor. More about executing a program is given in section 6.13.9.

Example 6.25: A simple script program

```
// A function to calculate the distance between two points.
function [dist]=calc_dist(x1, y1, x2, y2)
   dist=sqrt((abs(x2-x1))^2 +(abs(y2-y1))^2);
endfunction
// A function to calculate the area of a triangle
function [a]=calc_area(b, h);
   a=.5*b*h
endfunction

// Main program
d=calc_dist(-5,-4,-6,4);
```

```
disp(d," is the distance between two points");
a1=calc_area(6,4);
disp(sprintf("Area of a triangle is %f",a1));
```

Output

--> exec('C:\Users\Arvind\Documents\scilab_book_examples\chapter6\example1.sce', -1)
 The distance between the two points is 8.062258
 The area of the triangle is 12.000000

6.13.2 Function programs

Modular and reusable codes in Scilab are generally written as function programs, written in text files with .sci extension. A function file, invariably, contains only function definitions and do not directly execute Scilab statements. Once a function program file is loaded into Scilab workspace, all the functions written in the file are available for use either at the console prompt or in script files. The basic purpose of function programs is to extend the capability of Scilab by implementing new algorithms and make them available to other users. Any number of functions can be defined in a function file. All function definitions begin with a keyword **function** and end with a keyword **endfunction**. The syntax of a typical Scilab function is as follows:

>   **function [output arguments] = function_name (input arguments)**
>   **statement1**
>   **statement2**
>   **statement3**
>   **...**
>   **Statement_n**
> **endfunction**

The **function_name** variable is the name of the function, which is used to call the function. The variable naming rules, as described chapter 2, are applicable to name a function. A function can have zero or more number of input arguments and zero or more output arguments. By default, all the variables created in a function are local. Their scopes are limited to that function only and are destroyed at the end of the function. In a function, local variables have higher precedence than global variables with identical names. To maintain modularity, it is advisable not to use workspace variables directly in a function. If a workspace variable is required inside a function, it should be passed as its argument. Example 6.26 shows a simple function file with a few functions. To use the functions defined in Example 6.26, they must be loaded into Scilab memory with the help of **exec** command or using execute option of the Scilab editor, which are described in the next section. The interactive uses of the loaded functions are shown in the output section of the example.

It is not necessary to write functions in a file as functions definition can be typed directly at the command prompt. In this case, functions are automatically loaded in the memory and are available for use in the current session. However, at the end of the session or with the clear command, they are removed from the memory, and they are not available anymore. Further, their editing is also difficult. Hence, this way of defining a function is only suitable for simple and small functions. Example 6.27 shows interactive definition and use of a function.

Example 6.26: A simple function program

```
// Defining a few simple functions.
function [x, y]=myfun(a, b)
    x=a+b;
    y=a-b;
endfunction


function [dist]=cal_dist(x1, y1, x2, y2)
    dist=sqrt((abs(x2-x1))^2 +(abs(y2-y1))^2);
endfunction


function [area]=cal_area(b, h)
    area=.5*b*h;
endfunction
```

Output

```
--> exec('C:\Users\Arvind\Documents\scilab_book_examples\chapter6\example2.sci', -1)
--> who_user
 User variables are:
 cal_area  cal_dist  myfun
 Using 0 elements
 ans =
!cal_area !
!         !
!cal_dist !
!         !
!myfun    !
--> cal_area(3,4)
 ans =
  6.
--> cal_dist(1,2,5,6)
 ans =
  5.6568542
```

Example 6.27: Interactive definition of a function

```
--> function a=ak_sum(b,c)
  > a=b+c;
  > endfunction
--> ak_sum(1,2)
 ans  =

  3.
--> clear
--> ak_sum(1,2)

Undefined variable: ak_sum
```

6.13.3 Inline functions

Scilab has another facility to define very small functions, called inline functions, with the help of **deff** command. It also loads the function into the current workspace if used at the console command prompt. Inline functions are defined using the following syntax:

deff ('[out1, out2, ...] =function_name (in1, in2, ...)', text)

where **in1, in2**, … are input variables, **out1, out2**, … are output variables, and the **text** is a matrix of strings defining the body of the function. Example 6.28 shows the definition of an inline function written in a script file and the result produced when executed.

Example 6.28: An inline function definition and use

```
// Defining an inline function.
deff('[x,y]=myfun(a,b)',['x=a+b';'y=a-b'])
[x,y]=myfun(3,4)  // function call
```

Output

```
--> deff('[x,y]=myfun(a,b)',['x=a+b';'y=a-b'])
--> [x, y]=myfun(3,4)  // function call
 y  =
  -1.
 x  =
  7.
```

6.13.4 Global and local variables

By default, variables created in a function are local, i.e. their scope is limited to that function only, and they are killed after the function execution. A function can use all the variables created in the current workspace. In order to use a variable across functions, it must be explicitly declared global with the help of the **global** keyword in all the concerned functions separately. After this, any change to that variable, in any concerned function, is available to all the other functions declaring it `global`. Even if a variable is declared global in a function, it is not directly available in the current workspace. To make it available in the current workspace also, it must be declared global outside the functions in a script file or at the workspace command prompt. At the first encounter to a global variable declaration, by default, the variable is initialized to the empty matrix. Therefore, proper initialization of a global variable, preferably by an initialization function or at the command prompt, must be ensured for consistent results. Example 6.29 shows an example to create and use a global variable.

Once a global variable is created, it exists in memory even if it is cleared from the workspace by the clear command. To clear a global variable from the memory, the **clearglobal** command is used. Table 6.6 shows some commands related to the management of global variables with a brief description of each.

Example 6.29: Use of global variables

```
// A program illustrating the use of a global variable.
function A()
   global counter
   disp('In function A');
   counter = counter + 1
endfunction

function B()
   global counter
   disp('In function B');
   counter = counter + 1
endfunction

function printCounter()
   global counter
   disp(counter)
endfunction
```

```
global counter
counter = 0;    //Initialization of the global variable counter
A();
B();
A();
printCounter();
A();
B();
printCounter();
```

Output

```
-->
exec('C:\Users\Arvind\AppData\Local\Temp\SCI_TMP_3696_14677\untitled.sci',
-1)
 In function A
 In function B

 In function A
  3.
 In function A
 In function B
  5.
```

Table 6.6 Commands related to variables

Command	Description
who_user	Lists all the user created variables and functions in the current session.
isglobal('variable_name')	Checks if the specified variable is global. If the variable is global, it returns True (T) else returns False (F).
clearglobal	Kills all the global variables created in the current session.
clear	Clears the entire user created variables and functions present in the current workspace.

6.13.5 Recursive functions

Scilab supports recursive functions. A recursive function is a function that calls itself. The function calls itself a number of times, by changing the value of the parameter in every self-call and finally recursion stops in a condition that is solved directly. Recursion is useful in situations where problems can be formulated in terms of sub problems of the identical type. For example, the factorial of a number n can be recursively defined as: **n! = n × (n-1)!**. Example 6.30 shows an example of a recursive function.

Example 6.30: Factorial of a number using a recursive function

```
// A program to find factorial of a number using recursion.

function [y]=fact(x)
    disp(sprintf('Calling fact(%d)', x));
    if x == 1 then
        y=1
    else
        y=x*fact(x-1)
    end
endfunction
// Main program
y=fact(5);  // calling the function
disp(sprintf("Result: fact(5)=%d", y));
```

Output

```
--> exec('C:\Users\Arvind\Documents\scilabbook\fact.sci', -1)
Calling fact(5)
Calling fact(4)
Calling fact(3)
Calling fact(2)
Calling fact(1)
Result: fact(5)=120
```

6.13.6 Nesting of functions

Scilab allows nesting of functions, i.e. a function can be defined in the body of another function. The scope of the inner function is limited to the outer function only. Nested functions are useful when the nested function is required only within the defining function. This reduces the clutter of no more useful functions in the workspace. Any level of nesting is allowed in Scilab. The structure of the nesting of functions is as given below:

```
function [y] =outer_function(x)
    statements;
    function [z]=inner_function(p)
        statements;
    endfunction
endfunction
```

Example 6.31 shows the use of nested functions.

Example 6.31: Nested functions

```
//A program to illustrate the use of Nested functions.
function y=outer_fun(x)
    a=x+1;
    disp ("executing outer_fun");
    function y=inner_fun1(x)
        z=x+2;
        whereami (); // a library function to return the current line of the program
        function y=inner_fun2(x), y=x^2, disp ("Executing inner_fun2"), endfunction;
        y=inner_fun2(z);
    endfunction
    y=inner_fun1(a)+1
    disp (msprintf ('is function inner_fun1 exist? %s', string(isdef("inner_fun1"))));
    disp (msprintf ('is function inner_fun1 exist? %s', string(isdef("inner_fun2"))));
endfunction
// Main program
disp (outer_fun (2));
disp (msprintf ('is function inner_fun1 exist? %s', string(isdef("inner_fun1"))));
```

Output
executing outer_fun
whereami   called at line 3 of macro inner_fun1
inner_fun1 called at line 10 of macro outer_fun
outer_fun called at line 16 of exec_file
Executing inner_fun2
is function inner_fun1 exist? T

> is function inner_fun1 exist? F
> 26.
> is function inner_fun1 exist? F

6.13.7 Variable number of arguments in functions

Scilab allows variable number of input and output arguments in a function definition. This facilitates writing versatile functions. The keyword **varargin** is used to pass variable number of input arguments, whereas the keyword **varargout** is used for receiving the variable number of output arguments. The keywords **varargin** and **varargout** have these special meaning only if they are the last argument in the input and output arguments, respectively. In other situations, they are treated as simple arguments. It is not essential for a function to have any fixed number of arguments, i.e. a function may be defined with only variable number of arguments. However, if **varargout** is the only formal output of a function, the function must return at least one value assigned to **varargout**. In other situations, the **varargout** and **varargin** may be empty. The syntax for the variable number of arguments is as given below:

> **function [out1, out2, ..., outn, varargout] =function_name (in1, in2, ..., inn, varargin)**
>   **statements**
> **endfunction**

Inside the body of a function, variable input arguments are available as a list with the name **varargin**. The number of actual input and output arguments used in a function call can be determined inside the function by the function **argn (num)**. To get the actual number of input arguments, use **argn(2)** and to get the number of actual output arguments, use **argn (1)**. To get both simultaneously, use **[lhs, rhs] =argn (0)**. Here, **lhs** receives the total number of output arguments, whereas **rhs** receives the total number of input arguments. If a function has fixed arguments along with **varargout** argument, the variable output arguments is always returned as a list. Hence, the total number of output arguments is equal to the number of fixed arguments plus one. However, if the **varargout** is the only output arguments, they are returned as separate variables. Example 6.32 illustrates the above concepts with simple examples. As can be seen from the example, number of input arguments must be equal to or more than fixed input arguments to avoid error messages. Further, the number of the actual output arguments used in calling a function must be less than or equal to the maximum number of outputs expected to be returned by the function to avoid the error messages.

Example 6.32: Use of varargin and varargout arguments

```
// A program to illustrate some uses of varargin and varargout.
function [a, b, varargout] =fun1(x, y, varargin)
   a=x.^2;
   b=y.^3;
   varargout=varargin;
   [lhs, rhs] =argn (0);
   disp (sprintf ('No of input=%d, and No of output=%d', rhs, lhs));
endfunction

function [varargout]=fun2(x, varargin)
   n=length(varargin);
   varargout (1) =x.^2;
   for i=1: n
      varargout(i+1) =varargin(i).^2;
   end
   disp (sprintf ('Total no of input arguments= %d, and total no of output arguments=%d', argn(2),argn(1)));
endfunction
```

Output

```
--> [a,b,c]=fun1(1)
at line     3 of function fun1 ( C:\Users\Arvind\Documents\test6.sce line 3 )
Undefined variable: y
--> [a,b,c]=fun1(1,2)
 No of input=2, and No of output=3
 c  =
    ()
 b  =
    8.
 a  =
    1.
--> [a,b,c]=fun1(1,2,3,4)
 No of input=4, and No of output=3
 c  =
     c(1)
    3.
     c(2)
```

```
    4.
 b =
    8.
 a =
    1.
--> [a,b,c]=fun2(1)
 Total no of input arguments= 1, and total no of output arguments=3
 fun2: Wrong number of output argument(s): 1 expected.
--> [a,b,c]=fun2(1,2)
 Total no of input arguments= 2, and total no of output arguments=3
 fun2: Wrong number of output argument(s): 2 expected.
--> [a,b,c]=fun2(1,2,3)
 Total no of input arguments= 3, and total no of output arguments=3
 c =
    9.
 b =
    4.
 a =
    1.
--> [a]=fun2(1,2,3)
 Total no of input arguments= 3, and total no of output arguments=1
 a =
    1.
--> [a,b]=fun2(1,2,3)
 Total no of input arguments= 3, and total no of output arguments=2
 b =
    4.
 a =
    1.
--> [a,b,c,d]=fun2(1,2,3)
 Total no of input arguments= 3, and total no of output arguments=4
 fun2: Wrong number of output argument(s): 3 expected.
```

6.13.8 Multiple evaluation of a function

The **feval** function is used to evaluate a function with one or two arguments at multiple data sets given in vector form. The function is used in the following syntaxes:

[z]=feval (x, f)
[z]=feval (x, y, f)

where **x, y** are two vectors of real numbers, and **f** is a function handle which accepts either one or two arguments only. The return values of the function, i.e. **z**, can be real or complex numbers.

The expression **z = feval (x, f)** returns the vector **z** defined by $z(i) = f(x(i))$, and **z = feval (x, y, f)** returns the matrix **z** such as $z(i, j) = f(x(i), y(j))$, where **i = 1: length(x)** and **j = 1: length(y)**. Example 6.33 explains the concepts of the multiple evaluation of a function.

Example 6.33: Multiple evaluation of a function

//A program to illustrate the multiple evaluation of a function with single argument.
deff('[z]=f(x)','z=x^2')
feval (1:10, f)
//output
ans =
1. 4. 9. 16. 25. 36. 49. 64. 81. 100.
//A program to illustrate the multiple evaluation of a function with two arguments
deff('[z]=f (x, y)','z=x^2+y^2');
mat=feval (1:4,1:3, f)
Output
mat =
2. 5. 10.
5. 8. 13.
10. 13. 18.
17. 20. 25.

6.13.9 Executing a program file

A Scilab script or function program is executed with the help of either the **exec** or the **getd** commands. The **exec** command can be used directly at the command prompt or through the execute menu option of SciNotes (the Scilab integrated editor). Following are the syntaxes for using the **exec** function:

    exec (filename [,mode])
    ierr = exec(filename, 'errcatch' [,mode])

where filename is the program file name that is to be executed, mode is an integer which controls the mode of program execution, and 'errcatch' is a constant string which controls the way errors are handled. If the program file is not in the current directory, full path of the file must be provided. The various mode values are described in Table 6.7 along with the corresponding menu options if available.

If an error is encountered while executing a program and 'errcatch' flag is present in the exec command, Scilab issues no error message, aborts execution of the instructions and returns to command prompt after setting ierr equal to the error number, which may be used to determine the cause of the error. If 'errcatch' flag is not present, the first error encountered is displayed at the command prompt and the program execution stops. Example 6.34 shows the use of the exec command with different values of the mode.

Table 6.7: Various program execution modes

Mode	Description	Menu option
0	The new variable values in script files, outside any function, are displayed in the console window if the statements are not terminated by semicolons. If a statement contains more than one assignment separated by commas and finally terminated by a semicolon, all the assignments are displayed except the last one. Variables inside a function are not displayed even if not terminated by a semicolon.	No equivalent menu option
-1	The program file runs silently without displaying any variable values even if not terminated by semicolon. This is the default mode for function files.	Execute->file with no echo
1,3,5	Each line of the program is echoed at the prompt and executed. If a statement is not terminated by a semicolon, the result is also displayed. The function definitions are loaded in the memory. This is the default for script files.	Execute->file with echo
2	Statements are not echoed at the command prompt. Only the results are displayed if the statements are not terminated by semicolons.	No equivalent menu option
4,7	The new variable values are displayed if not terminated by semicolons and each line of instructions is also echoed. Further, the prompt changes to the pause prompt (>>) and waits for the carriage return to proceed and all the pause facilities are activated. This mode is useful for program debugging.	No equivalent menu option

| >7 | The mode values greater than 7 behave similar to mode=-1 | No equivalent menu option |

Example 6.34: Illustration of various modes of execution

```
//This program is saved as abc.sci in d:\test folder.
function [y]=f (a, b)
   y=a + b;
endfunction
a=10;
b=5
c=f (a, b)
```

Output

```
--> exec('d:\test\abc.sci',0)
 b =

   5.
 c =

   15.
--> exec('d:\test\abc.sci',1)
--> function [y] = f(a, b)
-->    y=a + b;
--> endfunction
--> a=10;
--> b=5
 b =

   5.
--> c=f(a, b)
 c =

   15.
--> exec('d:\test\abc.sci',2)
 b =

   5.
```

```
            c =

              15.

--> exec('d:\test\abc.sci',4)
>> function [y] = f(a, b)
>>     y=a + b;
>> endfunction
>>
>> a=10;
-->
>> b=5
 b =

   5.
>>
>> c=f(a, b)
 c =

   15.
>>
>>
--> exec('d:\test\abc.sci',-1) // nothing is displayed due to -1.
```

The command **getd** can be used to load and execute all the .sci files located in a folder. The syntax of the command is:

    getd (path)

where **path** is a string which stores the address of the folder whose .sci files are to be loaded. If the **getd** is called without any argument, all the .sci files in the current folder are loaded and executed. The **getd** command loads all the functions defined in various files and also executes the codes written outside the functions.

6.14 Error Handling

In large and complex programs, it is challenging to properly handle unexpected run-time conditions created due to data, such as operations not defined for the given data, division by zero, inverse of a singular matrix. Scilab can be set to take different actions to handle various error situations as listed in Table 6.8. The type of action suitable for a program is set with the help of **errcatch** function, which has the following syntax:

errcatch (n [,'action'] [,'option'])

where **n** is an integer and **action**, **option** are strings.

If the parameter **n > 0**, Scilab only traps the error corresponding to the error number equal to **n** and if **n < 0**, all errors are trapped. Scilab, internally, maintains an error code tables, named **error_table**, which contains unique codes for various errors and their descriptions. Table 6.8 gives a few, randomly selected, entries from the error-table (for more detail, see the Scilab help). The optional parameter action can be set to a value listed in Table 6.9 and Scilab error handling action is set accordingly. If the optional parameter option is set to **'nomessage'**, no error message is displayed in the console window. Example 6.35 illustrates some uses of the **errcatch** function for setting various error handling modes.

Table 6.8: A Few selected entry of the error_table

Error_code	Error message
1	Incorrect assignment.
4	Undefined variable.
5	Inconsistent column/row dimensions.
8	Inconsistent addition.
27	Division by zero.
28	Empty function.
74	Leading coefficient is zero.
144	Undefined operation for the given operands.

Table 6.9: Error handling approaches of Scilab

Action	Description
pause	In this approach, a pause is executed when an error occurs. This option is useful for debugging purposes. The **whereami** function can be used to locate the line causing the error and the code is corrected to avoid future occurrence of the error.
continue	In this approach, after recoding the cause of error, the current instruction is ignored, and the next instruction in the function or exec files is executed. It is possible to check if an error has occurred using the **iserror** function. The recorded error can be cleared by the **errclear** function.

kill	In this approach, all the codes and functions written after the error causing statement are killed and Scilab returns back to the console prompt. This is the default error handling mode of Scilab.
stop	In this mode, the current Scilab session is terminated. This is useful when Scilab is called from an external program.

Example 6.35: Uses of the errcatch function

```
// A program to illustrate various error handling approaches.
a='Error handling';
errcatch(144,"continue")
2/"foo"  // The line causing error 144, i.e. operation not defined for the data
disp(a) // Without the errcatch, this line would not be executed

errcatch(144,"pause")
2/"foo"
// Entered in the "pause" mode, type resume command to continue.

errcatch(27,'continue','nomessage')
b=2/0 // No error message is displayed, but b will not exist
c=100;
disp(c);

errcatch(-1,"kill") // Comes back in the normal mode and handle all the errors

disp(6+7);
d=2/"foo"; // Program terminates here.
disp(c); // This line is not executed
```

Output

```
-->exec('C:\Users\dell\AppData\Local\Temp\SCI_TMP_4256_\untitled.sci', -1)
2/"foo"  // The line causing error 144, i.e. operation not defined
   !--error 144
Undefined operation for the given operands.
check or define function %s_r_c for overloading.

 Error handling
2/"foo"
```

```
     !--error 144
Undefined operation for the given operands.
check or define function %s_r_c for overloading.

 -1->resume

  100.

  13.
d=2/"foo";
     !--error 144
Undefined operation for the given operands.
check or define function %s_r_c for overloading.
at line     19 of exec file called by :
\SCI_TMP_4256_\untitled.sci', -1
```

There are many diagnostic functions to locate the statement causing errors and their types. Table 6.10 lists the commonly used such functions.

Table 6.10: Error handling functions

Function	Description
error	Returns the error message corresponding to an error code.
lasterror	Returns the last recorded error message.
errclear	Clears the last error message.
iserror	Tests whether any error occurred after the last errclear call.

6.14.1 try-catch statement

The **try-catch** control instruction, a simple and powerful mechanism for error handling, helps to take alternative course of actions in the event of an error in the main program codes. The syntax of the **try-catch** statement is as given below:

try
    program_statements
catch
    error_handling_statements
end

When a **try-catch** control instruction is executed, only the **program_statements** written between the **try** and **catch** keywords are executed. However, if an error occurs during execution of any of these statements, the error is recorded, the remaining statements up to the **catch** keyword are skipped, and the statements between the **catch** and **end** keywords, i.e. **error_handling_statements**, are executed using the default error handling mode. The recorded error can be retrieved using the **lasterror** function. The statements between the **catch** and **end** keywords can be omitted if no alternative statements are given. Example 6.36 illustrates a use of the **try-catch** instruction. Similar to loops, **try-catch** statements can be nested as illustrated in Example 6.37.

Example 6.36: A use of a try-catch statement

```
// A program to illustrate a use of a try-catch statement.
function test_try(a)
   disp("START")
   mprintf ("\ta is %s\n", string(a));
   try
      disp ("Executing normal code")
      c=a+10; // Error when a is a string
      disp(c);
   catch
      disp ("Error occurred")
   end
   disp("END");
endfunction
// Main program
test_try(10);
test_try('a'); // Calling the function with an argument with wrong data type.
```

Output

STARTa is 10

Executing normal code

   20.
END

START
   a is a

```
Executing normal code

Error occurred
 END
```

Example 6.37: A use of nested try-catch statements

```
// A program to illustrate the nested try-catch structure.
function nestedtry(a, b)
  disp("START")
  try
     disp ("Executing the try 1 block.")
     t=10/b; // err when b=0
     try
        disp ("Executing the try 2 block.")
        z=a+1; // err when a is a string
     catch
        disp ("Error occurred in the try 2 block and handled by the catch 2 block.")
        [str, n] =lasterror ();
        disp (msprintf ("Error code: %d and error message: %s", n, str));
        errclear ();

     end
     disp ("Executing statements outside the try 2 block.")
  catch
     disp ("Error occurred in the try 1 block and handled by the catch 1 block.")
     [str, n] = lasterror ();
     disp (msprintf ("Error code: %d and error message: %s", n, str));
     errclear ();
  end
  disp("END")
endfunction
// Main program
clc;
nestedtry (1,1)
nestedtry ("a string",1)
nestedtry (1,0)
```

```
Output
START

Executing the try 1 block.

Executing the try 2 block.

Executing statements outside the try 2 block.

END

START

Executing the try 1 block.

Executing the try 2 block.

Error occurred in the try 2 block and handled by the catch 2 block.

Error code: 144 and error message: Undefined operation for the given operands.

Executing statements outside the try 2 block.

END

START

Executing the try 1 block.

Error occurred in the try 1 block and handled by the catch 1 block.

Error code: 27 and error message: Division by zero...

END
```

6.15 Program Debugging

As the size of a program increases, some bugs (logical errors) creep in the program. Debugging is a process of locating and correcting these errors. Prior to Scilab 6.0, there is no direct debugging tool available in Scilab. The programmers have to use the **pause**, **resume** and **abort** commands to debug the scripts and functions. However, Scilab 6 offers a full-featured debugger, without any graphical user interface. Currently, the tool is available for use at the command prompt and is not integrated with the IDE, i.e. SciNotes. However, it is expected that the tool will be integrated with SciNotes in the next release of Scilab. At the time of writing this book, some features of the debugger are not working properly. For example, there is no provision to debug script programs. However, a script program can be temporarily converted to a function program for the purpose of debugging. It is expected that these issues will be taken care of in the next release of Scilab.

The **debug** command, issued at the command prompt, is used to start the Scilab debugger tool. Once in the debug mode, the standard command prompt (-->) changes to the debug mode command prompt (**debug>**). After the debugging is complete, the **quit** command is used to return back to the standard command mode. Table 6.11 lists the commonly used debugging commands along with their shortcuts and brief descriptions. Example 6.38 illustrates the use of some debugging commands with the help of a simple program. The program consists of two functions: the test function and the funLarge function. The test function calls the funLarge function. Before debugging, the program is loaded in the memory. Once in the debug mode, four breakpoints are set: one default breakpoint for the test function, one default breakpoint for the funLarge function, one conditional breakpoint for the test function and one unconditional breakpoint for the funLarge function. After setting the breakpoints, the command **exec** is used to execute the test function, with its arguments, in the debug mode. Various debug commands are used to advance the execution, listing breakpoints and querying the variables. The debugging is ended with **quit** command.

Table 6.11: Debugging commands

Command	Shortcut	Description
abort	A	Aborts the execution of the program and returns to the debug prompt.
breakpoint	break	Adds a breakpoint in the specified function at the specified line number, along with a condition when the breakpoint will be enabled. If no line number is specified, the breakpoint is inserted at the first executable program line. If a condition is specified, a breakpoint becomes enabled only if the condition is **%t**. If no condition is specified, the breakpoint is enabled, by default. The line number specified in a breakpoint command is local to the function, i.e. the function header is treated as line 1 and the other statements are numbered sequentially, for which the breakpoint is being set. The syntax of the breakpoint is as given below: **breakpoint function_name, [line_number, condition]**

			For example, the command **breakpoint test1 4 "i = 5"** inserts a breakpoint at line number 4 in the function file test1.sce. The execution of the function halts at line 4, during debugging, only if the value of the variable **i** is equal to 5. Otherwise, the execution proceeds as normal.
continue	c		Resumes the execution of the program, which was halted by the last break point. The execution of the program halts again at the next breakpoint.
delete	del		Deletes all breakpoints currently set in various functions.
delete n	del		Deletes the specified breakpoint.
disable			Disables all breakpoints.
disable n			Disables the specified breakpoint.
disp	d		Displays the content of a variable. For example, the command **disp x** prints the content of the variable **x** at the command prompt.
enable			Enables all breakpoints.
enable n			Enables the specified breakpoint.
exec	e		Starts execution of a function in the debug mode and stops at the first active breakpoint. For example, the command **exec test** executes the function test in the debug mode. Before executing a function, it must be loaded into the current work space.
h	h		Lists all the debug commands available in the debug mode.
help	-		Opens the debug documentation page of Scilab help documentation.
print			Same as the **disp** command.
quit	q		Stops the debugger and returns to the standard command prompt.
run	r		Same as the **exec** command.
show	s		Shows all breakpoints.
show n	s		Shows the specified breakpoint.
stepin	in		When used at a statement containing a function call, the execution steps into the function to debug it. In other situations, it is equivalent to the **stepnext** command.
stepnext	next		Executes the current statement and halts the execution at the next statement. If the current statement contains a function call and the called function has enabled breakpoints, the execution enters into the called function and debugs it. If there is no breakpoint in the called function, the execution does not enter into the function for the debugging, and the function call is executed in the normal execution mode.

stepout	out		When used at a statement inside a called function, the subsequent statements, till the next breakpoint, of the called function are executed in the normal execution mode. If there is no breakpoint after the current statement in the called function, the execution halts at the next statement of the calling function. In other words, it bypasses the debugging of the remaining statements of the called function and resumes the debugging of the calling function.
where	w		Shows the call stack of the function.

Program 6.38: Debugging of a program

```
// A function program to illustrate the concepts of debugging.
function y=test(a, b)
  c=a+b;
  disp(c);
  for i=1:5
    disp(i);
  end
  x=funLarge(a,b);
  disp(x);
  y=x;
endfunction

function y=funLarge(a, b)
  if a>b then
    y=a;
  else
    y=b;
  end
endfunction
```

Debugging

--> exec('C:\Users\Arvind\Documents\test.sci', -1) // *Loads the function program in memory.*

--> debug // *Starts the debugging tool.*

debug> breakpoint test // *Inserts a breakpoint in the function test at the first line of the function.*
num enable   function line condition

```
0    true              test   -1
```

debug> break test 5 "i==2" // *Inserts a conditional breakpoint at line 5 of the function test.*
```
num  enable            function  line condition

0    true              test   -1
1    true              test    5  i==2
```

debug> break test 8 // *Inserts a breakpoint at line 8 of the function test.*
```
num  enable            function  line condition

0    true              test   -1
1    true              test    5  i==2
2    true              test    8
```

debug> break funLarge // *Inserts a breakpoint at the first line of the function funLarge.*
```
num  enable            function  line condition

0    true              test   -1
1    true              test    5  i==2
2    true              test    8
3    true              funLarge  -1
```

debug> show //*Lists all the breakpoints currently set in various functions and their details.*
```
num  enable            function name  line condition

0    true              test   -1
1    true              test    5  i==2
2    true              test    8
3    true              funLarge  -1
```

debug> exec test(3,7) // *Executes the function test in the debug mode.*
debugger stop on breakpoint(0) in function test line 2
>> c = (a + b)

break> disp a // *Execution halted at the first breakpoint. Showing the content of the variable a.*

219

3.

break> stepnext //*Executes the next line and halt.*
\>> disp(c)

break> stepnext // *Executes the next line.*

  10.
\>> for (i=(1:5)) do

break> continue
  1.
debugger stop on breakpoint(1) in function test line 5 // *Executing the conditional breakpoint.*
\>> disp(i)

debug> disp i

  2.

break> continue // *Continue to the next breakpoint.*

  2.

  3.

  4.

  5.
debugger stop on breakpoint(3) in function funLarge line 2
\>> if ((a > b)) then // *Halted at a breakpoint in the called function.*

debug> continue // *Continue execution till the next breakpoint.*
debugger stop on breakpoint(2) in function test line 8
\>> disp(x)

break> c // *Continue execution till the next breakpoint.*

   7.
ans =

   7.

debug> quit // *Quit debugging.*
Leave debugger.

--> debug

debug> s // *Lists all the breakpoints.*
num enable   function name line condition

0   true   test   2
1   true   test   5   i==2
2   true   test   8
3   true   funLarge   2

debug> del 2 // *Deletes the 2nd breakpoint.*
num enable   function line condition

0   true   test   2
1   true   test   5   i==2
2   true   funLarge 2

debug> disable 1 // *Disables the first breakpoint.*
num enable   function line condition

0   true   test   2
1   false   test   5   i==2
2   true   funLarge 2

debug> q
Leave debugger.

6.16 Scilab Code Conventions

The Code Conventions for the Scilab Programming Language recommends the following guidelines to write Scilab programs:

(a) Start each statement on a new line.
(b) Write no more than one simple statement per line.
(c) Break compound statements over multiple lines.

>For example, use:
>i = 0
>while i<5
> disp("i");
> i = i + 1;
>end
>
>rather than
>i = 0; while i<5 disp("i"); i = i + 1; end

Summary

- Scilab is a high-level programming language with matrices as the basic data processing unit. It has all the programming constructs and features, such as input/output, flow control, looping, data structures, user defined functions, and object oriented features, like the other popular computer programming languages have.
- Programs can be written as scripts or function programs. Scripts are mainly used for automation and functions for implementing new algorithms. The function programming makes programs more modular and reusable.
- Scilab has an IDE for program creation and execution.
- The functions **input**, **x_choices**, **x_choose**, **x_dialog**, **x_matrix**, **x_mdialog** are commonly used for interactively reading scalar and matrix data.
- The functions **disp** and **printf** are the primary functions for console output and the function **xstring**, with Latex formatting capabilities, is the primary function for writing text in a graphics window.
- For repeating certain porting of a program, **for** and **while** loops are used. Both support **continue** and **break** facilities.
- **if-elseif-else** and **select-case-else** statements are primary branching constructs.
- Scilab has functions for reading and writing data from text files, CSV files and Excel files.

- The **errcatch** function and **try-catch construct** are powerful mechanisms to handle run time errors.
- The console mode debugging is introduced in Scilab 6.0. In the older versions, **pause**, **resume** and **abort** facilities can be used to debug programs.

Key Terms

- branching structures
- **break**
- code conventions
- **continue**
- control structures
- current workspace
- data structures
- debugging
- escape characters
- file handling
- file reading
- file writing
- flow control
- flow of execution
- **for**
- formatted input
- formatted output
- function call
- function program
- global variable
- high-level programming language
- **if-else**
- importing data from Excel
- inline function
- interactive input
- Keywords
- local variable
- looping structures
- multiple evaluation of a function
- nested functions
- object oriented features
- output functions
- predefined variables
- reading/writing csv files
- recursive functions
- Scinotes
- script program
- **select-case-else**
- test expression
- **try-catch**
- user defined functions
- **varargin**
- **varargout**
- **while**

Exercise Problems

6.1 Get the lengths of three sides of a triangle and check whether the triangle can be formed or not.

6.2 Write a program to print all the even and odd numbers between a given range.

6.3 Write a program to print the second largest number among a list of numbers.

6.4 Write a program to plot a sine curve for a given set of wavelengths, amplitude and the number of cycles with facilities to choose the plot colour and line type. Use various interactive input facilities for giving parameters and choosing colours and line types.

6.5 Write a function sub-program to evaluate the following series

$$f(x) = x - \frac{x^3}{3!} + \frac{x^5}{5!} - \frac{x^7}{7!} + \cdots$$

6.6 Generate the first n terms (n>2) of Fibonacci numbers starting with 1 and 1 as the first two terms using recursive and non-recursive functions.

6.7 Write a program to list all the prime numbers between two given numbers.

6.8 Write a program to sort a given vector of numbers in ascending order using bubble sort method.

6.9 Write an inline function to calculate compound interest compounded quarterly.

6.10 Write a function program for summing variable number of input arguments.

6.11 Write a function to evaluate the following function for user specified values of x and y

$$f(x,y) = \begin{cases} x + y & x \geq 0 \text{ and } y \geq 0 \\ x - y & x \geq 0 \text{ and } y < 0 \\ x^2 + y^2 & x < 0 \text{ and } y \geq 0 \\ x^2 - y^2 & x < 0 \text{ and } y < 0 \end{cases}$$

6.12 Write a program for the following

$$S(n) = \sum_{i=1}^{n} \frac{1}{i^2 + 1}$$

6.13 Write a function to classify a flow according to the values of its Reynolds (Re) and Mach (Ma) numbers, such that if Re < 2000, the flow is laminar; if 2000 < Re < 5000, the flow is transitional; if Re > 5000, the flow is turbulent; if Ma < 1, the flow is sub-sonic, if Ma = 1, the flow is sonic; and, if Ma >1, the flow is super-sonic.

6.14 Write a function to calculate the area of different open-channel cross-sections of the following types, based on a selection performed by the user and the parameter values provided:

              1 - Trapezoidal
              2 - Rectangular
              3 - Triangular
              4 – Circular

6.15   Write a program to generate multiplication table of the numbers between a and b and display it in the console window and also write it into a file whose name is specified by the user.

Chapter 7
Numerical Methods Using Scilab

Learning Objectives

- Elementary introduction to numerical methods
- Writing programs for various numerical methods

In this chapter, Scilab is used to write a few illustrative programs to implement some numerical methods. Since the numerical method is widely used by scientists and engineers, it has been chosen to write sample programs to illustrate the potential of the Scilab programming facilities. As the complete coverage of the numerical method is out of the scope of the present book, Scilab programs are written for commonly used numerical methods along with a brief introduction of the selected methods. Moreover, there are many excellent books available on numerical methods.

7.1. Solutions of Algebraic and Transcendental equations

Many problems in science and engineering are formulated in the form of *f(x)=0*. For quadratic, cubical or bi-quadratic equations, close form analytical solutions are available in the terms of coefficients of equations, but for equations of higher complexities and involving transcendental expressions, such as $\cos(x) - 5x, 2x - \log(x), 2x - e^{2x}$, etc., algebraic methods are not available, hence numerical methods, such as the bisection method, Newton-Raphson method, etc., are used to find approximate solutions. In this section, some of the popular numerical methods to solve algebraic or transcendental equations are discussed briefly along with corresponding Scilab programs.

7.1.1. Bisection method

This method is based on the fact that for a continuous function *f(x)* between *a* and *b*, if *f(a)* and *f(b)* are of opposite signs, there exist at least one root between *a* and *b* for the equation *f(x)=0*. Without loss of generality, let us assume *f(a)* be positive and *f(b)* be negative. Then the root lies between *a* and *b* and its approximate value can be calculated by *x0 = (a + b)/2*. If *f(x0) =0*, it is concluded that *x0* is the root. Otherwise, the root lies between *a* and *x0* if the sign of *f(x0)* is negative else the root lies between *x0* and *b*. This results into a new range [*a1, b1*] whose length is half the previous range [*a, b*], i.e. the previous range is bisected, hence the name bisection method. The range bisection process is repeated till we get the desired accuracy. Figure 7.1 shows the concept of the method graphically. A Scilab program of the bisection method is shown in Program 7.1.

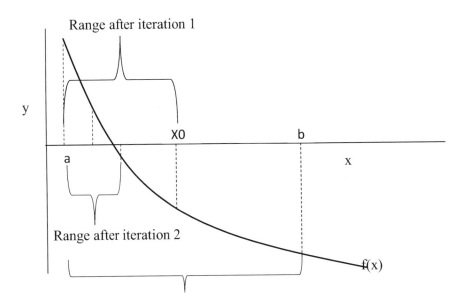

Fig. 7.1: Graphical interpretation of the bisection method

Program 7.1: A program of the bisection method

```
// A program to find a root of an equation using the bisection method.
//Input:
   // f = The function handle of the equation (written as a Scilab function) whose root is to be found.
   // (a, b) = The initial interval in which the root is to be found.
   // epsilon = The desired accuracy level of the root.
   // maxit = the maximum number of iterations to be performed in case the desired accuracy is not attained.
//Output:
   // root= Calculated root.
   // noit = The number of iterations performed to obtain the root.

//A function to implement the bisection method
function [root, noit]=ak_bisect(f, a, b, epsilon, maxit)
   // Check the presence of a root at the interval boundary
```

```
    if abs(f(a))<= %eps then
       root=a;
       noit=0;
       return;
    end
    if abs(f(b))<= %eps then
       root=b;
       noit=0;
       return;
    end
    // Verify the given initial interval to check the presence of a root in it.
    if f(a)*f(b)>0 then
       //Invalid initial interval. Generate an error message and return to the main Scilab window.
       root="invalid interval";
       noit=0;
       return;
    else
       // Valid initial interval.
       i=0;
       while i < maxit
          i=i+1;
          // Bisect the current interval.
          c=(a+b)/2;
          // Check the accuracy of the computed root with the desired accuracy.
          if (c <> 0 & abs((a-b)/c)< epsilon) | f(c)==0 then
             root=c;
             noit=i;
             return;
          end
          // Select the interval having the root for the next iteration.
          if f(c)*f(a) >= 0 then
             a=c;
          else
             b=c;
          end

       end
```

```
//The maximum number of iterations reached and no root with the desired accuracy is
found. Hence, returning the root obtained after performing the maximum number of
iterations.
        root=c;
        noit=i;
    end

endfunction
// The equation whose root is to be found
function [y]=f(x)
    y=x^2-3*x+2;
endfunction
// main program
[r, n] =ak_bisect(f,0.3,1.3,.001,50)
```

Output
n =
11.
r =
0.9997070

7.1.2. False Position method

For a continuous function f(x) between x0 and x1, if f(x0) and f(x1) are of opposite signs, there exists at least one root between x0 and x1 of the equation f(x)=0. In this method, the portion of the curve between x0 and x1 is replaced by a chord joining the two points, (x0, f(x0)) and (x1, f(x1)). The intersection point of the chord with x axis is taken as the approximation of the root of the equation, which can be calculated with equation 7.1.

$$x2 = \frac{f(x0)}{f(x1)-f(x0)}(x1 - x0) \qquad (7.1)$$

Depending on the sign of *f(x2)*, a new chord is generated between *(x0, f(x0))* and *(x2, f(x2))* if signs of *f(x0)* and *f(x2)* are opposite, otherwise the chord is generated between *(x1, f(x1))* and *(x2, f(x2)*. This process is repeated till the required accuracy of the root is not attained or a pre-decided number of iterations is reached. Figure 7.2 shows the graphical interpretation of the method. Program 7.2 implements the above method.

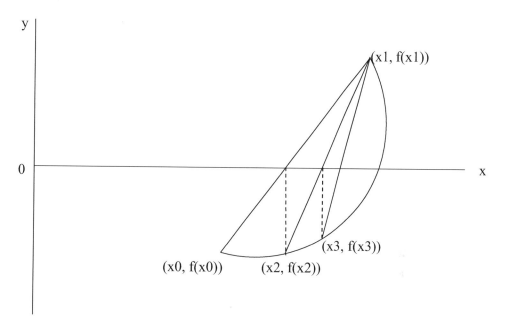

Fig. 7.2: False position method

Program 7.2: A program of the false position method

// A program to find the root of an equation using the false position method.
//Input:
  // f = The function handle of the equation (written as x0 Scilab function) whose root is to be found.
  // (x0, x1) = The initial interval in which the root is to be found.
  // epsilon = The desired accuracy level of the root.
  // maxit = the maximum number of iterations to be performed in case the desired accuracy is not attained.
//Output:
  // root= Calculated root.
  // noit = The number of iterations performed to obtain the root.
  //A function to implement the false position method
function [**root, noit**] = ak_false_position(**f, x0, x1, epsilon, maxit**)
  // Check the presence of a root at the interval boundary
  if abs(**f(x0)**)<= %eps then
    root=x0;
    noit=0;

```
        return;
    end
    if abs(f(x1))<= %eps then
        root=x1;
        noit=0;
        return;
    end
    // Verify the given initial interval to check the presence of a root in it.
    if f(x0) * f(x1)>0 then
        //Invalid initial interval. Generate an error message and return to the main Scilab window.
        root="invalid interval";
        noit=0;
        return;
    else
        // Valid initial interval.
        i=0;
        while i < maxit
            i=i+1;
            // Calculate the next better root.
            x2=x0-(x1-x0) * (f(x0)/(f(x1)-f(x0)));
            // Check the accuracy of the computed root with the desired accuracy.
            if (abs(f(x2))< epsilon) then
                root=x2;
                noit=i;
                return;
            end
            // Select the interval having the root for the next iteration.
            if f(x2)*f(x0) >= 0 then
                x0=x2;
            else
                x1=x2;
            end
        end
        //The maximum number of iterations is reached and no root with the desired accuracy is found. Hence, returning the root obtained after performing the maximum number of iterations.
            root=x2;
```

```
        noit=i;
    end
endfunction
// The equation whose root is to be found
function [y]=f(x)
    y=x^3-2*x-5;
endfunction
// main program
[r,n]=ak_false_position(f,2,3,.001,50);
disp(r,'r=',n,'n=');
```

Output

n=

    8.

r=

    2.0945181

7.1.3. Newton-Raphson method

The methods discussed above are slow in converging to high accuracy. Due to fast converging rate, Newton-Raphson method is generally used to further improve the roots obtained by the previous methods. Let x0 be an approximate root of $f(x) = 0$ and $x1 = x0+h$ be the correct root so that $f(x1) = 0$. Using Taylor's series, f(x0+h) can be expanded as given below:

$$f(x0 + h) = f(x0) + hf'(x0) + \frac{h^2}{2!}f''(x0) + \cdots = 0 \qquad (7.2)$$

Neglecting the second and higher order terms, we get

$$f(x0) + hf'(x0) = 0 \qquad (7.3)$$

From equation 7.3, we get

$$h = -\frac{f(x0)}{f'(x0)} \qquad (7.4)$$

Hence, the more accurate root can be written as

$$x1 = x0 + h = x0 - \frac{f(x0)}{f'(x0)} \tag{7.5}$$

This process is repeated till the desired accuracy of the root is obtained.

Geometrically, the method obtains a more accurate root (say *x1*) at the intersection of the tangent drawn on the curve at the point *(x0, f(x0))* and the x-axis. In the next iteration, the tangent is drawn at the point *(x1, f(x1))* and the new root is obtained at the intersection of the tangent and the x-axis. This process is repeated till the desired accuracy is obtained. Figure 7.3 shows the process with a diagram and Program 7.3 implements the method.

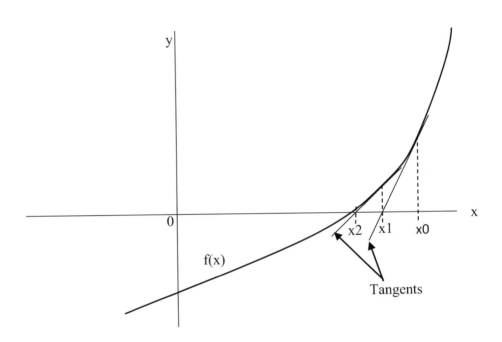

Fig. 7.3: Newton-Raphson method

Program 7.3: A Program for the Newton-Raphson method

// A program to find a root of an equation using the Newton-Raphson method.
//Input:
    // f = The function handle of the equation (written as a Scilab function) whose root is to be found.
    // fd = The derivative of the function f.
    // x0= The initial guess of the root.
    // epsilon = The desired accuracy level of the root.

// maxit = the maximum number of iterations to be performed in case the desired accuracy is not attained.
//Output:
// root= Calculated root.
// noit = The number of iterations performed to obtain the root.

```
function [root, noit]=ak_Newton_Raphson(f, fd, x0, epsilon, maxit)
    i=0;
    while i < maxit
        i=i+1;
        h=f(x0)/fd(x0);
        x0=x0-h;
        if abs(h)<=epsilon then
            root=x0;
            noit=i
            return;
        end

    end
    root=x0;
    noit=i
endfunction
```

// The following functions can be defined in other files or at the console window also
// The equation whose root is to be found
```
function [y]=f(x)
    y=x.^3-2*x-5;
endfunction
```
// The derivative function
```
function [y]=fd(x)
    y=3*x.^2-2
endfunction
[r, n] = ak_Newton_Raphson(f, fd,1,.0001,10)
```

Output
n =
8.
r =
2.0945515

7.2. Interpolation

Interpolation is the process of finding a function $f(x)$ from a given set of tabular values, (x_0, y_0), (x_1, y_1), (x_2, y_2), ..., (x_n, y_n), satisfying the relation $y=f(x)$ at the given values. If $f(x)$ is a polynomial, the process is called polynomial interpolation. In this section, a few popular polynomial interpolation methods are briefly described along with the corresponding Scilab programs.

7.2.1. Newton's formula for interpolation

For a set of (n+1) tabular values, (x_0, y_0), (x_1, y_1), (x_2, y_2), ..., (x_n, y_n) with equidistant x values, Newton's forward difference interpolation formula for interpolating at any arbitrary value of x, near the beginning of the tabular data, is given as follows (for derivation of the formulae, kindly refer any standard numerical method book):

$$y_n(x) = y_0 + p\Delta y_0 + \frac{p(p-1)}{2!}\Delta^2 y_0 + \frac{p(p-1)(p-2)}{3!}\Delta^3 y_0 + \cdots \\ + \frac{p(p-1)\ldots(p-n+1)}{n!}\Delta^n y_0 \quad (7.6)$$

Where Δ is the forward difference operation and its power shows the order of the difference, e.g. $\Delta y_0 = y_1 - y_0$, $\Delta^2 y_0 = \Delta y_1 - \Delta y_0$, $\Delta^3 y_0 = \Delta^2 y_1 - \Delta^2 y_0$ and so on. The value of p is calculated from the equation $x = x_0 + ph$, where $h = x_1 - x_0$. Program 7.4 implements the method.

Program 7.4: A program for the Newton's forward interpolation method

```
// A program for interpolation using the Newton's forward interpolation method.
// Input
    // x and y = A set of data points
    // xp= The value where interpolated value is required
// Output
    // yp = The interpolated value at xp

function [yp]=ak_Newton_Fwd_Int(x, y, xp)
    n=length(x);
    h=x(2)-x(1);
    p=(xp-x(1))/h;
    // Prepare forward difference table, dt
    dt=zeros(n,n);
```

```
    dt(:,1)=y';
    for i=2:n
        for j=1:n-i+1
            dt(j,i)=dt(j+1,i-1)-dt(j,i-1);
        end
    end
    // Calculate the interpolated value using the Newton's forward interpolation formula
    ysum=dt(1,1); // Initialize ysum with y0
    pvalue=1;    // Initialize pvalue to 1 to calculate p, p(p-1), p(p-1)(p-2) ...
    fvalue=1;    // Initialize fvalue to 1 to calculate factorial terms

    for i=1:n-1
        pvalue=pvalue*(p-i+1);
        fvalue=fvalue*i;
        ysum=ysum+pvalue*dt(1,i+1)/fvalue;
    end
    yp=ysum;
endfunction
//Example

x=[1891,1901,1911,1921,1931];
y=[46,66,81,93,101];
xp=1895;
yp=ak_Newton_Fwd_Int(x,y,xp);
s=msprintf("y(%d)=%8.2f",int(xp),yp);
disp(s);
```

Output

y(1895)=   54.85

Program 7.5: A program to generate a polynomial using the Newton's forward formula

```
// A program to find the form of an interpolating polynomial using the Newton's forward
interpolation.
// Input
   // x and y = A set of data points
// Output
   // yp = A polynomial of the form a0+a1 x+a2 x^2+ ...+an x^n
```

```
function [yp]=ak_Newton_Fwd_Int_poly(x, y)

    n=length(x);
    // Prepare forward difference table
    dt=zeros(n,n);
    dt(:,1)=y';
    for i=2:n
        for j=1:n-i+1
            dt(j,i)=dt(j+1,i-1)-dt(j,i-1);
        end
    end
    // Generate Newton's forward interpolation polynomial
    X = poly (0, "x");
    h = x(2) - x (1) ;
    p = (X-x (1) ) / h;
    dely0 = dt (1 ,:);

    Y = dt(1,1);

    for i = 2: length (y)-1
        t = 1;
        for j = 1:i-1
            t = t * (p-j +1) ;
        end
        Y = Y + t* dt(1,i)/ factorial (i-1);
    end
    Y = round (Y *10^2) /10^2;
    //disp (Y);
    yp=Y;
endfunction

//Example
x = 0:3;
y = [1 0 1 10];
[yp] = ak_Newton_Fwd_Int_poly(x,y)
disp(yp, "The form of the interpolated polynomial is:");
```

Output

> The form of the interpolated polynomial is:
>
> $1 - 2x + x^2$

7.2.2. Lagrange's interpolation formula

The major limitation of Newton's interpolation formula is that it cannot be used for non-equispaced data points (For example, [0,-12], [1,0], [3,12], [4,24]). For such data sets, Lagrange's interpolation formula is widely used for interpolation. The method is also applicable to equispaced data sets.

Lagrange's interpolation formula is given as below:

$$L_n(x) = \sum_{i=0}^{n} \frac{\pi_{n+1}(x)}{(x - x_i)\pi'_{n+1}(x_i)} y_i \quad (7.7)$$

where (x_i, y_i) is the ith data point of the given tabular data points, $n+1$ is the number of data points,

and
$$\pi_{n+1}(x) = (x - x_0)(x - x_1)(x - x_2) \ldots (x - x_i)(x - x_{i+1}) \ldots (x - x_n)$$

$$\pi'_{n+1}(x_i) = (x_i - x_0)(x_i - x_1) \ldots (x_i - x_{i-1})(x_i - x_{i+1}) \ldots (x - x_n).$$

Program 7.5: A program for interpolation using the Lagrange's method

```
// A program for interpolation using the Lagrange's method.
// Input
   // x and y = A set of data points
   // xp= X value where interpolated value is required
// Output
   // yp = The interpolated value at xp

function [yp]=ak_Lagrange_Int(x, y, xp)
   n=length(x);
   yp=0;
```

```
    for k=1 : n
        pi=1;
        // Calculate Numerator of Lagrange terms
        for i=1 : n
            if i <> k then
                pi =pi*(xp-x(i));
            end
        end
        pid=1;
        // Calculate denominator of Lagrange terms
        for j=1 : n
            if j <> k then
                pid=pid*(x(k)-x(j));
            end
        end
        //Sum Langrange terms
        yp=yp+pi*y(k)/pid;
    end
endfunction

//Example
x=[300 304 305 307];
y=[2.4771 2.4829 2.4843 2.4871];
xp=301;
[yp] = ak_Lagrange_Int(x,y,xp);
s=msprintf("The interpolated value at x= %f is %f",xp,yp);
disp(s);
```

Output

The interpolated value at x= 301.000000 is 2.478597

Program 7.7: A program to find the interpolating polynomial using the Lagrange's method

```
// A program to find the form of an interpolating polynomial using the Lagrange's method.
// Input
    // x and y = A set of data points
// Output
```

```
// yp = A polynomial of the form a0+a1 x+a2 x^2+ ...+an x^n

function [yp]=ak_Lagrange_Int_poly(x, y)
    n=length(x);
    yp=0;
    X=poly(0,'x');
    for k=1 : n
        pi=1;
        // Calculate Numerator of Lagrange terms
        for i=1 : n
            if i <> k then
                pi =pi*(X-x(i));
            end
        end
        pid=1;
        // Calculate denominator of Lagrange terms
        for j=1 : n
            if j <> k then
                pid=pid*(x(k)-x(j));
            end
        end
        //Sum Lagrange terms
        yp=yp+pi*y(k)/pid;
    end
endfunction

//Example
x=[0 1 3 4];
y=[-12 0 12 24];
[yp] = ak_Lagrange_Int_poly(x,y);
disp(yp, "The form of the Lagrange polynomial is:");
```

Output

The form of the Lagrange polynomial is:

                 2   3
 - 12 + 17x - 6x + x

7.3. Numerical Differentiation

Numerical differentiation is the process of finding the derivative of a function given in a tabular form. The process can use any of the interpolating polynomials (some popular interpolating polynomials are discussed in the previous section) for a given data set. In this section, the process is illustrated with help of Newton's interpolating polynomial as given below:

$$y = y_0 + p\Delta y_0 + \frac{p(p-1)}{2!}\Delta^2 y_0 + \frac{p(p-1)(p-2)}{3!}\Delta^3 y_0 + \cdots \quad (7.8)$$

Where $x = x_0 + ph$

The numerical differential formula for the above is

$$\frac{dy}{dx} = \frac{dy}{dp} \cdot \frac{dp}{dx} \quad (7.9)$$

$$\frac{dy}{dx} = \frac{1}{h}\left[\Delta y_0 + \frac{2p-1}{2}\Delta^2 y_0 + \frac{3p^2-6p+2}{6}\Delta^3 y_0 + \cdots\right] \quad (7.10)$$

The second order derivatives can be derived as below:

$$\frac{d^2 y}{dx^2} = \frac{d}{dx}\left(\frac{dy}{dx}\right) = \frac{1}{h^2}\left[\Delta^2 y_0 + \frac{6p-6}{6}\Delta^3 y_0 + \frac{12p^2+26p+22}{24}\Delta^4 y_0 + \cdots\right] \quad (7.11)$$

Similarly, the higher order derivatives can be obtained by successive differentiation as given above.

Program 7.8: A program to find the derivatives from tabular data using the Newton's forward interpolation

```
// A program to find the derivatives from tabular data using the Newton's forward
interpolation.
// Input
    // x and y = A set of data points
    // xp = A point where derivatives are calculated
// Output
    // yp = A polynomial of the form a0+a1 x+a2 x^2+ ...+an x^n

function [dydx]=ak_poly_derivative(x) // A function to evaluate the derivative
```

```
n=1:length(x)-1
c=x(2:$); // Extract the coefficients of the polynomial terms except the constant term
dydx=c.*n;
endfunction


// Main program
// input
clc;
x=1:.2:2.2;
y=round((%e^x)*10000)/10000; // Rounding to four decimal place accuracy
xp=2.0; // The point where the derivative is required
// Calculate the interpolative polynomial (refer interpolation section)
yp] = ak_Newton_Fwd_Int_poly(x,y);
// Get coefficients of the polynomial

disp(yp, "f(x)=","Interpolating polynomial");
ypc=coeff(yp);
// Calculate first order derivative
[dydx]=ak_poly_derivative(ypc);

disp(poly(dydx,"x","coeff"),"d f(x)/dx =");
p=poly(dydx,"x","coeff");
// Calculate the derivative at the specified point and display
disp(msprintf("First derivative of f(x) at x= %f is %f",xp, horner(p,xp)));

// Calculate second order derivative
[d2ydx2]=ak_poly_derivative(dydx);
disp(poly(d2ydx2,"x","coeff"), "d^2 f(x)/dx^2 =");
p1=poly(d2ydx2,"x","coeff");
disp(msprintf("Second derivative of f(x) at x= %f is %f",xp, horner(p1,xp)));
```

Output
Interpolating polynomial f(x)=   2   3   4   5 0.98 + 1.09x + 0.31x + 0.36x - 0.06x + 0.03x

```
d f(x)/dx =

                 2        3        4
1.09 + 0.62x + 1.08x - 0.24x + 0.15x

First derivative of f(x) at x= 2.000000 is 7.130000

d^2 f(x)/dx^2 =

                2        3
0.62 + 2.16x - 0.72x + 0.6x

Second derivative of f(x) at x= 2.000000 is 6.860000
```

7.4. Numerical Integration

For a set of tabular data points, numerical integration is to compute the finite integral between given interval by using some form of interpolating polynomials. Using Newton's forward interpolating polynomial, the numerical integration formula can be derived as follows:

Let the interval $[a, b]$ be divided into n equal subintervals such that $x_n = x_0 + nh$. Hence the integral becomes

$$I = \int_{x_0}^{x_n} y \, dx \qquad (7.12)$$

Substituting y with the corresponding Newton's forward interpolating polynomial, the integral becomes

$$I = \int_{x_0}^{x_n} \left[y_0 + p\Delta y_0 + \frac{p(p-1)}{2}\Delta^2 y_0 + \frac{p(p-1)(p-2)}{6}\Delta^3 y_0 + \cdots \right] dx \qquad (7.13)$$

Since $x = x_0 + ph$, dx can be substituted with hdp, hence the integral becomes

$$I = h \int_0^n \left[y_0 + p\Delta y_0 + \frac{p(p-1)}{2}\Delta^2 y_0 + \frac{p(p-1)(p-2)}{6}\Delta^3 y_0 + \cdots \right] dp \qquad (7.14)$$

Which on simplification gives

$$I = \int_{x_0}^{x_n} y\, dx = nh\left[y_0 + \frac{n}{2}\Delta y_0 + \frac{n(2n-3)}{12}\Delta^2 y_0 + \frac{n(n-2)^2}{24}\Delta^3 y_0 + \cdots\right] \quad (7.15)$$

From this general integral formula, various integral formulae are obtained by putting n=1,2, 3… etc. The most popular and widely used formulae are corresponding to *n=1* and *n=2*, commonly known as trapezoidal integral rule and Simpson's 1/3 rule, respectively.

7.4.1. Trapezoidal rule

Setting n=1 in the general integration formula (7.15) based on Newton's forward interpolation polynomial, all the differences higher than the first will vanish and the trapezoidal integration rule is obtained, which is give as below for the first interval $[x_0, x_1]$:

$$\int_{x_0}^{x_1} y\, dx = h\left[y_0 + \frac{1}{2}\Delta y_0\right] = h\left[y_0 + \frac{1}{2}(y_1 - y_0)\right] = \frac{h}{2}[y_0 + y_1] \quad (7.16)$$

Similarly, for the next interval $[x_1, x_2]$

$$\int_{x_1}^{x_2} y\, dx = \frac{h}{2}[y_1 + y_2] \quad (7.17)$$

The similar rule is obtained for the other interval also. For the last interval, the rule is

$$\int_{x_{n-1}}^{x_n} y\, dx = \frac{h}{2}[y_{n-1} + y_n] \quad (7.18)$$

Combining all these intervals together, the formula for the trapezoidal rule becomes

$$\int_{x_0}^{x_n} y\, dx = \frac{h}{2}[y_0 + 2(y_1 + y_2 + y_3 \ldots + y_{n-1}) + y_n] \quad (7.19)$$

Geometrically, in this rule, the portion of the curve *y=f(x)* in each interval is replaced by a straight line joining the data points of the corresponding interval. With straight lines, the shape of each interval looks like a trapezium, hence the name trapezoidal rule.

7.4.2. Simpson's 1/3 rule

This rule is obtained by putting *n=2* in the general integration formula (7.15), which is equivalent to replacing the portion of the curve *y=f(x)* between two consecutive intervals by a second order polynomial. Thus, for the first two consecutive intervals, i.e. $[x_0, x_1]$ and $[x_1, x_2]$, the integration formula becomes:

$$\int_{x_0}^{x_2} y\, dx = 2h\left[y_0 + \Delta y_0 + \frac{1}{6}\Delta^2 y_0\right] = \frac{h}{3}[y_0 + 4y_1 + y_2] \qquad (7.20)$$

Similarly, for the next two consecutive intervals, i.e., $[x_2, x_3]$ and $[x_3, x_4]$, the integration formula becomes

$$\int_{x_2}^{x_4} y\, dx = 2h\left[y_2 + \Delta y_2 + \frac{1}{6}\Delta^2 y_2\right] = \frac{h}{3}[y_2 + 4y_3 + y_4] \qquad (7.21)$$

And finally, for the last two consecutive intervals, i.e., $[x_{n-2}, x_{n-1}]$ and $[x_{n-1}, x_n]$, the integration formula becomes

$$\int_{x_{n-2}}^{x_n} y\, dx = 2h\left[y_{n-2} + \Delta y_{n-2} + \frac{1}{6}\Delta^2 y_{n-2}\right] = \frac{h}{3}[y_{n-2} + 4y_{n-1} + y_n] \qquad (7.22)$$

On combining all the formulae together, the final integration formula becomes

$$\int_{x_0}^{x_n} y\, dx = \frac{h}{3}[y_0 + 4(y_1+y_3+y_5 + \cdots +y_{n-1}) + 2(y_2+y_4+y_6 + \cdots +y_{n-2}) + y_n] \qquad (7.23)$$

Since this rule uses two consecutive intervals to derive the formulae, the rule requires the division of the integration interval into an even number of subintervals of equal width h.

Program 7.9: A program for numerical integration using trapezoidal and Simpson's 1/3 rule

```
// A program to calculate integration using trapezoidal and Simpson's 1/3 rule.
// Input
   // x and y = A set of data points
// Output
   // I = The value of integration

// Function for the trapezoidal method
function [I]=ak_integration_trap(x, y)
h=x(2)-x(1);
I=h*(y(1)+2*sum(y(2:1:$-1))+y($))/2;
endfunction

// Function for the Simpson's 1/3 rule
function [I]=ak_integration_simp(x, y)
h=x(2)-x(1);
I=h*(y(1)+4*sum(y(2:2:$-1))+2*sum(y(3:2:$-1))+y($))/3;
endfunction
```

```
//Example 1
clc;
x=7.47:.01:7.52;
y=[1.93 1.95 1.98 2.01 2.03 2.06];

[I]=ak_integration_trap(x,y);
disp(I, "Integration using the trapezoidal method");
[I]=ak_integration_simp(x,y)
disp(I, "Integration using the Simpson''s 1/3 rule");

//Example 2
x=0:.125:1;
y=1 ./(1+x);
[I]=ak_integration_trap(x,y);
disp(I, "Integration using the trapezoidal method");
[I]=ak_integration_simp(x,y)
disp(I, "Integration using the Simpson"s 1/3 rule");
```

Output

Integration using the trapezoidal method
 	
    0.09965
 	
Integration using the Simpson's 1/3 rule
 	
    0.0928333
 	
Integration using the trapezoidal method
 	
    0.6941219
 	
Integration using the Simpson's 1/3 rule
 	
    0.6931545

7.5. Solution of Linear Systems of Equations

There are two approaches to solve a linear system of equations: direct and iterative methods. In direct methods, the matrix inversion method and the Gauss elimination and backward substitution method are very popular. In iterative methods, the Jacobi and Gauss-Seidel Methods are very popular. In this section, a brief introduction of these methods is presented and Scilab programs are developed for the same.

7.5.1. Matrix inversion method

Following is the general representation of n linear equations in n unknowns:

$$\left.\begin{matrix} a_{11}x_1 + a_{12}x_2 + \cdots + a_{1n}x_n = b_1 \\ a_{21}x_1 + a_{22}x_2 + \cdots + a_{2n}x_n = b_2 \\ \cdots \\ a_{n1}x_1 + a_{n2}x_2 + \cdots + a_{nn}x_n = b_n \end{matrix}\right\} \quad (7.24)$$

The matrix representation of the above equation is

$$AX = B$$

where $A = \begin{bmatrix} a_{11} & a_{12} & \cdots & a_{1n} \\ a_{21} & a_{22} & \cdots & a_{2n} \\ & & \cdots & \\ a_{n1} & a_{n2} & \cdots & a_{nn} \end{bmatrix}, X = \begin{bmatrix} x_1 \\ x_2 \\ \cdots \\ x_2 \end{bmatrix}$ and $B = \begin{bmatrix} b_1 \\ b_2 \\ \cdots \\ b_2 \end{bmatrix}$ (7.25)

If inverse of matrix A (denoted by A^{-1}) exists, then the solution of the system of equations can be found from the following relation:

$$X = A^{-1}B$$

Program 7.10: A program for the matrix inversion method to solve the system of equations

```
// A Program to solve a system of equations using the matrix inversion method.
//Input:
    // a = the coefficient matrix of the system of equations
    // b = the right side constant vector of the system of equations
//Output:
    // x= the solution vector
```

```
//A function subprogram for the matrix inversion method to solve the system of equations
function [x]=ak_Linear_System_Matrix(a, b)
    try // to handle the situation when the inverse of the matrix does not exist
        a_inv=inv(a);
        x=a_inv*b;
    catch
        disp(lasterror());
        x=[];
    end

endfunction

//Main Program
a=[3 1 2;2 -3 -1;1 2 1];
b=[3;-3;4];
[x] = ak_Linear_System_Matrix(a,b);
```

Output

x =

   1.
   2.
 - 1.

7.5.2. Gauss elimination method

The Gauss elimination method is a two-step process. In the first step, the system of equations is reduced to an equivalent upper triangular system, using matrix row operations. In an upper triangular system, the number of unknowns in any equation is one less than its previous equation and the last equation contains only one unknown, i.e. coefficients of all the other unknowns are zero. In the second step, starting from the last equation which contains only one unknown, the value of the last unknown is determined. The determined unknown is back substituted in the second last equation which contains only two unknowns. This process is repeated for all the remaining equations to determine the values of all the unknowns. Without loss of generality, the above steps are illustrated for a system of three equations (given in equation 7.26).

$$\begin{aligned} a_{11}x_1 + a_{12}x_2 + a_{13}x_3 &= b_1 \\ a_{21}x_1 + a_{22}x_2 + a_{23}x_3 &= b_2 \\ a_{31}x_1 + a_{32}x_2 + a_{33}x_3 &= b_3 \end{aligned} \quad (7.26)$$

The augmented matrix of the above equation is given below:

$$\begin{bmatrix} a_{11} & a_{12} & a_{13} & b_1 \\ a_{21} & a_{22} & a_{23} & b_2 \\ a_{31} & a_{32} & a_{33} & b_3 \end{bmatrix} \quad (7.27)$$

To eliminate x_1 form the second and third equations, the following row operations are performed on the second and third rows of the augmented matrix, respectively:

$$R'_2 = R_2 - \frac{a_{21}}{a_{11}} R_1 \text{ and } R'_3 = R_3 - \frac{a_{31}}{a_{11}} R_1$$

where R_1, R_2 and R_3 are the original rows of the augmented matrix and R'_2 and R'_3 are the revised second and third rows of the revised augmented matrix.

The revised augmented matrix is as given below after the previous operations:

$$\begin{bmatrix} a_{11} & a_{12} & a_{13} & b_1 \\ 0 & a'_{22} & a'_{23} & b'_2 \\ 0 & a'_{32} & a'_{33} & b'_3 \end{bmatrix} \quad (7.28)$$

Similarly, to eliminate x_2 from the third equation, the following operation is performed on the third row of the revised augmented matrix:

$$R''_3 = R'_3 - \frac{a'_{32}}{a'_{22}} R'_2$$

This results into the following upper triangular augmented matrix:

$$\begin{bmatrix} a_{11} & a_{12} & a_{13} & b_1 \\ 0 & a'_{22} & a'_{23} & b'_2 \\ 0 & 0 & a''_{33} & b''_3 \end{bmatrix} \quad (7.29)$$

From the final augmented matrix, the values of the unknowns are calculated as given below:

$$\left.\begin{aligned} x_3 &= \frac{b''_3}{a''_{33}} \\ x_2 &= \frac{b'_2}{a'_{22}} - \frac{a'_{23}}{a'_{22}} x_3 \\ x_1 &= \frac{b_1}{a_{11}} - \frac{a_{12}}{a_{11}} x_2 - \frac{a_{13}}{a_{11}} x_3 \end{aligned}\right\} \quad (7.30)$$

It is clear that the method fails if any of the diagonal elements of the triangular matrix vanishes. However, the method can be modified by rearranging the rows to get non-vanishing diagonal elements. Even after rearranging the rows, if it is not possible to achieve non-vanishing diagonal elements, it indicates that the matrix is singular and there exists no solution of the system of equations.

Program 7.11: A program for the Gauss elimination method to solve the system of equations

```
// A Program to solve a system of equations using Gauss elimination method.
//Input:
   // a = the coefficient matrix of the system of equations
   // b = the right side constant vector of the system of equations
//Output:
   // x= solution vector

//A function subprogram for the Gauss elimination method to solve the system of equations
function [x]=ak_Linear_System_Gauss_E(a, b)
   try
      Aug=[a,b];
      n=length(b);
      for j = 1:n -1
         for i = j +1: n
            Aug (i,j:n+1) = Aug (i,j:n +1) - Aug (i,j) / Aug(j,j) * Aug (j,j:n+1);
         end
      end
      // Backward Substitution
      x = zeros (n ,1) ;
      x(n) = Aug(n,n +1) / Aug(n,n);
```

```
        for i = n -1: -1:1
            x(i) = (Aug(i,n +1) -Aug (i,i+1:n)*x(i +1: n))/ Aug (i,i);
        end

    catch
        disp(lasterror());
        x=[];
    end

endfunction

//Main Program
a=[2 1 1;3 2 3;1 4 9];

b=[10;18;16];
[x] = ak_Linear_System_Gauss_E(a,b)
```

Output
x =
7.
- 9.
5.

7.5.3. Iterative method

In general, one should use direct methods to solve a system of equations. However, for a large system of equations having a large number of zeroes, it is advantageous to use iterative methods, such as the Jacobi method. The Jacobi method rewrites the system of equations (equation 7.31) in the form as shown in equation 7.32 and starts from an approximate solution, normally all the unknowns are assigned zero in the beginning. Using the new form of the equations, the new values of the unknowns are determined, and the process is repeated till the required accuracy of the solution is found.

    In the Jacobi method, for the calculation of the new value of any unknown, only old values of other unknowns available at the beginning of the current iteration are used. However, if the latest values of unknowns are used in the calculation of any unknown as soon as they are available, the solution process coverages faster. This modified iterative method is known as Gauss-Seidel method.

The iterative form of the system of equations 7.31 is shown in equation 7.32 for the Jacobi method where $(x_1^i, x_2^i, x_3^i, \ldots, x_n^i,)$ are the current approximations of the unknowns and $(x_1^{i+1}, x_2^{i+1}, x_3^{i+1}, \ldots, x_n^{i+1},)$ are the new computed values in the next iteration. Before writing the iterative form, the equations should be arranged in such a way that the diagonal elements do not vanish and as for as possible, the diagonal elements should have large absolute values. Equation 7.33 shows the iterative form of the equations for the Gauss-Seidel method.

$$\left.\begin{aligned}
a_{11}x_1 + a_{12}x_2 + \cdots + a_{1n}x_n &= b_1 \\
a_{21}x_1 + a_{22}x_2 + \cdots + a_{2n}x_n &= b_2 \\
&\cdots \\
a_{n1}x_1 + a_{n2}x_2 + \cdots + a_{nn}x_n &= b_n
\end{aligned}\right\} \quad (7.31)$$

Jacobi method

$$\left.\begin{aligned}
x_1^{i+1} &= \frac{b_1}{a_{11}} - \frac{a_{12}}{a_{11}}x_2^i - \frac{a_{13}}{a_{11}}x_3^i - \cdots - \frac{a_{1n}}{a_{11}}x_n^i \\
x_2^{i+1} &= \frac{b_2}{a_{22}} - \frac{a_{21}}{a_{22}}x_1^i - \frac{a_{23}}{a_{22}}x_3^i - \cdots - \frac{a_{2n}}{a_{22}}x_n^i \\
x_3^{i+1} &= \frac{b_3}{a_{33}} - \frac{a_{31}}{a_{33}}x_1^i - \frac{a_{32}}{a_{33}}x_2^i - \cdots - \frac{a_{3n}}{a_{33}}x_n^i \\
&\cdots \\
x_n^{i+1} &= \frac{b_n}{a_{nn}} - \frac{a_{n2}}{a_{nn}}x_1^i - \frac{a_{n3}}{a_{nn}}x_2^i - \cdots - \frac{a_{nn-1}}{a_{nn}}x_{n-1}^i
\end{aligned}\right\} \quad (7.32)$$

Gauss-Seidel Method

$$\left.\begin{aligned}
x_1^{i+1} &= \frac{b_1}{a_{11}} - \frac{a_{12}}{a_{11}}x_2^i - \frac{a_{13}}{a_{11}}x_3^i - \cdots - \frac{a_{1n}}{a_{11}}x_n^i \\
x_2^{i+1} &= \frac{b_2}{a_{22}} - \frac{a_{21}}{a_{22}}x_1^{i+1} - \frac{a_{23}}{a_{22}}x_3^i - \cdots - \frac{a_{2n}}{a_{22}}x_n^i \\
x_3^{i+1} &= \frac{b_3}{a_{33}} - \frac{a_{31}}{a_{33}}x_1^{i+1} - \frac{a_{32}}{a_{33}}x_2^{i+1} - \cdots - \frac{a_{3n}}{a_{33}}x_n^i \\
&\cdots \\
x_n^{i+1} &= \frac{b_n}{a_{nn}} - \frac{a_{n2}}{a_{nn}}x_1^{i+1} - \frac{a_{n3}}{a_{nn}}x_2^{i+1} - \cdots - \frac{a_{nn-1}}{a_{nn}}x_{n-1}^{i+1}
\end{aligned}\right\} \quad (7.33)$$

Program 7.12: A program for the Jacobi method to solve a system of equations

```
// A Program to solve a system of equations using Jacobi method.
//Input:
    // a = the coefficient matrix of the system of equations
    // b = the right side constant vector of the system of equations
    // epsilon = the desired accuracy of the roots
    // maxit = the maximum number of iterations
//Output:
    // x= solution vector

//A function subprogram for the Jacobi method to solve a system of equations
function [x, noit]=ak_Linear_Sys_Jacobi(a, b, epsilon, maxit)
    try
        aug=[a,b]; // Creating augmented matrix
        [r,c]=size(a);
        for i=1:r-1 // Pivoting equations according to the leading diagonal
            [m n]=max(abs(aug(i:$,i)),'r');
            index=n+i-1;
            aug=swap(aug,i,index)
        end
        a=aug(1:r,1:r);
        b=aug(1:r,$);
        i=1:r+1:r*r;
        ad=diag(a);
        a(i)=0;
        c=sum(abs(a),'c'); // Testing for the convergence of the solution
        d=abs(ad);
        if sum(d<c) then
            disp("Warning: The iterative method may not converge as the coefficient matrix is not a strictly dominant diagonal matrix" );
        end

        x=zeros(r,1);
        for i=1:maxit // Iterative process
            y=x;
            x=b-a*x;
            x=x./ad;
            z=abs(y-x);
```

```
            if (max(z)< epsilon) then // Termination condition
               break;
            end
            noit=i;
        end


    catch
        disp(lasterror()); // Error reporting
        x=[];
    end

endfunction
function [a]=swap(a, i, j)
    t=a(j,:);
    a(j,:)=a(i,:);
    a(i,:)=t;
endfunction

//Main Program
a=[-1 -1 -2 10;10 -2 -1 -1;-2 10 -1 -1;-1 -1 10 -2];
b=[-9;3; 15; 27];
epsilon=.005;
[x,n] = ak_Linear_Sys_Jacobi(a,b, epsilon,200)
disp(x, "The solution of the equations:");


a=[2 1 1;3 2 3;1 4 9];
b=[10;18;16];
[x,n] = ak_Linear_Sys_Jacobi(a,b, epsilon,200)
disp(x, "The solution of the equations:");


a=[-4 5;1 2];
b=[1;3];
[x,n] = ak_Linear_Sys_Jacobi(a,b, epsilon,200)
disp(x, "The solution of the equations:");
```

Output

The solution of the equations:

  0.997536
  1.9975488
  2.9975616
 - 0.0024768

Warning: The iterative method may not converge as the coefficient matrix is not a strictly dominant diagonal matrix

The solution of the equations:

10^{76} *

 - 2.0973642
 - 3.0393587
 - 3.0116694

Warning: The iterative method may not converge as the coefficient matrix is not a strictly dominant diagonal matrix

The solution of the equations:

  1.0027756
  0.9988898

Program 7.13: A program for the Gauss-Seidel method to solve a system of equations

```
// A Program to solve a system of equations using Gauss-Seidel method.
//Input:
    // a = the coefficient matrix of the system of equations
    // b = the right side constant vector of the system of equations
    // epsilon = the desired accuracy of the roots
    // maxit = the maximum number of iterations
//Output:
    // x= solution vector

//A function subprogram for the Gauss-Seidel method to solve the system of equations
```

```
function [x, noit]=ak_Lin_Sys_Gauss_Siedel(a, b, epsilon, maxit)
    try
        aug=[a,b]; // Creating augmented matrix
        [r,c]=size(a);
        for i=1:r-1 // Pivoting equations according to the leading diagonal
            [m n]=max(abs(aug(i:$,i)),'r');
            index=n+i-1;
            aug=swap(aug,i,index)
        end
        a=aug(1:r,1:r);
        b=aug(1:r,$);
        i=1:r+1:r*r;
        ad=diag(a);
        a(i)=0;
        c=sum(abs(a),'c'); // Testing for the convergence of the solution
        d=abs(ad);
        if sum(d<c) then
            disp("Warning: The iterative method may not converge as the coefficient matrix is not a strictly dominant diagonal matrix" );
        end

        x=zeros(r,1);
        for i=1:maxit // Iterative process
            y=x;
            for j=1:r
                x(j)=(b(j)-a(j,:)*x)/ad(j);
            end

            z=abs(y-x);
            //disp(x');
            if (max(z)< epsilon) then // Termination condition
                break;
            end
        noit=i;
        end

    catch
```

```
      disp(lasterror()); // Error reporting
        x=[];
      end

endfunction
function [a]=swap(a, i, j)
    t=a(j,:);
    a(j,:)=a(i,:);
    a(i,:)=t;
endfunction

//Main Program
a=[-1 -1 -2 10;10 -2 -1 -1;-2 10 -1 -1;-1 -1 10 -2];
b=[-9;3; 15; 27];
epsilon=.005;
[x,n] = ak_Lin_Sys_Gauss_Siedel(a,b, epsilon,200)
disp(x, "The solution of the equations:");


a=[2 1 1;3 2 3;1 4 9];
b=[10;18;16];
[x,n] = ak_Lin_Sys_Gauss_Siedel(a,b, epsilon,200)
disp(x, "The solution of the equations:");


a=[-4 5;1 2];
b=[1;3];
[x,n] = ak_Lin_Sys_Gauss_Siedel(a,b, epsilon,200)
disp(x, "The solution of the equations:");
```

Output

The solution of the equations:
 	
   0.9994268
   1.9996752
   2.9997566
  - 0.0001385
 	
Warning: The iterative method may not converge as the coefficient matrix is not a strictly dominant diagonal matrix

> The solution of the equations:
>
> $10^{101} *$
>
>   5.0376995
>   18.755915
> - 28.831314
>
> Warning: The iterative method may not converge as the coefficient matrix is not a strictly dominant diagonal matrix
>
> The solution of the equations:
>
> 0.9982653
> 1.0008674

Summary

- The numerical method is widely used by scientists and engineers for solving wider varieties of complex problems.
- The **bisection**, **Newton-Raphson** and **false position** methods are popular methods for finding roots of transcendental and algebraic equations.
- The **Newton's interpolation formula** and **Lagrange's interpolation formula** are widely used for interpolations for uniformly and non-uniformly spaced data, respectively.
- The **trapezoidal integral rule** and **Simpson's 1/3 rule** are popular methods for numerical integration.
- The **Gauss-elimination**, **Jacobi** and **Gauss-Seidel** methods are very popular methods for solving a system of linear equations.

Key Terms

- algebraic equations
- approximate solution
- backward substitution
- bisection method
- Jacobi method
- Lagrange's method
- linear system of equations
- matrix inversion method

- epsilon
- false position method
- Gauss elimination method
- Gauss-Seidel method
- interpolation
- Iteration
- Newton's forward interpolation
- Newton-Raphson method
- numerical differentiation
- roots
- Simpson's 1/3 rule
- transcendental equations

Exercise Problems

7.1 Write a program to find a real root of the equation $x^3 + x^2 - 100 = 0$, starting with x=3, accurate up to 4 decimal places, using the iterative method.

7.2 Write a program to find a real root of the equation $3x - \cos(x) - 1 = 0$, using the Newton-Raphson method.

7.3 Write a program to find the dominant eigenvalue of a matrix using the power method.

7.4 Write a program for interpolation near the end of a set of tabulated data using the Newton's backward difference formula.

7.5 Write a program for interpolation from an unequal interval data set using the Newton's divided difference formula.

7.6 Write a program to fit a straight line for a given set of data using the least square method.

7.7 Write a program to fit a second degree parabola for a given set of data using the least square error method.

7.8 Write a program to evaluate $\int_0^4 e^x dx$ using the Trapezoidal, Simpson's one-third and Simpson's three-eight rules.

7.9 Write a program to find the numerical solution at x=1.4 for the equation $\frac{dy}{dx} = y^2 + x^2, y(1) = 0$ with h=0.1, using the Runga-Kutta fourth order method.

Appendix-I
List of commonly used functions

Bitwise operations

bitand	Performs bitwise AND operations
bitcmp	Gets bitwise complement
bitget	Gets the value of a bit at the specified position
bitor	Performs bitwise OR operations
bitset	Sets the value of a bit at the specified position
bitxor	Performs bitwise XOR operations
isequalbitwise	Performs bitwise comparison of arguments

Complex Numbers

complex	Creates a complex number
conj	Calculates complex conjugate of the argument
imag	Gets imaginary parts of complex numbers
imult	Multiplies the argument by i(iota), i.e. $\sqrt{-1}$
isreal	Returns true if the argument contains only real numbers
real	Returns the real part of the argument

Discrete mathematics

factor	Returns factors of the integer argument
factorial	Calculates factorial of the argument
gcd	Calculates the greatest common divisor of the arguments
lcm	Calculates the least common multiple of the arguments
perms	Returns all permutations of the vector argument
primes	Returns all the prime numbers between 1 and the argument

Elementary matrices

diag	Extracts the specified diagonal elements of a matrix, or create a matrix form the diagonal elements
eye	Creates an identity matrix of the specified size
ind2sub	Returns the matrix subscript values of specified size from a vector
linspace	Creates a linearly spaced vector for a given range
logspace	Creates a logarithmically spaced vector for a given range
meshgrid	Creates a 2D meshgrid from two vectors
ndgrid	Creates a multidimensional grid from vectors
ones	Creates a matrix of the specified size with all elements set to 1
testmatrix	Generates special matrices, such as Hilbert, Franck, etc
zeros	Creates a matrix of the specified size with all elements set to 0

Log - exp - power

exp	Calculates the element-wise exponential matrix of a matrix
log	Calculates the natural logarithm of the argument
log10	Calculates the base 10 logarithm of the argument
log1p	Computes with accuracy the natural logarithm of its argument added by one
log2	Calculates the base 2 logarithm of the argument
polar	Calculates the polar form of a real square matrix
sqrt	Calculates the square root of the argument
sqrtm	Calculates the matrix square root of the square matrix argument

Floating point operations

ceil	Rounds up the arguments
clean	Cleans matrices (rounds small entries to zero)
double	Converts the arguments from integer to double precision representation
fix	Rounds the arguments towards zero
floor	Rounds the arguments down
format	Formats the argument for printing and display

isinf	Checks for infinite entries in the argument
isnan	Checks for "Not a Number" entries in the argument
nearfloat	Gets the nearest next floating-point number from the argument
nextpow2	Returns the next higher, say n, power of 2 such that the argument $<=2^n$
round	Rounds the arguments to the nearest integers

Matrix manipulation

flipdim	Flips the specified dimension of the argument matrix in a specified block size. The block size must divide the selected dimension.
matrix	Reshapes a vector or a matrix to a different size matrix
permute	Creates an equivalent matrix of the shape of a matrix according to the specified permutation of the dimensions of the argument matrix.
pertrans	Returns a matrix that is mirror of the argument matrix along its 2 diagonal, i.e. the simultaneous permutation and transposition operations are applied to the argument matrix.
repmat	Returns a larger matrix of the specified replications of the argument array
resize_matrix	Creates a new matrix with a different size
squeeze	Removes singleton dimensions of a hyper-matrix

Matrix operations

abs	Returns a matrix consisting of the absolute values of the elements of the argument matrix
cumprod	Returns the cumulative product of the elements of the argument array
cumsum	Returns the cumulative sum of the elements of the argument array
max	Returns the maximum of the argument array, either row wise, column wise or the maximum of the whole array
min	Returns the minimum of the argument array, either row wise, column wise or the minimum of the whole array
norm	Returns the matrix norm of the argument matrix

prod	Returns the product of the argument array elements, either row wise, column wise or the whole array
sum	Returns the sum of the argument array elements, either row wise, column wise or the whole array
tril	Returns the lower triangular part of the argument matrix
triu	Returns the upper triangle part of the argument matrix

Search and sort

find	Returns the indices of true elements in a Boolean vector or matrix
dsearch	Classifies and labels the elements of a matrix into specified bins and returns labeled matrix, the number of elements in each bin and the number of elements outside the specified bin.
Gsort	Sorts a matrix either row wise, column wise or the complete matrix
Vectorfind	Searches either rows or columns in a matrix for a matching vector of the same data type
intersect	Returns a vector of the common elements of the two argument vectors / matrices, or returns common rows or columns of the argument matrices
setdiff	Returns a vector consisting of the elements of the first argument which do not belong to the second argument
union	Returns a vector that is union of the argument vectors/matrices
unique	Returns a vector consisting of unique elements of the argument vectors/matrices

Trigonometric functions

Acos	Computes the element wise inverse cosine (in radians) of the argument
acot	Computes the element-wise inverse cotangent of the argument.
acsc	Computes the element-wise inverse cosecant of the argument
asec	Computes the element-wise inverse secant of the argument
asin	Computes the element wise inverse sine of the argument
atan	Computes the element wise inverse tangent of the argument
cos	Computes the element wise cosine of the argument

sec	Computes the element-wise secant of the argument
sin	Computes the element wise sine of the argument
sinh	Computes the element wise hyperbolic sine of the argument
tan	Computes the element wise tangent of the argument

Miscellaneous functions

and	Performs the element wise logical AND operation on the arguments
cat	Concatenates the argument arrays
cell2mat	Converts a cell array into a matrix
cellstr	Converts strings vector (or strings matrix) into a cell array of strings
isempty	Checks if a variable is an empty matrix or an empty list
isequal	Checks the equality of the arguments
isvector	Checks if a variable is a vector
pmodulo	Calculates the positive arithmetic remainder modulo
ndims	Returns the number of dimensions of the argument
nthroot	Calculates the nth real root of the argument
or	Performs the element wise logical AND operation on the arguments
sign	Returns a matrix consisting of the signs (1 for positive, -1 for negative and 0 for zero) of the elements of the argument
size	Returns the dimensions of the argument
rand	Generates a matrix consisting of random numbers (uniform or normal)
length	Returns the number of elements in a vector

Variables related functions

clear	Kills all the user defined workspace variables
clearglobal	Kills all the user defined global variables
Isdef	Checks the existence of variables
Isglobal	Checks if the variable is global
who	Lists all the variables of the current workspace
who_user	Lists all the user defined variables
type	Returns the type of a variable

exists   Checks the existence of variables and returns 1 if a variable exist and 0 if not

Strings functions

evstr	Returns the result of the evaluation of a matrix of character strings
grep	Finds matches of a string in a vector of strings
strcat	Concatenates character strings
strchr	Find the first occurrence of a character in a string
strcmp	Compares character strings
strcmpi	Compares character strings (case insensitive)
string	Converts a matrix into a matrix of strings
strncpy	Copies the specified number of characters from a character string, starting from the beginning of the string
strrev	Returns the reverse of a character string or matrix of character strings
strsplit	Splits a string into a vector of characters or sub-strings
strstr	Locates a substring in a string
strtod	Converts a string to double

Made in United States
Orlando, FL
04 February 2023

29511824R00169